The Great Demographic Reversal

Charles Goodhart · Manoj Pradhan

The Great Demographic Reversal

Ageing Societies, Waning Inequality,
and an Inflation Revival

Charles Goodhart
London School of Economics
London, UK

Manoj Pradhan
Talking Heads Macro
London, UK

ISBN 978-3-030-42656-9   ISBN 978-3-030-42657-6   (eBook)
https://doi.org/10.1007/978-3-030-42657-6

Cover image: © ducu59us shutterstock.com

This Palgrave Macmillan imprint is published by the registered company Springer Nature Switzerland AG
The registered company address is: Gewerbestrasse 11, 6330 Cham, Switzerland

Preface (April 4 Version)

In this book, we focus on the effects of demography and globalisation on longer run trends in finance and the real economy. Such trends are usually slow-moving and operate at the global, rather than national, level. Since the concern of most macroeconomic analysis is on developments at the cyclical frequency and at the national level, we believe that the importance of these factors has been largely overlooked. Our global and structural focus has provided us with more than enough material for quite a long book.

We do not, indeed we could not, try to encompass all the other myriad issues that will affect our longer-term economic future, such as climate change and technological developments, largely because many others, much more expert than ourselves, have taken up such subjects. And there are the 'unknown unknowns', which will probably become the dominant influence on all our future lives.

Our main thesis is that such demographic and globalisation factors were largely responsible for the deflationary pressures of the last three decades, but that such forces are now reversing, so that the world's main economies will, once again, face inflationary pressures over the next three, or so, decades. The question, which we have been most frequently asked, is 'Just when will the point of inflexion from deflation to inflation occur?' When we were writing this book in 2019, we had to answer that we did not know to within five years, or so.

That was, of course, before the coronavirus pandemic hit in early 2020; the occurrence of such a pandemic being a 'known unknown'. The overall impact of the pandemic will be to accelerate the trends we have outlined in this book. China will become more inward-looking and less deflationary globally, and inflation itself will rise much earlier and faster than we had anticipated. Because of the importance of this to the issues that we raise in our book, our publisher kindly agreed to allow us to append a short epilogue (postscript) to the book.

This is primarily an empirical book and could not have been completed without the invaluable research assistance and insights into the data by Patryk Drozdzik and Bo Tang, and Marina Emond's organisation and preparation of our manuscript. We are indebted to them for their tireless work. We would like to thank Pratyancha Pardeshi for her help in our early work on these themes.

Data, however, need to be transformed, mainly by theory, into narratives to be comprehensible and persuasive. For that, of course, we are beholden to many who have preceded us, for example, the literature kicked off by Bill Phillips in Chapter 8 on the relationship between slack in the labour market and wages growth, and the work on inequality undertaken by Branko Milanovic in Chapter 7. We are particularly grateful to Carol Jagger for correcting an error in our work on Dependency and Dementia and to Camilla Cavendish for her guidance in Chapter 4, and to Carol Jagger and her co-authors, for permission to reproduce Tables from the PACSim modelling study; and Chris Lynch and Alzheimer's Disease International for permission to reprint Tables from various World Alzheimer Reports. The insights we gleaned from the conference convened by the Global CEO Initiative on Alzheimer's Disease were most helpful. Our thanks go to George Vradenburg and Drew Holzapfel, and separately to Natalia Shelvey. Similarly, we are grateful to Michael Devereux and his co-authors for permission to reprint the whole Executive Summary from their paper on Destination-Based Cash Flow Taxation, and for his helpful comments on our draft. We also thank Benoit Mojon and Xavier Ragot for help with participation data.

Besides these, we also thank:

- The Bank of England for permission to reprint a Figure from G. Gutiérrez and S. Piton (2019), and two Figures from the July 2019 Financial Stability Report.
- The Federal Reserve Bank of St Louis for permission to reprint a Figure from R. Hernández-Murillo, et al. (2011).
- Taylor and Francis for permission to reprint a Figure from G. Meen (2005).
- The London Institute of Banking and Finance for permission to reprint some paragraphs from L. Mayhew in *Financial World* (2019).

- The Banco de España for permission to reprint a Table from Y. Aksoy, et al. (2015).
- Rightslink for permission to reprint a Table from M. Heise (2019).
- Brookings for permission to reproduce a Figure from L. Rachel and L. H. Summers (2019).
- Marketplace Copyright for permission to reprint Paragraphs and Figures from W. Gbohoui, et al. (2019).
- The American Economic Association for permission to reproduce two Figures from D. H. Autor (2019); reproduced with the permission of the American Economic Association Papers & Proceedings.
- Statista for permission to reprint one of their Figures.
- The High Pay Centre for permission to reproduce one of their Figures.

More generally our thanks are due to Hyun Shin for encouraging us to write this extended book. We are especially grateful to Haizhou Huang for carefully reading the whole book, and for greatly improving our chapter on China. Similarly, our thanks go to Takatoshi Ito-San for help with our chapter on Japan. We have been fortunate to have had helpful publishers in Palgrave Macmillan, particularly in the persons of Tula Weis, Rachel Sangster, Lucy Kidwell and Azarudeen Ahamed Sheriff.

But above all our greatest debt is to Miffy Goodhart and the Pradhan family, who cannot remember when previously we have been so inattentive, and have still forgiven us.

London, UK

Charles Goodhart
Manoj Pradhan

Contents

Abbreviations

ACE	Allowance for Corporate Equity
ADL	Activities of Daily Life
AE	Advanced Economies
AEA	American Economic Association
AFD	Alternative for Germany
AGM	Annual General Meeting
AI	Artificial Intelligence
AIG	American International Group
BEPS	Base Erosion and Profit Shifting
BIS	Bank of International Settlements
BLS	Bureau of Labour Statistics
BoA	Bank of America
BoJ	Bank of Japan
CAR	Capital Adequacy Ratio
CBI	Central Bank Independence
CBO	Congressional Budget Office
CEO	Chief Executive Officer
CFAS	Cognitive Function and Ageing Study
CPI	Consumer Price Index
CSI	Cyclically Sensitive Inflation
DBCFT	Destination-Based Cash Flow Taxation
ECB	European Central Bank
ELB	Effective Lower Bound
ELSA	English Longitudinal Study of Ageing
EME	Emerging Market Economies

EQ	Emotional Quotient
FDI	Foreign Direct Investment
FRB	Federal Reserve Board
FRED	Federal Reserve Economic Database
FT	Financial Times
FTSE	Financial Times Stock Exchange
FX	Forex
G10	Group of 10
GDP	Gross Domestic Product
GFC	Great Financial Crisis
GFCF	Gross Fixed Capital Formation
GGM	General Gaidar Model
HH	Household
HIC	High-Income Countries
IBC	Indian Bankruptcy Code
ICE	Intercontinental Exchange
IMF	International Monetary Fund
LHS	Left Hand Side
LMIC	Low- and Middle-Income Countries
LTI	Loan to Income
LTIP	Long-Term Incentive Plan
LTV	Loan to Value
MAC	Migration Advisory Committee
METI	[Japan] Ministry of Economy, Trade and Industry
MFN	Most Favoured Nation
MITI	[Japan] Ministry of International Trade and Industry
MMSE	Mini-Mental State Examination
NAIRU	Non-Accelerating Inflation Rate of Unemployment
NBER	National Bureau of Economic Research
NFC	Non-Financial Corporation
NHS	[British] National Health Service
NICE	Non-Inflatiory with Continuous Expansion
NLW	National Living Wage
NRU	Natural Rate of Unemployment
NUM	[UK] National Union of Mineworkers
OBR	Office for Budget Responsibility
OECD	Organisation for Economic Cooperation and Development
ONS	Office for National Statistics
O-FDI	Outbound Foreign Direct Investment
p.a.	Per Annum
PACSim	Population Ageing and Care Simulation
PBoC	People's Bank of China
PNTR	Permanent Normal Trade Relations
PSC	Private Sector

QE	Quantitative Easing
R&D	Research and Development
RHS	Right Hand Side
RMB	Renminbi
RoE	Return on Equity
RPA	Rural Payment Agency
RPI	Retail Price Index
SOE	State-Owned Enterprises
SSA	Sub-Saharan Africa
TARP	Troubled Asset Recovery Program
TU	Trade Union
UAW	[USA] Union of Auto Workers
UE	Unemployment
UN	United Nations
UR	Unemployment Rate
USD	US Dollar
VAT	Value Added Tax
WAP	Working Age Population
WAR	World Alzheimer Report
WEF	World Economic Forum
WHO	World Health Association
WTO	World Trading Organisation
ZLB	Zero Lower Bound

List of Diagrams

List of Tables

1

Introduction

The rise of China and demography created a 'sweet spot' that has dictated the path of inflation, interest rates and inequality over the last three decades. But the future will be nothing like the past—and we are at a point of inflexion. As that sweet spot turns sour, the multi-decade trends that demography brought about are set for a dramatic reversal.

Many of our conclusions are controversial. Neither financial markets nor policymakers are prepared for a significant rise in inflation and wages, or a rise in nominal interest rates. Our other predictions are more benign—productivity will rise and labour will reclaim a greater share of national output, reducing the inequality that has led to so much social and political upheaval.

Regardless of whether we are right or wrong, the effects of the 'Great Demographic Reversal' will be pervasive across finance, health care, pension systems, and both monetary and fiscal policies.

Of one thing we are sure, the future will be nothing like the past.

© The Author(s) 2020
C. Goodhart and M. Pradhan, *The Great Demographic Reversal*,
https://doi.org/10.1007/978-3-030-42657-6_1

1.1   The Demographic 'Sweet Spot': How the Fundamental Forces of Demography, China and Globalisation Shaped Our Economies in Recent Decades

1.1.1   The Rise of China…

The single most important economic development over the years from 1990 to 2018 has been the rise of China and its integration into the global trading economy. Chairman Deng Xiaoping reversed Mao Zedong's disastrous policies during the 1980s by combining socialist ideology with an opening to pragmatic market economics, using the slogan 'socialism with Chinese characteristics'—that led to China's eventual inclusion in the World Trading Organization (WTO) in 1997. The integration of China into the global manufacturing complex by itself more than doubled the available labour supply for the production of tradeable products among the advanced economies (AEs). So we start the rest of this book with a Chapter on China, Chapter 2.

The increase in the working age population (WAP, aged 15–64) in China outstripped the combined increase in Europe and the USA from 1990 to 2017 over fourfold—China saw an increase of over 240 million while in the latter two WAP increased by less than 60 million and mostly in the USA. The participation of the working age population also tilted the scales heavily in China's favour. On the one hand, workers migrated aggressively from rural to urban China—the latter's share of total population increased by over 23 percentage points (pp hereafter), or 370 million between 2000 and 2017. In the USA meanwhile, the participation rate (share of labour force to population) declined by over 4pp during the same time—had it stayed steady, the unemployment rate would have been higher before the pandemic struck.

1.1.2   …and the Re-integration of Eastern Europe

But there was yet another boost to the world's effective labour supply, arising from the collapse of the USSR, following the fall of the Berlin Wall in 1989. This brought the whole of Eastern Europe, from the Baltic States, through Poland down to Bulgaria, also into the world's trading system. The population of working age in Eastern Europe rose from 209.4 million in 2000 to 209.7 million in 2010 and is now projected to be 193.9 million in 2020.

These two politico-economic developments, the rise of China, and the return of Eastern Europe to the world trading system, provided an enormous positive supply shock to the available labour force in the world's trading system. The opportunity to take advantage of such newly available workers was reinforced by a general acceptance of economic liberalism during these decades, reducing barriers to international trade, with the trade rounds in Uruguay in 1986 and Doha in 2001. As a result, globalisation surged ahead, with trade flows over the years 1990 until 2017 growing by 5.6% per annum, compared to the growth of world GDP of 2.8%. In 2004, the share of world manufacturing output produced by China was 8.7%; by 2017, it had reached 26.6%.

But the integration of China and Eastern Europe was not the only factor leading to a dramatic rise in the availability of labour. The global supply of labour was further boosted by two other demographic features, both domestic in origin in the advanced economies (henceforth AEs).

1.1.3 Benign Demography in the AEs

The first of these demographic features is the continuing fall in the dependency ratio during these years, i.e. a rise in the number of workers, defined as those 15 to 64, relative to dependents. And the second is the rise in the proportion of women in the working age group taking paid jobs.

The dependency ratio improved because the birth rate, which had soared after World War II, then began to decrease quite sharply during the 1950s and onwards. Life expectancy, on the other hand, only began its long upwards trend rise rather later. The baby boomers were an important part of this dynamic as they began entering the labour force from the late 1960s onwards and only started to retire in the decade following 2010. During the period 1970–2010, the decline in the number of young relative to the working force outweighed the rise in the number of retirees (Table 1.1), except in Japan and the UK. At the same time, a number of social and economic developments raised the proportion of women working in the labour force (Table 1.2, USA, UK, France, Germany, Japan).

Combining these two factors, the rise of China, globalisation and the reincorporation of Eastern Europe into the world trading system, together with the demographic forces, the arrival of the baby boomers into the labour force and the improvement in the dependency ratio, together with greater women's employment, produced the largest ever, massive positive labour supply shock. The effective labour supply force for the world's advanced economy trading system more than doubled over these 27 years, from 1991 to 2018 (Diagram 1.1).

Table 1.1 Percentage of young and retirees in the population

	USA	UK	Germany	Japan	China
Young					
1970	28	24	23	24	40
2010	20	17	14	13	19
Change 1970–2010:	−8	−7	−9	−11	−21
2010	20	17	14	13	19
2019	19	18	14	13	18
Change 2010–2019:	−1	1	0	0	−1
Retiree					
1970	10	13	24	7	4
2010	13	17	21	22	8
Change 1970–2010:	3	4	3	15	4
2010	13	17	21	22	8
2019	16	19	22	28	11
Change 2010–2019:	3	2	1	6	3

Source UN Population Statistics

Table 1.2 Participation of women in the labour force

	USA	UK	Germany	France	Japan
1990	56.2	52.0	45.2	46.3	50.1
2010	57.5	55.5	52.8	50.9	48.7
2019	55.8	57.1	55.3	50.2	51.4
Change: 1990–2019	−0.4	5.1	10.0	3.9	1.3

Source World Bank

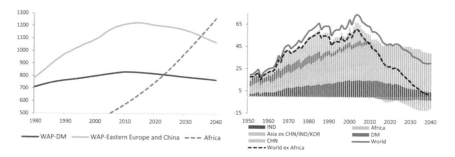

Diagram 1.1 An ageing world: working age population (Mil) is falling; working age population growth (yearly increase) is slowing (*Source* UN Population Statistics)

1.1.4   The Economic Effects Have Been Dramatic

The last 30 odd years from the beginning of the 1990s to the present have been extraordinary for the global economy (Chapter 3). When such a positive supply shock to labour occurs, the inevitable result is a weakening in the bargaining power of the labour force. Especially in advanced countries, a fall in real wages has seen the economic position of unskilled labour as well as semi-skilled labour suffer relative to capital, profits and managerial and skilled labour remuneration.

Both a symptom of labour's declining bargaining power and a further cause of it have been the steady decline in private sector trades union membership. This has been a common factor in most AEs. Diagram 1.2 gives the data on this for the major AEs.

No wonder that the deflationary forces have been so strong. During these 28 years, prices of durable manufacturing goods tended to fall regularly in most advanced economies, though perhaps slightly less so in more recent years. In contrast, services inflation in developed market economies, having initially fallen quite sharply in the 1980s, tended to stabilise from the 1990s onwards at nearer 2%, though perhaps declining slightly in the last few years. Obstfeld (2019) displays a diagram similar to our Diagram 1.3 in his 'Global Dimensions of US Monetary Policy'.

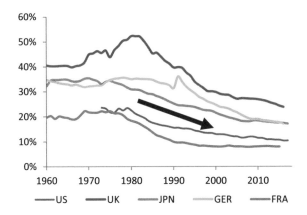

Diagram 1.2 Trade union density has been falling for decades now (*Source* OECD)

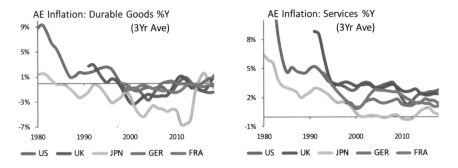

Diagram 1.3 Advanced economies inflation: Durable goods and services (year on year = %Y, averaged over 3 years = 3Yr Ave) (*Source* BLS, ONS, national sources)

These deflationary forces have been so aggressive that they have caused inflation to remain at, or more recently below, Central Bank targets, mostly set at about 2% over the decades from 1990 onwards. Even massively expansionary monetary policies and fiscal policies which have resulted in the largest and most persistent rise in public sector debt ratios ever during periods of general peacetime (apart from Germany—see Table 1.3 and Diagram 1.4) have had little success in reflating the global economy.

Finance has recorded some of the strongest effects of demographic change. Interest rates have trended steadily downwards, at least until about 2017/2018 (Diagram 1.5). With inflation remaining low, this has meant that real interest rates, i.e. after adjustment for the current inflation rates, have also been falling. Falling interest rates have led to rising asset prices. Despite some interruption from the Great Financial Crisis (GFC) over 2008/2009, this too has been happening, notably with equity and housing prices.

Table 1.3 General government debt to Gross domestic product ratio

	1990	2000	2010	2017
USA	62.0	53.1	95.7	105.2
UK	27.2	37.0	75.6	87.5
Germany	41.0	58.9	80.9	63.9
France	35.4	58.6	85.1	96.8
Japan	64.3	137.9	207.9	237.7
China	N/A	22.8	33.7	47.0

Source IMF Global Debt Database

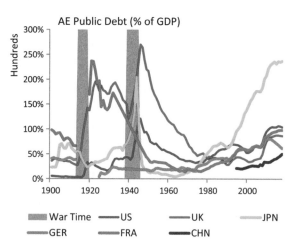

Diagram 1.4 Advanced economies public debt (% of Gross Domestic Product) is going to rise even further (*Source* IMF)

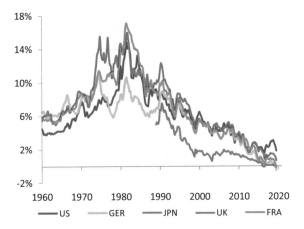

Diagram 1.5 Long-term government bond yields: 10-year maturity (*Source* Federal Reserve Economic Database – FRED hereafter)

1.1.5   Social Effects: Winners, Losers and Inequality

The gainers from all this have been those with capital, both embodied and human in the advanced countries, and workers in China and Eastern Europe. Thus, the ratio of the wages of an American worker to a Chinese worker, and of a French to a Polish worker, have been narrowing sharply, as shown in Table 1.4. There are many more Chinese than Americans, so, just as income inequality *within* particularly the advanced countries has tended to worsen, income inequality *between* countries and in the world as a whole has been improving. Inequality, as measured by the ratio of the income of the top 10% to the bottom 90%, has tended to worsen within most countries, as has wealth inequality. This is recorded in much more detail in Chapter 7.

The rise in income and wealth inequality, and the slow rate of growth of real wages among the less skilled, had led an increasing proportion of voters in many advanced countries to lose faith in their political institutions, and to believe that the elite has ceased to care about them. For the first time since World War II, many, perhaps most, of the populations in our countries do not see any strong likelihood of an improvement in either their or their children's economic well-being over future decades. For this bleak outlook, they largely blame globalisation and competition from abroad, including the offshoring of manufacturing production, competition from immigrants taking up unskilled jobs in their own countries, and the failure of the elite to respond to their concerns. The result has been a rise in political populism and a crisis of economic liberalism.

There was no political backlash before the GFC in 2008 because rising inequality within countries was offset by the general economic well-being of

Table 1.4 Ratio of the wages of workers: USA/China; France/Poland

	USA/China	France/Poland
2000	34.6	3.9
2001	30.6	3.3
2002	27.4	3.5
2003	25.0	4.0
2004	22.9	4.2
2005	20.4	3.8
2006	18.1	3.7
2007	15.2	3.5
2008	12.2	3.0
2009	10.8	3.7
2010	9.7	3.3
2011	8.4	3.3
2012	7.5	3.4
2013	6.7	3.4
2014	6.3	3.3
2015	6.0	3.4
2016	5.9	3.4
2017	5.6	3.2
2018	5.1	2.9

Source National Sources

these years, often described as the 'Great Moderation'. Indeed, in many ways, these were the best 15(plus) years for general economic success in the history of the world. Growth was steady, unemployment was low, inflation was stable and more people taken out of poverty than in any prior equivalent period. As Mervyn King stated (2003), these were the NICE years (Non-Inflationary with Continuous Expansion). Naturally, this counterbalanced the worsening developments in inequality within the advanced countries.

But once the GFC hit, the benign offset disappeared. Worsening inequality was reinforced by an actual drop in real wages in most AEs. The population tended to mistakenly perceive the bail-outs of banks and the effect of expansionary monetary policy on asset prices as examples of the elite looking after their own, and not responding to the worsening conditions of the majority of workers.

If the rise of China and massive positive labour shock that the world has had to absorb seem as compelling to you as they do to us, why is this focus not commonly highlighted in general macroeconomic analysis? A basic problem is that most financial, macroeconomic and policy discussion relates to forecast developments over the course of the next two, or at the most three, years. During such a relatively short time period, the underlying trends, as represented by demographic factors and the effects of globalisation, generally move too slowly and steadily to affect the key features of the short-run, cyclical forecasts. Except in rare cases, such underlying trends become dominated by short-run shocks and policy responses.

A related failing is that the factors that dominate short-term forecasting are then given too large a role when it comes to constructing a long-term view, while the slow-moving factors like demographics that surely dominate long-term change are still given too small a role.

1.2 The Great Reversal Is Now Starting—The Sweet Spot Turns Sour

But, regardless of the shortcomings of the literature, these long-run trends end up dominating the underlying fundamental conditions for our economies. Globalisation and demographic shocks have led to an extraordinarily deflationary trend over the last 30 years. The decades from the 1970s to 2000 saw the baby boomers swell the ranks of the labour force, while demographic trends improved the dependency ratio.

But the future will not be like the past. Indeed, in many crucial respects there will be a major reversal of past trends.

1.2.1 The Sweet Spot Is Turning Sour

Over the next three or four decades, the steady decline in birth rates, starting in the 1950s in many advanced economies, notably in Europe, to below the rate at which the population is self-sustaining, will bring about a sharp reduction in the growth of the labour force in many countries. There will be an absolute decline in the labour force in several countries—in the key economies of Japan, China and most of North Asia as well as several in continental Europe, such as Germany, Italy, Spain and Poland. Meanwhile, extensions to the expectation of life, with improvements in morbidity and mortality rates, will lead to a rapid increase in the number of retirees over 65. All this is set out in some detail in Chapter 3 on 'The Reversal of Demography'.

1.2.2   Care for the Aged Raises Economic Costs Dramatically

We are particularly enthusiastic about Chapter 4. It attempts to address a shortcoming of the literature by introducing a cross-disciplinary study of demography that integrates the medical perspective on ageing with the economics of the sharply increasing incidence of physical dependency and dementia. This chapter explores the medical progress in, and estimates of, the cost of detection, treatment of and caring for those afflicted by dementia.

Unlike the dominant diseases of our age, dementia does not curtail lifespans. Rather, it incapacitates those who are afflicted and therefore involves a large use of resources to care for them. Whereas medical science has made remarkable steps in treating cancer and cardiovascular diseases, both of which tended to kill quite quickly, there has been very little improvement in the treatment of dementia. Nor is the care of the old a field in which the new technological advances, of robotics and AI, are likely to be of great help. Of course, all this could change, and it is almost certain that governments will shift the balance of research funding of medicine towards the treatment of mental decay. But at the moment, if we try to extrapolate past trends into the future, the outlook for health expenses, care homes and carers is worrying. The fiscal implications of the worsening dependency ratios are severe and concerning (Diagram 1.6).

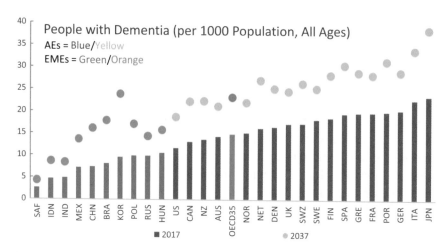

Diagram 1.6   The number of people with dementia (per 1000 population, all ages) will rise sharply across the advanced economies (*Source* OECD Health Statistics 2017)

1.2.3 Slowing Globalisation

The further slowing of globalisation will reinforce ageing just as globalisation energised falling dependency ratios in the past. Globalisation is likely to slow because of two headwinds.

First, China faces not only a sharp decline in the number of those entering the labour force, but is also reaching the end of internal migration from the farming community in the western provinces to the manufacturing sector in the east (Chapter 2). Moreover, globalisation in the guise of enhanced cross-border flows of goods and services, the migration of people, and capital flows is under increasing political threat as resurgent nationalism becomes politically more popular.

Second, while manufactured goods and some services can be produced elsewhere and then 'shipped' to their destination, this is virtually impossible when it comes to looking after the elderly. Advanced nations will therefore be increasingly reliant on their own resources, particularly the shrinking pool of their own labour force.

1.2.4 Economic Effects

We then go on to explore first the broad economic effects (Chapter 3), and then the effects on inflation (Chapter 5), real interest rates (Chapter 6) and inequality (Chapter 7). Chapter 4 plays a dual role, explaining both the economic effect of ageing and also demonstrating the severity of the impact of ageing on the great demographic reversal.

What, then, are the main economic effects?

First, the declining growth rate of the labour force will necessarily reduce the growth of real output, unless there is an unexpected and quite remarkable surge in productivity. Growth rates generally cannot be expected to recover, if at all, beyond the disappointingly slow levels of the years since the GFC (Chapter 3).

Second, our highest conviction view is that the world will increasingly shift from a deflationary bias to one in which there is a major inflationary bias (Chapter 5). Why? Put simply, improvements in the dependency ratio are deflationary, since workers produce more than they consume (otherwise it would not be profitable to employ them in the first place), while dependents consume but do not produce. The sharp worsening in the dependency ratios around the world means that dependents who consume but do not produce will outweigh the deflationary workers. The inevitable result will be inflation.

With the supply of labour shifting down, standard economics suggests that their bargaining power will increase, and that real wages and the relative income share of labour will start rising again. While this will have beneficial effects on inequality within countries, it will be inflationary as unit costs rise. Add on top of this an increasing tax burden on workers (which we explain below), and they may well raise their wages demands in order to secure a desired real wage *after taxation*. While Milton Friedman (e.g. 1968) and other eminent economists argued that workers would not be subject to money illusion (i.e. that they would bargain for a desired level of real wages in the light of their expectations of future inflation), will this also apply to taxation? If tax rates should have to rise significantly to finance pensions and medical expenses, will workers start to bargain for post-tax real wages? We would think so, and if we're right, it would lead to yet further upwards pressures on inflation.

Third, real, inflation-adjusted interest rates, particularly at the longer end of the yield curve, may rise (Chapter 6) because of the behaviour of ex-ante (expected) savings and investment. That the elderly will dissave is not controversial. Those who believe real interest rates are likely to fall or stay low clearly believe that investment will fall even further below savings—we disagree. There are (at least) two reasons to believe that investment will remain more buoyant than many believe. First, the demand for housing will remain relatively steady as the elderly stay in their houses and new households create demand for new construction. Second, the corporate sector is likely to invest in capital in a way that raises the capital-labour ratio, in order to boost productivity. In net terms, we believe savings are likely to fall by more than investment, lowering the real interest rate.

As in the case of inflation, financial markets are not pricing in much by way of nominal interest rates rising over the next decade and more.

Finally, we believe that inequality will now fall (Chapter 7). As the wave of populism and the success of nationalist right-wing parties have demonstrated, inequality within economies has risen to critical levels, even though inequality across nations has actually fallen thanks to the rise of China and Asia. We consider four explanations for the trend of rising inequality: (i) ineluctable trends of the kind that Piketty (2014) and others have espoused, (ii) technological change, (iii) concentration and monopoly power and (iv) globalisation and demography. We disagree the most with the first and find more merit in the other arguments. The most fundamental explanation for the rise in inequality can be traced back to the global surge in labour—and hence its reversal will also lead to a decline in inequality.

So more and more of us will live longer lives, but where are the resources which will enable the aged to consume after retirement going to come from, even if we abstract from the extra medical burden? There are three main alternatives, discussed at greater length in Chapter 6.

The first is that the age of retirement should be raised a lot, with people in future expected to work into their 70s. But, as described later in the book, there is no sign of retirement ages yet being significantly increased (with the exception that women's retirement ages are being raised into line with those of men). Moreover, there are quite a large number of more manual occupations where physical strength declines to an extent that makes continuing to work past a particular age inappropriate, e.g. firemen, policemen, construction workers, etc. Though against that, one may remark that farming is a physical activity, and many farmers continue to be active well into their 70s.

The second alternative is that workers finance their own retirement by saving more. This latter depends on the expected generosity of state pensions and the myopia of those in work. It is very difficult at age 25 to envisage oneself surviving to (say) 85 and visualise the consumption needs of an aged person, and yet the likelihood of doing so is high. Certainly, the less the expected generosity of state pensions and the longer the expected duration of retirement, the greater individual savings rates will tend to be. Again, an important example is China, where the absence of a welfare state and the collapse of reliance on younger family members (as a result of the one-child family, where there is one grandchild for every four grandparents), has led in the past to very high personal savings rates. But in the West there has been relatively little sign, yet, of personal savings rising to meet the need to smooth lifetime consumption rates, even though the difference between life expectancy and retirement age has risen dramatically. Perhaps this is due to an expectation that the state will provide, or perhaps it is due to myopia.

An added complication is that the age of having children has increased in many advanced countries. With children remaining at home for longer, the years during which workers can save for their retirement, with no children to support, will decrease. The hope is that the savings that the children incur on what they would have otherwise paid for rent can then form part of household savings in the future—whether that pans out remains to be seen.

The third channel is for the state to tax workers, and use the funds to transfer the resources to the old, both for medical support and pensions. A key question is how the state will see the balance between higher taxes on those currently working, including workers of all levels of skill, managers, rentiers and capitalists, and the generosity of pensions. If one should assume that tax rates will remain constant at present levels, then the massive rise in the numbers of the old would mean that the relative generosity of pensions would have to decrease sharply, partially balanced by increased savings rates from those of working age. We do not believe that this is the right assumption to make, though it lies behind the assumption of interest rates remaining low over future decades in several other related studies of long-run demographic outcomes. Instead, we think that a better assumption is that pensions will go up in real terms in line with the rate of growth of real GDP, with the implication that the tax burden arising from pensions will rise in line with the ratio of aged to the total population. There are several reasons why we prefer this assumption to that in which tax rates are held constant. First, the pensions of the aged have generally been protected despite the slow growth of real output in recent years. Second, the old represent a major voting bloc, and they are more likely to vote than the young. The rising share of elderly voters in the electorate will provide a potent constituency for keeping pensions rising in line with real output. Note that promises to maintain or increase pensions have often been a significant part of the manifestos of populist political parties, e.g. in Italy in 2018. If we are correct in assuming that pension levels will rise with real GDP, and thus become an increasing fiscal burden, as the number of aged increase, then the tax burden on workers will inevitably have to increase.

1.3   Where Could We Be Wrong?

We are fully aware that our conclusions and projections are controversial. Quite naturally, they have been questioned along many different dimensions. We take these very seriously and allocate Chapters 8–11 to address them.

In Chapters 8 and 9, we discuss two counterarguments that are often put forward to rebut our view. The more prominent of these, Chapter 9, is that such a decline in the labour force has already been in evidence in Japan for over a decade, and that there have been no signs yet of any upwards pressure of wages, inflation or real interest rates there. Many consider Japan to be the blueprint for ageing and are therefore sceptical that our conclusions will hold for the global economy if none of them were in evidence in Japan. The second is that the recent relationship between unemployment and wage, or price, inflation, commonly known as the Phillips curve, Chapter 8, has not yet shown any tendency for wage rates to rise as unemployment falls, in a large number of advanced economies. Indeed, unemployment has declined in many of our countries to the kind of levels that would have probably generated wage inflation in the last century, but there is as yet little sign of any resultant upsurge in wages. The Phillips curve has recently seemed flat, i.e. as unemployment falls, nominal wage growth remains more or less constant at low levels. In many countries, it is not much higher than 2%, though the USA and the UK are seeing wage growth around 3 and 4% respectively, but only when labour shortages are already apparent in sectors like construction.

In the case of Japan, we argue that the decline in the Japanese labour force occurred at a time when the rest of the world was swimming in labour. Japanese businesses took advantage of the growing pool of labour overseas to offshore production to China and other parts of Asia. In other words, the 'true' available labour supply in Japan was Asian or even global, rather than purely Japanese. When seen through an overseas lens, the behaviour of Japan Inc. is quite dynamic and measured to maximise productivity. Our view stands contrary to the conventional view of a dormant corporate sector weighed down by deleveraging. What *is* in stark contrast is the scenario that confronts the world today. As the labour market tightens in China and the bulk of the global economy, such offshoring will become more difficult.

More generally we argue that the huge positive labour supply shock to the global economy has made labour so weak that their bargaining power has been significantly reduced. This has meant that the level of unemployment at which inflation starts to accelerate has probably declined quite sharply by several percentage points. To use a technical term, the non-accelerating inflation rate of unemployment (NAIRU) has gone down significantly. For example, the proportionate membership of trade unions in the private sector has declined sharply in most countries. But as labour becomes scarce again, it will recover its mojo. How quickly and how sharply this reversal may occur is yet to become clear.

Milton Friedman (e.g. 1968) popularised the concept of the Natural Rate of Unemployment (NRU). But the NRU is not constant. Perhaps the best definition of it is the rate that makes labour willing to accept that rate of growth of real wages that its own increasing productivity makes available. It then follows that the weaker is labour's bargaining power, the lower will be the NRU. As labour power, and TU membership, has fallen, so has the NRU. This is discussed further in Chapter 8.

The declining bargaining power of labour then goes a long way to explain the falling labour share of income in AEs and the stagnant nominal and real wages there, as also argued in Krueger (2018) (Luncheon Address on 'Reflections on Dwindling Worker Bargaining Power and Monetary

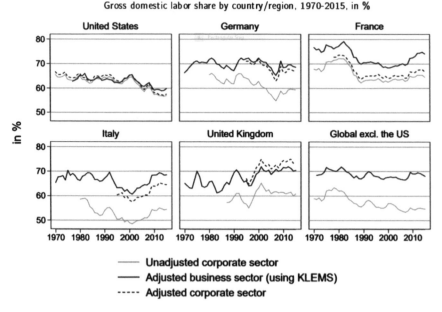

Diagram 1.7 Labour share of income in advanced economies (*Source* Bank of England Staff Working Paper No. 811)

Policy', at August, 2018, Jackson Hole Conference, pp. 267–282), also see Diagram 1.7.[1]

Others, rather than arguing against our results, have suggested that they may be much weaker in net terms because of other mitigating dynamics. There are, of course, several mitigants to our view that the reversal of demographic factors will shift global trends from deflation to inflation over the next thirty years. We have already mentioned two of these, which are included in Chapter 10, notably the possibility of a considerable further rise in retirement ages, and the possibility that the relative generosity of state pensions will decline in future, in order to limit an otherwise rise in tax burden. But in that same chapter we discuss another possible mitigant, which is that, rather than reversing, globalisation could take another turn. While birth rates have been going down sharply in most of the advanced countries, this has not been so in much of the Indian subcontinent, and particularly not so in Africa. There

---

[1]While it is generally accepted that the share of corporate value going to labour has been steadily declining in recent decades (see Schwellnus et al. 2018; IMF 2017), Gutiérrez and Piton (2019), state that this is not so for four main European countries (France, Germany, Italy, UK). Here, unlike the USA where the downwards trend remains clear, they claim that, after appropriate statistical adjustments, the labour share has remained roughly constant.

will be a massive rise in the available working population in these parts of the world. Just as the production of goods was shifted from the West into China over the last three decades, could a similar shift lead to the production of goods moving to the Indian subcontinent and, particularly, to Africa, where the rate of growth of the working population in countries like Nigeria and the Congo will be quite remarkable over the next few decades? There is also, of course, the possibility of further waves of migration from these poor countries into the richer countries in America, Europe and Asia. But the political, social and economic problems caused by mass migration are so severe, that the only viable alternative would be to take capital and management to the workers in these poor countries, rather than having them migrate to the rich countries. We shall argue that while such a new direction for globalisation is possible, we nevertheless think it somewhat unlikely.

Ironically, very few use a line of argument that we do believe is a potent and immediate roadblock, but one that will have to be dealt with in one way or another—the debt trap and how to get out of it (Chapters 11 and 12 respectively). The deflationary bias over recent decades, reinforced by the Global Financial Crisis (GFC), has led to massively expansionary monetary policies, with interest rates, both nominal and real, coming down to historically exceptionally low levels. This has, as was intended, led to a dramatic increase in debt ratios, both in the public and private sectors. The main exception in recent years has been the reduction in the leverage ratios of banks, whose dangerous level in 2007/2008 was a major factor in causing the GFC, and household leverage in countries where this sector has gone through a housing crisis. Although debt ratios have risen dramatically, there is not enough concern about leverage. That's because debt service ratios have not risen along with debt ratios, thanks to an almost exact inverse correlation between rising debt ratios and declining interest rates. This is set out in Chapter 11.

At the same time, these low interest rates have, naturally, enhanced asset prices. Sometimes the monetary policies of Central Banks have been accused of exacerbating inequality. But if Central Banks had not expanded, other policies being held constant, unemployment would have been worse, which normally hurts the poorest most. So Central Bank policies have, on balance, probably reduced income inequality. The alternative policies that some suggest would have been greater reliance on expansionary fiscal policies. But not only have public sector debt ratios grown faster over recent decades than in any other previous peacetime period, but also the outlook for expenditures relating to health and pensions is such that projections of future budgetary conditions are worrying, to say the least, see Diagrams 1.8 and 1.9.

And, if we are right, future inflationary pressures will drive up interest rates, adding yet further to fiscal problems.

In effect, we are in a debt trap. Debt ratios are so high that increases in interest rates, especially at a time in low growth, may drive exposed borrowers into an unsustainable state. As a result, the monetary authorities cannot raise interest rates, either sharply or quickly, without running into the danger of

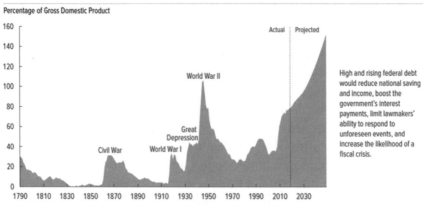

The extended baseline generally reflects current law, following CBO's 10-year baseline budget projections through 2029 and then extending most of the concepts underlying those baseline projections for the rest of the long-term period (in this case, through 2049).

Diagram 1.8 US federal debt held by the public was projected to rise sharply even before the pandemic (*Source* Congressional Budget Office)

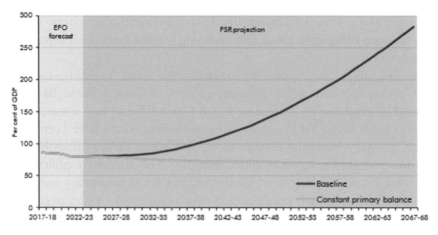

Diagram 1.9 Projections of UK public sector net debt (*Source* The Office for Budget Responsibility)

provoking another recession, which itself would make everything worse. But that will leave interest rates, and the accompany flood of liquidity, sufficiently expansionary (accommodating, in Central Bank speak) that debt ratios are likely to increase even further.

The inevitable question then is, how do we escape this debt trap? In Chapter 12, we discuss a variety of mechanisms for escaping the debt trap, notably growth, unexpected inflation, default, jubilee debt cancellation, debt restructuring or a shift away from debt finance towards equity finance. We demonstrate that all these alternatives have problems, except for growth, which, alas, is likely to remain sluggish at best. Of course, what would be nice would be to raise productivity, but its growth has been disappointingly weak during the period since the GFC, for reasons that remain unclear. The idea that there are available structural supply-side policies that could painlessly raise productivity is, alas, a fantasy. If robotics and AI and other tech wizardries can help to improve productivity per head, so much the better. The concerns about the world running out of jobs are likely to be unfounded—there will be more than enough jobs looking after the old!

1.3.1 How Could All of This Leave Policy and Policymakers Unscathed?

Over the last few decades, central bankers have been the best friends of Ministers of Finance, while central bankers themselves have achieved rock star status. As the Ministers of Finance have presided over continuing deficits and rising debt ratios, the interest burden has been held down by simultaneous falls in interest rates. Central Bank policy has eased the path for politicians. No wonder that Central Bank independence has not been subject to much serious criticism, except in relation to their more unconventional monetary policies, which have seemed to blur the boundaries between monetary and fiscal policies.

Central Banks have been in the driver's seat thus far. Before the onset of the GFC, Central Banks gave their inflation targeting regimes most of the credit for the persistent disinflation. After the crisis, Central Banks have been criticised for not being able to raise inflation, but their unconventional measures have helped raise asset prices to the benefit of investors and home-owners. If we are right in our thesis, then much of the disinflation of the prior decades should be attributed to demographics, putting the efficacy of monetary policy in dictating the path of inflation into even greater question than it has been in the post-crisis period.

The main thesis of this book is that the great demographic reversal will shortly raise inflation and interest rates. With public sector debt ratios at high levels, and continuing worsening pressures from demography, the aims and objectives of Ministers and Central Banks may soon cease to be comfortably aligned and may come into conflict. Moreover, the effect of quantitative easing (QE) has been drastically to shorten the average duration of public sector debt (including the cash liabilities of the Central Bank). The implication of this is that when interest rates go up, this will have an even quicker effect in raising the interest burden that the Minister of Finance has to face. So, Chapter 13 argues that Central Bank independence (CBI) will come under even greater threat in the future than it has been recently.

Our final chapter, Chapter 14, not only reviews and summarises our arguments, but also describes and emphasises our differences with most current mainstream analysis. We believe that the mainstream view of the longer-term future is plain wrong.

2

China: An Historic Mobilisation Ends

Did globalisation lead to the ascent of China or did China's rise lead to globalisation? It is not an easy question, and the turn in the fortunes of both over the last half a decade will not make it easier to answer either.

For most of the history of the last two millennia, China was a dominant force in the world in both innovation and growth. Its workforce has been trained in efficiency through guilds and the absorption of innovation that initially came mostly from within China's own borders. That culture of training and organisation allowed China to absorb technology from outside its border with a discipline that few advanced economies could match, aided by an administration that remains more single-minded and unencumbered than any other.

If there is a case to be made for China driving globalisation, its demography would be a key foundation. The ratio of China's population to the world's has actually fallen since 1955. Thus, it is not the relative size of China's population, but the accelerated rate at which its labour force integrated into the global economy that has mattered.

China benefitted asymmetrically relative to the rest of the world during its multi-decade re-engagement with the global economy. Part of the reason behind the asymmetry lies in China's starting point of an abundant and cheap supply of labour and very little capital and technology available to each worker. Yet, the other part was surely the economic strategy of China's administration to direct domestic savings and global capital into investment within China's special economic zones.

A series of frictions supported this asymmetry. Global capital was largely prevented from accessing China's financial markets, while the early returns

© The Author(s) 2020
C. Goodhart and M. Pradhan, *The Great Demographic Reversal*,
https://doi.org/10.1007/978-3-030-42657-6_2

from China's financial markets were not attractive enough for overseas investment to chase. As a result, global capital flowed into physical investment. Strict capital controls allowed China to maintain a competitive global advantage. That same strategy allowed financial repression to be pursued at home in order to direct the domestic pool of saving towards state-owned enterprises (SOEs) with government-owned banks as the conduit.

China's contribution to global disinflation of the last 35 years and its coming reversal needs to be understood through the lens of history and an understanding of its growth model in the global context.

China's historic mobilisation is best seen through two perspectives, the sequence of historical events and the evolution of its growth model. Together, they allowed China's vast labour force to integrate into the global economy at an unprecedented pace.

2.1   Three Acts of History that Shaped China's Place in the World

China's ascent in the global economy can be traced back to three events and periods. The earliest of these events was Deng Xiaoping's 'socialism with Chinese characteristics', particularly the second phase starting in 1992.

The first phase of this drive started in 1978 with reforms to agriculture, an invitation to private enterprises to re-enter the Chinese economy, and the creation of special economic zones (including the Pearl River Delta that we discuss below) where foreign investment was allowed. Though price controls were lifted for urban industries, the economy was still dominated by fairly inefficient state-owned enterprises (SOEs hereafter).

It was in the second phase that privatisation of SOEs began, when small, medium and even some large SOEs were closed or sold to the private sector. The private sector showed dramatic growth in this period, but large SOEs remained monopolies in sectors considered to be key to national interests (including banking). Growth in both phases in Diagram 2.1 shows the success of these strategies, surging to double digits with every new phase of reforms. The exception appears to be the latest slowdown, where China's transformation has been described more as improvement in the quality of growth rather than an outright, sustained rise in the growth rate itself.

The success of the second phase is evident in the bilateral trade deficit of the USA with China. Though the deficit grew dramatically from 1978 to 2000, much of the widening occurred in the 1990s, not the 1980s.

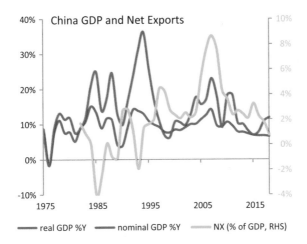

Diagram 2.1 Reforms and exports have led to sustained surges in growth (*Source* IMF)

Inbound FDI (i.e., foreign direct investment) also mirrors that pattern. A decade after the opening up of the economy, FDI was less than USD 5 billion in 1990. By the late 1990s, FDI was threatening to reach USD 50 billion, only for the last few years of that decade to see FDI slowing down again.

The end of the late 1990s was eerily similar to where China stands today. Then, like now, it seemed that China's reforms were losing steam. Growth had persistently slowed down and even that was widely considered to be overestimated. SOEs were inefficient and inventories were high. Then, like now, the widening trade deficit was widely seen as evidence of China's mercantilist, or at least of its asymmetric treatment of accessing export markets, while denying others access to its domestic markets.

By all accounts, the first phase of 'socialism with Chinese characteristics' began opening up China and it was during the second phase starting in 1992 that China integrated more rapidly with the global economy. By the end of the 1990s, there were clear concerns about the boost from those reforms running out of steam. Even though many of domestic and external metrics appeared unbalanced, China's leaders sought a new boost to growth. It was under such domestic and global scrutiny that China's leadership sought World Trade Organisation (WTO) accession.

A second set of events were the treaties that further integrated China into the global economy: WTO accession and US Congressional approval for PNTR (Permanent Normal Trade Relations, the equivalent of Most Favoured Nation) status for China, both in 2000.

The time between China gaining WTO membership and the global financing crisis finally cemented China's position in the world as an economic, and hence political, superpower. The strength of the global economy, the euphoria around the 'commodity supercycle' and emerging markets, and praise for the benefits of globalisation were all derivatives to varying extents of China's expansion over that period.

China became a WTO member after 14 years of negotiations. Its accession was granted conditional upon a long list of liberalisation and opening-up measures (set mostly by the US) to allow greater access to, and see greater transparency in, China's markets. China was, in broad terms, required to:

- Lower its tariffs to under 10% within five years and reduce tariffs on some agricultural imports almost to zero.
- The reduction or elimination of non-tariff barriers.
- The opening up of some key sectors including telecommunication and banking.
- Protecting global intellectual property rights.

Examining the stringent nature of the conditions imposed on China (more stringent than any in the past and on most applicants since), Lardy (2001) questions somewhat why China's leadership sought and accepted WTO membership. However, the quantum and quality of China's growth in the decade following WTO accession justifies the Chinese leadership's strategy in pursuing greater access to foreign markets.

Towards the end of that decade, there were clear signs that China's reforms were losing steam. Growth had fallen every year for most of the 1990s from a very high level, inventory accumulation had risen to worrisome levels and the inefficiency of SOEs was an open topic of discussion. In 1999, four large asset management companies (in effect, so-called bad banks) were set up to take on the large quantum of non-performing loans from the banking sector. Ma and Fung (BIS 2002) estimate that the total size of the non-performing loan problem at the four big state-owned banks could have 'amounted to RMB 3.4 trillion (USD 410 billion) or around 42% of the big four banks' loans outstanding at the end of 2001. This is comparable to the recent peak levels of 40% to 60% for Korea and Indonesia'. Since the four banks accounted for 65% of the total loan portfolio of the banking sector, the economy-wide size of the problem could have been closer to RMB 5.75 trillion (or just over 50% of GDP in 2001) if pro-rated across the loan portfolio for all of China's banking sector. The similarities of capital misallocation and non-performing assets to the situation that confronts China today are unmistakeable and it is clear, when seen in this light, why China's leadership pursued WTO membership despite a long list of conditions.

A cursory glance at the conditions listed earlier suggests that China has done well in reducing headline tariff barriers and has opened up many parts of its economy to entry by foreign firms. Yet those were sectors in which it lacked domestic capabilities. Where domestic capabilities were prevalent or acquired, non-tariff barriers have remained in place and generally made it difficult for foreign firms to prosper in China.

The US, on the other hand, had to make no new market access concessions. Most WTO members provide other members with MFN (Most Favoured Nation) status. If the US had not afforded China this status, WTO membership would have still gone through, but with a complicated relationship with the US.

Pierce and Schott (2012) document the 'surprisingly swift decline in US manufacturing employment' over the 2000s (see Diagram 2.2), identifying the removal of the threat of future tariffs against China as the key driver of that decline. That changed, according to the authors, when the US Congress approved a Permanent Normal Trading Relations (the US equivalent of the MFN) status on China in 2000 and eliminated the threat of tariffs in the future. Without a friction like tariffs to justify the onshore presence of manufacturing jobs, the production of many goods left US shores for China. The authors identify goods that used to be produced in the US, that were later imported from China. They find that the largest declines in manufacturing employment were felt in the production lines for these goods. That manufacturing value-added continued to rise despite the decline in manufacturing employment was caused by US companies engaging in cross-border reallocation of production and employment. Europe, on the other hand, had given

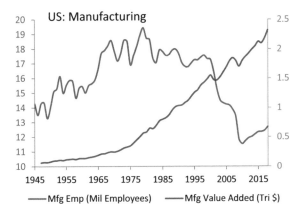

Diagram 2.2 "The surprisingly swift decline in US manufacturing employment" (*Source* Bureau of Economic Analysis)

China MFN status much earlier and did not see such declines in manufacturing after China joined the WTO. Presumably then, a relocation of manufacturing jobs from Europe (and others) to China had happened earlier, though likely at a much slower pace.

In a nutshell, China benefitted asymmetrically from WTO inclusion. Its entry on an MFN basis to the US market around the same time led to a decline in manufacturing employment there at a rate that had not been seen in previous decades. Both point to the conclusion that China's labour force integrated with global capital and global trade in a very rapid manner, adding to the considerable demographic tailwinds from which the world was already benefitting.

The third event was China's response to the Great Financial Crisis. China's aggressive response to the onset of the Great Financial Crisis was a major factor in preventing the collapse of the global economy. Diagram 2.3 shows that China's credit growth in the aftermath of the crisis rose by 35%. A policy impulse of that size quite naturally buoyed global growth, commodity prices and emerging market economies. In the years that followed, all the trends that China and emerging markets had seen before the crisis not only held steady, but even accelerated. These economies were seen as a viable alternative as an engine of growth to the advanced economies. For the period between 2007 and 2012, that was both mathematically and economically true—emerging markets dominated the contribution to growth.

The year 2012, however, marked the beginning of the end of China's demographic contribution to the world. Unsustainable credit growth is usually seen as borrowing from the future. The prior surge of credit in China

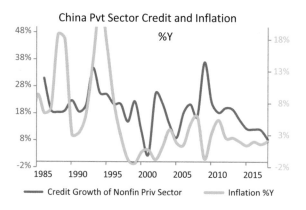

Diagram 2.3 China credit growth surged in the early 90s and after the Great Financial Crisis (*Source* Bank of International Settlements, IMF)

then brought forward a slowdown that would otherwise have been a few years further into the future. Over 2014–2015, China's manufacturing and property sectors saw a major slowdown. Along with the coincident slowdown in emerging markets and global manufacturing, China's slowdown contributed to the dramatic fall in oil prices from nearly $150 a barrel to $27 in 2015 and a collapse in global trade.

The cyclical fall in China's manufacturing and property sector was impossible to ignore, but there is too little understanding about the impact it had on the structure of China's economy. That is because the role of the manufacturing sector is very different in advanced economies versus emerging ones.

2.2   Centralisation of Economic Power, Decentralisation of Political Power

'Unlike economies as a whole, manufacturing industries exhibit strong unconditional convergence in labor productivity. Despite strong convergence within manufacturing, aggregate convergence fails due to the small share of manufacturing employment in low-income countries and the slow pace of industrialization'. Dani Rodrik, 2011, 'Unconditional Convergence in Manufacturing', NBER Working Paper.

Why is this important? The intuition behind these results is that manufactured goods are impossible to differentiate by their geographical origin. Regardless of where they are manufactured, these goods are usually tradeable, must match a global standard of quality, and must be cost-efficient relative to producers in other regions. If an economy manages to enlarge the share of the manufacturing sector in its economy at an early stage of its development, its labour productivity will converge with global standards faster and consistently.

China's growth strategy for many decades was designed to direct domestic and global resources to accelerate manufacturing and investment. Its basic advantage was its massive and heavily underutilised supply of labour, a lot of which had resided in its interior, rural regions.

The earlier phase of China's growth strategy was one of economic centralisation—where a singular monetary policy was deployed with the sole purpose of driving rapid capital accumulation. Over the last decade, particularly after the Great Financial Crisis, that strategy changed to one of decentralisation.

A key difference between AEs and EMEs is that capital is cheap and labour is expensive in the AEs while the opposite is usually true in the EMEs. In order to accumulate capital rapidly, the cost of capital has to either fall, or be intentionally distorted.

In the earlier stage of China's growth strategy, monetary policy was designed to dramatically lower the cost of capital. During this phase, it was the state players that were the tip of the spear even though the private sector grew rapidly. SOEs, state banks, and modern, state-directed industrial policy were all an integral part of China's growth strategy during its ascent. On the other hand, provinces were given considerable power, particularly those that were home to China's special economic zones. Governors of these provinces and the leaders of SOEs came to be some of the most powerful men in China during its expansion.

Every aspect of the production function was actively employed. Land, labour, capital and technology all played a strong role in China's great mobilisation.

Land: The special economic zones epitomise China's industrial policy. Land was heavily subsidised and businesses were given all the help they needed to set up and operate businesses efficiently. Infrastructure including power and distribution networks was prioritised.

The Pearl River Delta in Guangzhou province is the best known and most successful of these economic zones. Since 1978, nearly 30% of all foreign investment has gone to this region, and its growth rate has exceeded national growth by over 3% on average. Starting as a collection of villages amidst a rural landscape even by the mid-1980s, the World Bank describes the Pearl River Delta as the largest urban area in the world today. Its 9 biggest cities house a population of just less than 60 million.

Labour: A historic rural–urban migration provided a seemingly endless supply of cheap labour to the urban areas and the economic zones.

China's 'Hokou' registration system allowed this migration to occur without too much of a burden on the urbanising areas. The Hokou system essentially provides a passport for urban citizens. Migrants without credentials can reside in urban areas for work but they do not have access to most urban services including health care and education. As a result, the cost of migration does not pass on to the administration of these urban centres. It has resulted in only the workers themselves moving in search of work while families stayed in the rural habitat where they can access their local services. Without the Hokou system, rural workers might have sold their land and moved at a much faster pace to the urban areas, resulting in a significant excess supply of urban labour and, perhaps, of rural land as well.

In any event, rural–urban migration happened slowly but consistently over decades, resulting in a steady supply of cheap labour.

Capital: Most emerging markets accumulate capital when its cost falls because of global forces or is forcefully lowered through policy-led distortions. China recouped the benefits of both. The multi-decade, global decline in nominal and real interest rates has already been documented. The domestic cost of capital was lowered through three mechanisms.

First, China dealt with the 'impossible trinity' by imposing strict capital controls, allowing the exchange rate to be fixed and domestic monetary policy to be independent of global monetary conditions. The 'impossible trinity' dictates that an economy has to choose two out of the trio of free capital flows, a fixed exchange rate and monetary independence—having all three is not possible. As just one example of how this would work, consider China under a fixed (or heavily controlled) exchange rate. If China's central bank (the People's Bank of China, hereafter the PBoC) sets interest rates at a very low level, then the fixed exchange rate makes it attractive for China's residents to seek higher interest rates outside. With capital free to move in and out quickly, there would have been large capital outflows and that would have put enough pressure on the exchange rate that it could no longer remain fixed. But if capital is not free to flow in and out of China, then the exchange rate can remain fixed and the PBoC can set interest rates to suit the needs of the domestic growth strategy. And it did.

Besides strict capital controls on financial flows both in and out of the country, the PBoC intervened heavily in foreign exchange markets to prevent the inflows of investment funds from raising the value of the Renminbi. Over 2001–2015, the PBoC intervened regularly in foreign exchange markets, the intervention peaking at nearly 18% of GDP in 2007 according to official estimates, resulting in a massive accumulation of central bank reserves. Such a sustained intervention allowed the exchange rate to remain steady at a level that delivered China's exports a considerable advantage. As a result, the trade balance (the difference between exports and imports) grew rapidly (Diagram 2.4).

Second, households faced financial repression at home and saw their savings effectively transferred from households to banks to SOEs. The implicit tax they paid was used to subsidise the growth of SOEs.

How did China manage to do this? China's interest rate market was effectively insulated from the rest of the world, thanks to the restrictions on capital controls. Within China, the PBoC dictated the rate at which banks (dominated by government-owned banks) could borrow and lend, and it controls the flow of credit in the economy even today.

Interest rates were set well below the rate of growth and the rate of inflation. While the economy grew on average by around 10% over 1990–2010,

Diagram 2.4 Capital inflows were offset at the border, leading to huge foreign exchange reserves (*Source* IMF)

the inflation-adjusted deposit rate over the same period averaged −3.3% (for a 1.4% average for the nominal deposit rate versus an average annual inflation rate of 4.75%). Let alone receiving protection against inflation on their deposits in the banking sector, the inability to participate in China's growth through financial investment at home or abroad was a double-digit, inflation-adjusted penalty on households. Households had very few means of protecting themselves financially; buying houses was the investment of choice. Household leverage rose as a result.

In other words, low interest rates were effectively a tax on households. As household savings were collected by banks and redirected towards SOEs, the tax on households effectively became a subsidy for SOEs with banks acting as a conduit.

But why did households continue to put their money in banks rather than in other financial assets? The choices for households to protect their savings were designed to be, and remain, extremely limited. Buying foreign assets remains an option for an extremely small and wealthy segment of the population, and equity ownership too remains limited among the population. China's average household had effectively only two ways of storing wealth, in houses and bank accounts.

Nabar (2011, IMF) finds a negative correlation between urban savings and the decline in real deposit rates. When banks fail to protect household savings, households tend to save more, not less, in order to achieve a 'target', whether that is for education or the purchase of a home. China's household savings have also been linked to the lack of a social safety net, and importantly in the context of this book, to the life cycle of a population that is saving for retirement.

Third, as we have argued earlier, global capital was partly directed towards, and in part attracted to, investing in physical rather than financial assets. Subsidised land and infrastructure, cheap labour, an extremely competitive exchange rate and access to advanced economy markets (particularly after WTO accession) encouraged multinationals to use China as a manufacturing base.

Know-how: The West provided much of the know-how and the physical capital in exchange for cheap and plentiful labour, and business-friendly conditions. Capital goods embed the newest vintage of technology, and newer vintages of capital capture a newer vintage of technology. The flow of physical capital, particularly in manufacturing, brought along with it the newer vintages of technology to China. Additionally, multinationals brought along with them state-of-the-art methods to combine labour, capital and the technology embedded in that capital.

China's regulations allow foreign firms to operate in certain key sectors in China only if they form joint ventures with Chinese firms. Jiang et al. (VoxEU, April 2018) find evidence that considerable technology transfers from foreign firms occurred, not only to their Chinese joint venture counterparts, but also to other local firms operating in the same industry. Regardless of whether these transfers were intended or were simply 'digested', the end result was the transfer or technology and know-how from foreign firms to local ones on a consistent basis.

China's integration into the global economy benefitted China vastly. As we argued above, global capital was mostly restricted in its access to China's financial markets. Instead, physical capital was encouraged to enter China. The transfer of technology and access to credit allowed China's SOEs as well as the private sector to grow rapidly.

All of that should have resulted in a huge current account deficit for China, which would have reflected the surge in investment. Except that China's savings were even larger—the financial repression encouraged high household savings, high enough to finance domestic investment and push national savings higher than investment and create a current account surplus.

The capital that entered China was met by the PBoC in the foreign exchange markets through a massive sterilisation effort to prevent the Renminbi from appreciating. The PBoC purchased US dollars in the foreign exchange market equivalent to 18% of GDP by 2007. As a result of these purchases, China's FX reserves grew dramatically, as mentioned earlier, to just below USD 4 trillion. These hard currency reserves were assets and needed to be invested. Under the stewardship of the State Administration of Foreign Exchange, China's official agency for managing reserves, hard currency reserves were invested almost entirely in the deep and liquid asset markets in the advanced economies. The bulk of that investment was in US Treasury securities.

Global capital thus flowed 'uphill', from China (and most of North Asia) to the advanced economies, helping create what the Federal Reserve's ex-Chair Ben Bernanke termed the 'global savings glut'. The excess of desired savings over desired investment in the AEs was driving the equilibrium real interest rate lower by itself, since the dependency ratio improved in the 1980s. The injection of excess savings from China and North Asia served to push interest rates even lower.

The US consumer, fabled for needing no encouragement to spend, got some help nevertheless. Falling interest rates raised the value of asset prices, including housing. The sharp decline in manufacturing employment in the 2000s, mentioned earlier, went largely unnoticed at the time because construction employment growth was rampant. The surge in consumption during the 2000s added fuel to the fire as imports grew strongly, and the bilateral current account balance between the USA and China widened substantially before the crisis.

Central banks misinterpreted these global, demographic trends for the success of their inflation targeting regimes which were introduced from 1990. The over-confidence of central banks in their ability to control inflation, volatility and financial stability contributed to the under-regulated rise of house prices. The rest, as they say, is history.

2.3   China's Great Reversal

China's greatest contribution to global growth and globalisation is past us. The current account surplus peaked in 2007 and it will now move into a deficit over time. Nominal GDP growth topped out in 2012 at around 18% and fell very sharply to just over 5% in 2015 before recovering somewhat. Investment growth and the property sector mirrored this fall but have remained in a much more subdued, post-crisis-type state since then. Its stock of hard currency reserves still stands at USD 3 trillion but could fall further as the current account moves into deficit territory.

China's working age population has been shrinking (Diagram 2.5), a reflection of its rapidly ageing population. The internal migration that had provided a seemingly endless supply of labour to the industrial zones has reached the 'Lewis turning point', a point at which the surplus rural

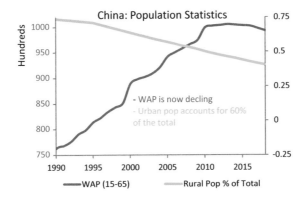

Diagram 2.5 China's working age population is shrinking; Urban population is now 60% of the total (*Source* National Bureau of Statistics)

labour supply no longer provides a net economic benefit through migration (discussed further below).

On the capital side, China's phase of rapid capital accumulation in the sectors that are connected to the global manufacturing supply chain has already drawn to a close. The collapse in the manufacturing complex and the property sector back in 2014–2015 has been followed by consolidation and capacity cutting rather than in more capital accumulation.

Globally, China's demographic reversal comes at a time when the social tide has turned against globalisation. That means global incentives are not aligned towards continued physical inflows of capital into China. Financial flows too were small, but the inclusion of China into the Bloomberg Barclays Aggregate Global Index will force index-tracking asset managers to buy Chinese bonds to the tune of around USD 150 billion. China will become second only to Japan in the index and will dwarf the holdings dedicated to its emerging market peers. It is, nevertheless, unlikely that physical investment will start growing again because of these inflows, thanks to the low rate of return on offer—something we discuss in greater detail below.

With labour and capital flows both constrained, China has now turned to upgrading technology as a means of sustaining growth and compensating for the contracting supply of labour. Without the influx of foreign firms and with the current intense scrutiny around the acquisition of technology by Chinese firms in foreign markets, the transfer of technology that was present in the past will no longer be in place.

That does not mean Chinese firms are not innovative or innovating—quite the opposite. China has some of the most innovative firms in telecommunications (where a significant number of 5G licenses have come from the likes of Huawei and Xiaomi), electrical power and even electric vehicles.

The easier path of technology transfer is no longer available for two reasons. First, foreign technology is harder to acquire both within and outside China. Second, the starting point of China's firms has improved to a point where reaching up towards the global standard no longer means a huge rise as it did in the past. Innovation thus has to be created at home, and of a magnitude that is quite large. That is the part that looks like a tall task.

The emphasis on innovation and technology will suit the already-educated urban population, but it will act against the 'flying geese' model, (a strategy to move investment to rural areas) that the administration hopes, or hoped, would materialise. Innovation naturally requires highly educated and trained workers. That is the kind of labour that already resides in the developed, coastal regions of China, not the type of labour supply that is available in the underdeveloped, interior regions of China. It is highly unlikely that these highly technical industries, China's best bet for productivity gains in the future, will move to the interior of China.

In theory, a global pool of educated workers could at least partially offset some of the risks we have mentioned here. However, since every major manufacturing economy among the AEs and EMEs is going through a similar demographic transition, the global demand for such skilled labour is likely to intensify. Within China itself, the educated labour force already resides on the coast, close to the production hubs, and in the urban areas.

In fact, rather than looking inward for growth, China's 'One Belt, One Road' initiative is more promising as an outward-looking strategy. More specifically, it would export to other economies the prospective excess capacity created by the lack of economically viable demand for infrastructure within China. That initiative has been heavily backed not just by China but also by many of the countries through which the project passes. More recently, serious questions have been raised about the profitability and financing of this ambitious plan. In a world where growth has been meagre, we doubt there will be enough activity to make the One Belt One Road initiative sustainable. China's ability to create growth for itself from this venture is, therefore, limited.

Could the capital account lead to a change in the direction of the current account? Should the capital account move into a persistent deficit, then the current account would be pushed back into surplus. However, it is not clear what direction the capital account will take. On the one hand, China's households hold too much of their wealth at home and have been trying to hold more foreign assets. At the same time, the flows associated with the investments in the 'One Belt One Road' drive should also mean persistent outflows. On the other hand, opening up the financial sector and access to China's financial markets will provide incentives to global investors to allocate funds to China's assets. How strong these trends will be is open to question.

Agarwal et al. (2019) argue that just 10% of China's bank deposits moving to buy foreign assets would mean USD 2 trillion of funds flowing to markets offshore. The history of capital account liberalisation, however, shows that freeing up household flows is the least predictable and hardest to control part of capital flows. As a result, such a move is usually one of the last changes in the process of capital account liberalisation. There are questions around the viability and financing of the Belt and Road Initiative and the speed with which it can be implemented. As we have stated earlier, the return on China's assets has been modest and uncertain, which means that the willingness to invest heavily in China will be dampened. The direction of net capital flows and therefore of the current account remains uncertain at best.

The change in China's economic fortunes was accompanied by a radical change in its growth strategy.

Around a decade ago, the growth strategy in China switched from a centralised one of promoting growth to one of decentralisation of economic decisions. Three clear changes define the strategy of decentralisation: (i) the whole-hearted pursuit of a consumption-based model of growth, (ii) a greater role for the private sector aided by deregulation and (iii) a change in the role of SOEs pursuing a cut in excess capacity and excess leverage with the aim of raising productivity.

The second and third goals are already on display. Excess capacity in several industries has been cut dramatically (steel is the poster child), debt is slowly being converted to equity (more on that in Chapter 12), and consolidation among SOEs is collectively already raising profitability. The role of the private sector has increased dramatically. Over the last ten years, the private sector contributed for over 60% of GDP, over 70% of tax revenue, over 80% of innovations, and over 90% of employment.

What will China's new growth profile look like? Consumption, investment and debt. There is, however, a greater balance to China's future growth than a picture of consumption-led growth conveys. Contrary to popular perception, consumption growth and the services that cater to consumption are already leading the next leg of China's structural slowdown, taking over after a huge adjustment in the role of investment in the economy. On the investment side, the beleaguered manufacturing and property sectors will focus on raising productivity and show the kind of discipline that most post-crisis survivors do. China's corporate debt carries a much lower risk of default than many believe, but its resolution does not bode well for the consumption-led model of growth.

Lessons from Japan: 'History never repeats itself, but it often rhymes' is a quote often attributed to Mark Twain, and he might well have been talking about the similarities between Japan's transition and China's ongoing transformation. Chapter 9 tracks Japan's evolution in much greater detail. For our purposes, suffice it to say that the collapse of Japan's investment growth in the early 1990s also led to a significant slowdown in consumption growth. However, for every year that consumption growth remained just above 0% but investment growth remained negative, consumption became a larger share of GDP. That was a mathematical rebalancing, not an economic one. Over that period, Japan's corporate sector repaired itself and raised manufacturing productivity by investing abroad rather than at home, and reallocating labour away from manufacturing and towards services (Diagram 2.6).

In both Japan and China, the labour market is incapable of acting as a shock absorber—because of long-standing cultural norms in Japan and because of social-stability reasons in China. As a result, other parts of the economy have to adjust more than they otherwise would.

Can Japan's lessons be applied to China? China is clearly very different, not least because it is at a much earlier stage of development than Japan was. That means there are still plenty of inefficiencies within its borders and policies that it can reform and raise productivity—that's how developing economies catch up with advanced ones. However, given the inability of the labour market to rapidly adjust, the nature of the evolution is likely to be similar. Consumption-led growth will be a disappointment but the investment side of the economy will perform better than many think. Debt will be a drag as it is digested (as we explain further below), but it is unlikely to bring about a crisis now, or in the future. Like Japan, China's transition

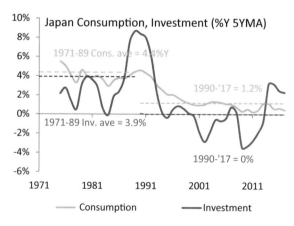

Diagram 2.6 Like Japan, China will see a mathematical rebalancing (*Source* IMF)

to consumption-led growth is likely to be a mathematical, not economic, rebalancing.

Consolidation in the manufacturing sector, particularly among SOEs. The 'hard landing' of China's manufacturing and property sectors in 2014–2015 marked a seminal moment in China's growth transition. Capacity in the manufacturing sector was addressed in a severe manner, particularly in the steel sector. In other areas of manufacturing, SOEs were involved in a consolidation of capacity through a freeze on further investment or through mergers.

Large-scale layoffs, however, were not a valid option for SOEs because of social considerations and the risk of political damage. The 1989 Tiananmen Square protest was not to be repeated, which meant the labour market could not bear the brunt of the adjustment. For example, even though a substantial portion of the credit extended by state-owned banks to SOEs was linked to excess capacity, both banks and SOEs were reluctant to write them off. Even if banks could be recapitalised by the government, SOEs that wrote down substantial loans would not receive any further funding, and would probably have to lay off a substantial part of the workforce. Instead, banks 'evergreened' the loans granted to SOEs and allowed them to stay operational. The presence of 'zombie' firms in China is therefore at least partly a function of societal and political constraints. Instead of mass layoffs, workers voluntarily left for jobs in urban areas in the gig economy, or were let go in small numbers when SOEs merged.

With capacity already having been cut, the slow release of labour from the manufacturing sector will actually raise the capital/labour ratio in the manufacturing sector and hence productivity.

Consumption, however, is likely to remain subdued. As the labour force and population growth go into reverse, overall growth will slow down. Household savings are likely to fall, with consumption directed to ageing- and health-related services, in the absence of a full and proper social safety net. This may happen either directly, or indirectly via the government. The social contract, that the Communist Party must abide by, may require the administration to provide these services in a subsidised manner. In this case, the upside risks to inflation may come from higher wages to offset the resultant tax on workers, or through the higher inflation that may be needed to reduce the burden of higher healthcare nominal spending.

Neither the healthcare-related increase in wages or inflation, nor the increase in wage growth due to China passing the Lewis point, are confidence-inspiring. The kind of sustainable increases in wage growth that would have led to a robust consumption cycle do not appear to be available.

The sharp decline in manufacturing investment is likely to lead to subdued productivity growth that rises only very slowly. As workers move from the manufacturing to the services sector, they will be moving to a sector that usually is more labour-intensive but has lower productivity growth, as has been the case in AEs elsewhere. Both dynamics will keep real wage growth under pressure.

China's debt is far less likely to lead to a crisis, but it will constrain future credit growth to the private sector.

It is a widely held view now that China's leverage has reached unsustainable levels and that a chunk of it has been used to back assets whose performance won't be good enough to service the debt. The most hawkish view in this regard probably comes from the PBoC. Could that really be true? There is no way to be sure, but consider that the PBoC's campaign against shadow banking started in 2017, but continued right through 2018 and 2019, even though President Trump's trade war was launched and intensified. Despite the worsening economic situation in China in late 2019, the PBoC continued to constrain the flow of funds from the shadow banking sector to the housing sector. In essence, the PBoC appears to be strongly committed to the process of deleveraging, stepping back from this aggressive stance only when economic conditions have deteriorated too much and warrant some accommodation. The PBoC's deleveraging drive and the path of China's economy continue to create concerns about a debt crisis at some point in the future.

The conventional wisdom about China's debt is misguided.

First, simply cancelling debt doesn't work in most places, but it does in China. Generically, even if debt is held domestically, debt cancellation is hard because debt is a liability for someone and an asset for someone else. Cancelling debt helps the debtor but shocks the wealth and future income of the creditor. In the aftermath, debtors don't ramp up lending, chastened by their experience, but creditors curb spending aggressively. The result is a sharp negative shock to overall spending, which is why debt cancellation isn't costless by any means (Chapter 11 deals with this issue in greater detail).

A quick look at Japan's debt profile is informative. Japan's government debt cannot be cancelled even if it is domestically held. Why? Because the 'leakage' via households is too big. The enormous stock of government debt is held almost entirely domestically, with a huge chunk held by pension funds. Let's say Japan's government decides to cancel its debt. That would impair the asset side of the balance sheet of Japan's pension funds, which would make it virtually impossible for them to service the liabilities that are due to the household sector. Shocked by the loss of future retirement income, households would raise their savings immediately and the 'paradox of thrift' would then lead to a consumption collapse and push Japan into a depression. Thus, the 'leakage' of Japan's debt cancellation via household spending is just far too big.

In China, both sides of leverage are on the same balance sheet (i.e. the government's) since so much of the corporate debt in question was issued by state-owned banks to SOEs. The 'leakage' (i.e. labour employed by SOEs) is smaller. China's state-owned banks have issued debt to domestic state-owned enterprises. If banks were to cancel the debt, it would create two issues. First, banks would have to take a hit to their capital in a discrete step—we will address this point just below. Second, it would be difficult to lend any more to SOEs. The SOEs would have to cut down operations and possibly fire a substantial part of their workforce. That's the problem—this could lead to social unrest which the authorities do not want.

Fixing the labour 'leakage': Manufacturing and property in China (i.e. 'Old China') hard-landed back in 2015. Since then, activity in Old China has been range-bound at best, and falling in the aftermath of the campaign against shadow banking and a trade war in 2018 and 2019. Labour is moving to the cities and into the myriad services that the gig economy is creating. Once the ranks of labour in the SOEs thin out (a process that is already underway but will still take years to reach critical mass), cancelling the debt will cause far fewer negative spillovers.

Second, debt-equity swaps are ongoing, but will take some time to make a dent in debt levels. Debt-equity swaps are our preferred solution to leverage (see Chapter 12). Cancelling part of the debt can risk putting the value of the entire stock of debt into question, whereas these swaps allow bank capital to be written down in a series of steps rather than in one discrete step. Unfortunately, like many other proposed 'solutions', these cannot be implemented aggressively either. Lenders are not necessarily keen to recognise a loss on their loans, and creditors are certainly not enthusiastic about it. However, the macroeconomic reason for a glacial pace of executing these swaps is the impact on incremental lending and employment. Once these swaps are executed, banks will no longer have to 'evergreen' old loans, and macroeconomic stability will improve. However, questions around the solvency of SOEs, which will still need to borrow to continue their operations, will rise. Many may then be forced to restructure their operations, and shed labour much faster. If done aggressively and all at once, the result would be mass unemployment and political stress. Thus, a gradual implementation is the best we should expect.

Third, the price for accruing a large stock of debt will be paid via a shortage of credit for consumption and for businesses in the services sector. Even though debt-equity swaps allow for a much smoother deleveraging, they will eat up bank capital as the value of swapped equity is slowly written down to match the realised value of the non-performing assets that had been financed by the debt in the first place. While bank capital is being eaten away, and while real wage growth finds lower support from capital accumulation, the ability and willingness of banks to lend will be lower. Thus, even though consumers and the private sector account for an increasingly larger share of the economy, they will not be able to draw upon future earnings to consume or grow faster today.

In summary, the future holds a much weaker path for the Chinese consumer, but a stronger rebound in productivity (particularly for the SOEs that work aggressively to reduce non-performing assets and loans). Debt run-off is likely to reinforce these trends—it will not create a crisis, but it will constrain the flow of credit in the future as banks digest the excesses of the past.

For China, the implications of everything we have discussed are threefold.

First, China will no longer be a global disinflationary force. If anything, demographic pressures and the Lewis turning point imply that inflationary pressures, with which the economy has never had to deal until now, could materialise and catch us off-guard.

Second, falling savings related to the ageing population and to the end of financial repression will push the current account into deficit. The capital account, as we discussed earlier, could push the current account back into surplus, but it is not clear how the contrasting flows in household wealth, financing of the Belt and Road Initiative and foreign investment within China will play out in net terms. Without the persistent 'uphill' flows of capital that China's earlier current account surplus had engendered, USA and global bond yields (and in turn asset prices) will see a reversal of the support from this source they had in the past.

Third, China's ability to introduce labour-saving and productivity-enhancing technology depends on the not-inconsiderable innovations that can be generated at home. Without the help of foreign firms transferring technology, and with political sensitivities around the acquisition of foreign technology firms by Chinese firms, an organic improvement in technology will be more difficult.

3

The Great Demographic Reversal and Its Effect on Future Growth

3.1 The Demographic Sweet Spot.... Slowly Turning Sour

We start by showing in this section how the demographic sweet spot of the last 35 or so years will now turn sour in the global industrial complex. China's shrinking workforce will stand in sharp relief to the historic surge in the global workforce it helped to create over the past decades. Then in Sect. 3.2, we will discuss the effects of this on output, leaving the discussion of the effects on inflation to Chapter 5, the discussion of the effects on interest rates to Chapter 6, and on inequality to Chapter 7. All of the data in this chapter comes from the UN Population Database (unless stated otherwise).

The 'sweet spot' will now disappear quite fast: The global dependency ratio is at a point of inflexion, and the rate of its ascent is predicted to steepen for almost every advanced economy and many key emerging ones right about now—especially China and Germany (see Diagram 3.3). Having grown fast between 1970 and 2005, the global working age population will now grow much less rapidly. In the advanced economies and North Asia, it will show outright declines at the same time as the ratio of workers to the elderly worsens greatly.

Fertility rates that have been stable in the advanced economies since the 1980s, in many cases below the self-sustaining rate, are not rising (see Diagram 3.1), but life expectancy continues to increase (Diagram 3.2). As a result, the retiring baby boomers will live longer but there is not enough local birthing to create an offset for the surge in the ranks of the elderly in those economies.

© The Author(s) 2020
C. Goodhart and M. Pradhan, *The Great Demographic Reversal*,
https://doi.org/10.1007/978-3-030-42657-6_3

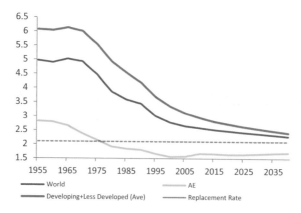

Diagram 3.1 Fertility (children per woman) is falling sharply in the EMEs, having already fallen in the AEs

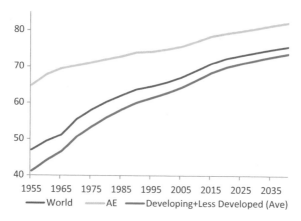

Diagram 3.2 Life expectancy at birth (years) is rising globally (*Note* AEs include high-income countries; EMEs include low and middle-income countries)

In the emerging market economies, life expectancy is quickly catching up with that of the advanced economies (and in places like Korea, that catch-up has already been realised) but there are significant disparities in the fertility profile among countries. The fertility rate in China, Korea and Russia is now at levels seen in the advanced economies. By sharp contrast, economies outside North Asia and Eastern Europe are still witnessing a steady decline in the fertility rate from much higher levels. By itself, this means their dependency ratios will worsen much later than in the advanced economies, providing some local relief in these economies against the global trend of ageing.

As a result, dependency ratios are set to rise sharply in the AEs, and even more sharply in some EMEs in North Asia and Eastern Europe. While Japan

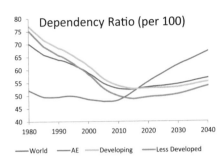
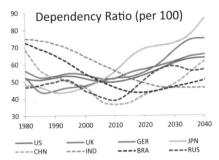

Diagram 3.3 Dependency ratios rising in the AEs, mixed among the EMEs (per 100)

is widely known for its population headwinds, Germany's dependency ratio will become a significant retardant in the coming decades. The trough of the dependency ratio in both Japan and Germany occurred in the 1990s and was followed by a trough in the USA and UK around 2010. Around the same time as the USA, China and Russia also saw their dependency ratios bottom out too, followed by Korea. Only India's inflexion is still a long way off (Diagram 3.3) among the large EMEs—a point we will return to later.

Notably, it is the worsening ratio of workers to the elderly (the 'old-age dependency ratio') that is responsible for the rise in the overall dependency ratio in the AEs, North Asia and Eastern Europe.

United Nations Report: World Population Ageing 2015

The report provides an excellent snapshot of how different the world will look over the next few decades and where the biggest changes will occur.

The pace of world population ageing is accelerating: Projections indicate that the proportion aged 60 years or over globally will increase more than 4 percentage points over the next 15 years, from 12.3% in 2015 to 16.5% in 2030, compared to the 2.3 percentage point increase in the share of older persons that occurred between 2000 and 2015.

Overwhelming rise of the over-60s: Between 2015 and 2030, the number of people in the world aged 60 years or over is projected to grow by 56%, from 901 million to 1.4 billion, and by 2050, the global population of older persons is projected to more than double its size in 2015, reaching nearly 2.1 billion.

In 2015, one in eight people worldwide was aged 60 years or over. By 2030, older persons are projected to account for one in six people globally. By the middle of the twenty-first century, one in every five people will be aged 60 years or over.

Oldest-old growing the fastest: Globally, the number of people aged 80 years or over, the 'oldest-old' persons, is growing even faster than the number of older persons overall. Projections indicate that in 2050 the oldest-old will number 434 million, having more than tripled in number since 2015, when there were 125 million people over age 80.

The proportion of the world's older persons who are aged 80 years or over is projected to rise from 14% in 2015 to more than 20% in 2050.

Home to the elderly: Where in the world is the population greying the fastest? Between 2015 and 2030, the number of elderly over 60 is expected to grow by 71% in Latin America and the Caribbean, followed by Asia (66%), Africa (64%), Oceania (47%), Northern America (41%) and Europe (23%).

In terms of levels, the ageing process is most advanced in high-income countries. Japan is home to the world's most aged population, as 33% were aged 60 years or over in 2015, followed by Germany (28%), Italy (28%) and Finland (27%).

By 2030, older persons are expected to account for more than 25% of the populations in Europe and in Northern America, 20% in Oceania, 17% in Asia and in Latin America and the Caribbean and 6% in Africa.

In 2050, 44% of the world's population will live in relatively aged countries, with at least 20% of the population aged 60 years or over, and one in four people will live in a country where more than 30% of people are above age 60.

3.2   The Demographic Cycle: Uniform Geographically, Lopsided Economically

The World Bank provides a useful classification of the demographic cycle by splitting economies into those where the demographic dividend has already passed by to those that have yet to live through theirs. The four sets of economies—pre-dividend, early-dividend, late-dividend and post-dividend—capture a global economy in demographic transition.

The differences in fertility and longevity among these economies help explain their labels. Countries with high fertility rates and low longevity are the ones that have yet to reap their demographic dividend. The expected fall in fertility rates and the increase in longevity, following the pattern in the rest of the world, will create the demographic dividend in the future. By contrast, post-dividend economies are the ones where fertility rates have plummeted and remain near their lows, and longevity too has converged to the global peak (Diagram 3.4).

At first glance, the current distribution of countries across these categories is fairly widely spread—which seems to paint a promising picture for the global demographic landscape. In fact, however, world population growth in 2040 will be higher than in the developed economies or in our categorisation

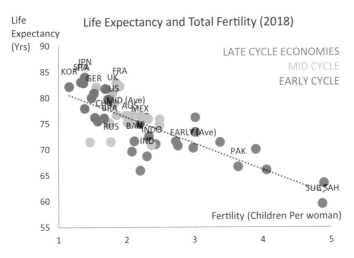

Diagram 3.4 Life expectancy (in years) and the geographical distribution of the demographic dividend (*Source* World Bank)

of the emerging economies, because there is yet another category of countries, defined as least-developed regions and countries, mostly in Africa, where population growth is predicted by the UN to remain much higher through 2040.

We have split our countries into three categories (sometimes also treating China (CHN) and India (IND) separately) namely: 'Early' (some additional dividends going forward), 'Middle' (getting worse but nothing extreme) and 'Late' (ageing visibly). The groups are set out in Table 3.1.

There is a rather clear split between the three groups in terms of population size (50, 25, 25), see Table 3.2 and Diagrams 3.5 and 3.6.

Unfortunately, the current relatively even population distribution belies a lop-sided economic distribution of economies along the demographic cycle.

Table 3.1 Country groupings by state of the demographic cycle

Groupings	
Early cycle	India, Pakistan, Bangladesh, Sub-Saharan countries, Mexico, Egypt, Argentina, Algeria, Iraq, Afghanistan, Uzbekistan, Venezuela, Nepal, Yemen, Myanmar, Philippines, Guatemala, Ecuador, Kazakhstan
Middle cycle	USA, Brazil, Vietnam, Turkey, Iran, Colombia, Canada, Sri Lanka, Saudi Arabia, Peru, Malaysia, Australia, Russia, Ukraine, UK, France, Morocco, Indonesia
Late cycle	China, Japan, Germany, Thailand, Italy, Korea, Spain, Poland, Romania, Chile, Holland

Note The grouping of Sub-Saharan countries includes about 50 economies

Table 3.2 Populations in early-, mid-, and late-cycle countries (2019, Mil.)

Early	3540	49%
Middle	1666	23%
Late	1966	27%
Total	7172	

The sample covers 90% of the world population

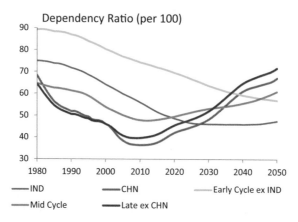

Diagram 3.5 Dependency ratio (per 100) in the different demographic cycles, % of world population

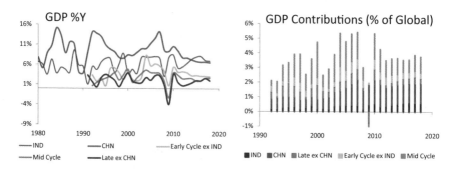

Diagram 3.6 Gross domestic product contributions (% of global) in the different demographic cycles

Most ageing economies (i.e. post-dividend and late-dividend stage) are the richer ones. The concentration of economic power thus rests heavily in the hands of economies that are ageing and have already 'used up' their demographic dividend, as shown in Table 3.3.

Most worryingly, it is not just the share of global GDP that the ageing economies dominate, they also account for the lion's share of global growth

Table 3.3 Share of growth of countries at different stages of demographic cycle

2012–2018 period	GDP Growth	Contributions to Global GDP growth	% of Global GDP in PPP terms
Early cycle economies	4.9	27	21
Mid-cycle economies	2.4	28	41
Late cycle economies	4.5	45	38

over the last 15 years. If we extend that timeline over the last 35 years, the picture does not change appreciably.

The danger facing the global economy is precisely that the economies that have dominated global growth are facing the biggest demographic challenges. And that means even if the world as a whole still faces substantial population growth going forward, the economies that shaped global growth for the last 35 years are the ones which bear the brunt of the demographic headwinds. Put differently, if demography is to leave only a scar on the global economy, then the economies that have done very little for global growth in the past few decades are the ones that must do much, much more in the future. Seen from this perspective, it should be clear that the disruption from technology that many fear so much in the advanced economies is actually an imperative without which the damage to global growth could well be far worse.

3.3   Output Growth

The rate of growth of output depends, naturally, on the interaction of the rate of growth of those working and their increasing productivity. As described earlier in Sect. 3.1, the rate of growth of the potential working population, ex India/Africa, is now set to decline, sharply in many cases. Unless this is offset either by a sharp rise in the share of the potential population that participates as workers (including retirees continuing to work), or by an offsetting rise in productivity per worker, the growth of output must fall, and the current rate of growth of output has already been disappointing despite the demographic reversal having barely begun.

We start by reviewing participation rates and continue by considering the future course of productivity. Mojon and Ragot (BIS 2019) have shown how the participation rates of those aged 55–64 have risen in many European countries, though not so much in the USA and Japan, and how the unemployment rates in almost all these countries of that age group are a major component of, and highly correlated with, total unemployment.

One of the conclusions of their study is that the participation of those in this age group (55–64) is more wage elastic than for the young, a factor causing the Phillips curve to become more horizontal, an issue taken up again in Chapter 8. On the other hand, there is a hint in Diagram 3.7 below that it may become much more difficult to raise such participation rates much above 65%, than it was to go from 40% to 65%. If so, then any further increases in participation must come from those aged over 65. In Diagram 3.7, we show participation rates for those aged 55 to 64, and over 65 for the USA, UK, Germany, France and Japan.

There is also a question about what kind of work the elderly could do, or want to do, (see Maestas and Jetsupphasuk 2019). While they can hardly expect to do some manual jobs (and most sports), nevertheless the average age of farmers in the UK is over 65, and farming requires more manual effort than most jobs. In Diagram 3.8, we plot the proportion of those over 65 still working against the generosity of the State pensions, as a percentage of final salary. For a discussion of the participation of seniors in the US workforce, see Button (2019).

It is both clear from this diagram, and natural, that the participation rate of the old will be a negative function of the generosity of pension benefits. Thus, some proportion of the likely cutback in growth can be clawed back by raising the retirement age and by reducing the ratio of pension to normal working wage. But effective retirement ages have only just recently begun to rise, and still grudgingly, usually by less than the rise in life expectancy, see Diagram 3.9.

In any case, how much could, and should, this route be followed? It used to be treated as almost axiomatic that the older one became, the less productive one would become. Indeed, many have explained part of the slower recent

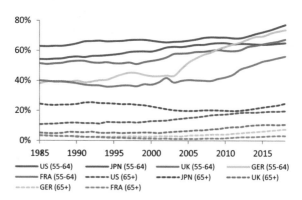

Diagram 3.7 Participation rate (% of population) has already risen sharply in the 55–64 year cohort in the AEs

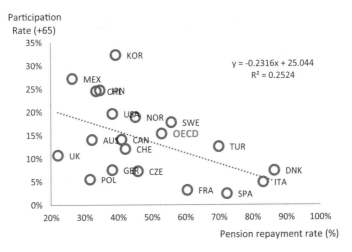

Diagram 3.8   Pension repayment rate and the participation rate are inversely correlated

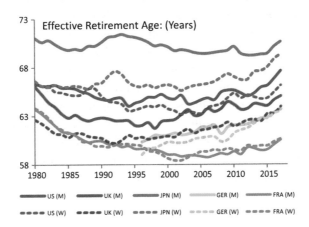

Diagram 3.9   Effective retirement age (years) has risen by less than life expectancy

slowing of productivity gains as due to the ageing of the 'baby-boom' cohort. But as discussed in greater length in Chapter 10, this view is being reconsidered. Even if productivity does not, in fact, suffer from higher participation of the elderly, there could be a problem over promotion. If we pressurise the old to continue in work, will it cause blockages for the young? Next, a comfortable retirement is perceived as part of inter-generational equity and fairness. Finally, the old have typically had a much higher propensity to vote than the young. It is politically risky to seek to remove benefits from the old that they had perceived as their just reward. Even Putin, whose command over the political system in Russia has been formidable, was forced to backtrack on his plans to make pension arrangements less favourable (BBC News, August 29, 2018). Also, see Börsch-Supan et al. (2014) for the backlash against labour market reforms targeting higher participation rates among the elderly. And note the difficulties that Macron faced in reforming French retirement and pension arrangements in France in late 2019.

There are plans to raise the official retirement age in many countries. In some cases, this is long overdue, especially in some cases for public servants, e.g. in Brazil. But considerations of the combination of (possibly) declining productivity with rising political hostility for pressurising the over 65s (soon the over 70s) back into regular paid employment make us doubt whether the increasing participation of the old can serve to offset more than a small proportion of the effect of a declining rate of growth of the regular workforce.

So, if we are to maintain, let alone to increase, growth rates from present, somewhat disappointing, trends, what would be needed would be a significant increase in the rates of growth of productivity per worker. Meanwhile, the pre-pandemic combination of sluggish output growth and strong labour markets means that the trends in the growth of productivity per worker have been dismal. In order to maintain overall growth rates, there needs to be a strong recovery in the rates of growth of output per worker.

This may seem daunting, but there are several glimmers of hope. First, as shown in Table 3.4, the rate of growth of productivity per worker in Japan, where the workforce has already been declining for a decade, has been better in recent years than in most other advanced countries. The harder it becomes to find and hire qualified workers, the more employers will be forced to raise the productivity of those that they can attract and maintain in order to remain competitive; we revert to this point in Chapter 5.

Table 3.4 Percentage change in gross domestic product per hour worked

	USA (%)	Germany (%)	UK (%)	France (%)	Japan (%)
2010	2.8	2.5	2.2	1.3	3.3
2011	0.2	2.1	0.3	0.9	0.2
2012	0.3	0.6	−0.5	0.2	0.9
2013	0.4	0.8	0.3	1.4	2.1
2014	0.4	1.0	0.2	1.0	0.1
2015	0.8	0.6	1.7	0.8	1.5
2016	0.3	1.4	−0.6	0.1	0.3
2017	1.0	0.9	0.8	1.0	0.9
% change since 2010	*6.2*	*10.3*	*4.3*	*6.7*	*9.6*

Source OECD

Next, some of the sluggish growth of productivity per worker in the last few decades may be due to a combination of technology, shifting jobs from semi-skilled to unskilled, as discussed subsequently in Chapter 7 on 'Inequality and the Rise of Populism', and, perhaps, the growing participation of older workers. Such trends in technology may, or may not, persist, and it may become increasingly hard to raise participation rates among the elderly without running into greater social and political problems. Finally, an ageing population tends to consume services, such as care and medicine, where productivity increases are harder to obtain than in manufacturing, see Cravino et al. (2019).

Thus, our reasonably confident expectation is that output growth, ex India and Africa, will slow markedly over coming decades, perhaps to about 1% p.a. In this respect, Japan is the trailblazer. Japan's growth has averaged 0.87% since 1999. Other advanced countries will do well if they can match this record over the next twenty years until 2040.

4

Dependency, Dementia and the Coming Crisis of Caring

4.1 Introduction

The implications of worsening future dependency ratios, as outlined in the previous chapter, become even more severe when the effects of ageing on health are considered. Increasing life expectancy implies that a growing proportion of this ageing population will become incapacitated with dementia and other causes of dependency, such as Parkinson's and arthritis, often with multimorbidity,[1] and will need care. Care involves personal and emotional support. Robots cannot provide this, though they may be of some support in physical and monitoring activities. As a result, an increasing portion of the labour force, from within the family or not, will be redirected to looking after the elderly. The introduction of Biogen's Aducanumab and, perhaps, China's Oligomannate, has given specialists in the field some reason for cautious optimism, but it is clear that detection, diagnosis, cure and policy are all lagging far behind the medical successes of other fields, e.g. hip replacements, cataract operations, etc. Note that in the health literature, dependency is defined as being in need of outside care and assistance, whereas in the macroeconomic literature dependency just relates to certain specific age groups, irrespective of their physical condition.

---

[1]Thus Kingston et al. (2018a, p. 3) note that, 'Over half (54.0%) of the population aged 65+ in 2015 have two or more diseases. As expected, multi-morbidity increases with age: in 2015, from 45.7% for those aged 65–74 to 68.7% for those aged 85+; and over time: to 64.4% in 2025 and 67.8% in 2035, for those aged 65+'.

© The Author(s) 2020
C. Goodhart and M. Pradhan, *The Great Demographic Reversal,*
https://doi.org/10.1007/978-3-030-42657-6_4

Table 4.1 Percentage of medical dependents in the aged population: UK, 2015

		Total population	Dependents	Percentage
Young–Old	65–75	5276	1621	30
Old	75–85	3130	1539	49
Old–Old	85+	1318	1023	78

In the three sections of this chapter, we discuss the forthcoming troubling forecasts for the incidence of dependency and dementia; in Sect. 4.3 its estimated costs and in Sect. 4.4 some macroeconomic consequences.

4.2   Ageing Is Hazardous

The onset of dementia, of which Alzheimer's is the most common and best-known type, makes its sufferers increasingly incapable of carrying out the normal activities of daily life (ADL) and therefore in need of care and assistance. The prevalence of dementia increases exponentially with age. One would be extremely unlucky to get dementia before reaching the age of 65, but the risk score of dementia for those over 85 is four times higher than those aged 75 or those showing ApoE4 positivity, the next two highest scoring risk factors (Kivipelto et al. 2006; Norton et al. 2014). Dementia is one of the several causes of dependency, alongside, for example, arthritis and Parkinson's, which also increase with age. In the paper by Kingston et al. (2018b), the prevalence of dependency, represented by the proportion of those with low, medium and high dependency, relative to their total population, i.e. plus the independents, was as follows (Table 4.1).[2]

Our societies today are still relatively young, compared to what is to come, and are well aware of cancer and heart disease. In such cases, mortality often occurs relatively early, even very rapidly. There are few patients with either disease that suffer at a high level of intensity for many years, even decades—but that is exactly what dementia often does to patients and carers. Most of us are, and society certainly is, unaware of what an ageing future holds. Perhaps that's why there is too much optimism and too little caution about the persistent increases in life expectancy, absent a medical miracle in the treatment of dementia (and Parkinson's).

In the World Alzheimer Report (Patterson 2018, p. 41), there is the following quote,

---

[2]Of course, the dividing line between those with mild cognitive impairment, e.g. forgetting names, and with low dependency is fuzzy, but the Population Ageing and Care Simulation model (PACSim) for the UK, from which these data were taken, is state of the art.

"A third of babies born now in Japan," Kenji Toba told me, "will live to 100 years. The risk of dementia in a centenarian in Japan is 99%. Everyone has to understand 'it's my story'. Not your story. 'Cognitive decline is my story.'"

Getting to the 100-year life, (Gratton and Scott 2016; Scott 2019), is not such a good outcome if it just means more years of dementia.

The World Health Organization (WHO) would argue that the 99% forecast is not a certainty—that at least some cases of dementia are preventable. Its latest campaign identifies lifestyle factors that reduce the risk of dementia. That campaign faces an uphill battle, given low public awareness and hence the limited political desire to tackle the problems caused by dementia. The World Alzheimer Report's (2019) survey of around 70,000 people across 155 countries suggests that: (i) 1 in 4 people think there is nothing that can be done to prevent dementia, (ii) 2 in 3 people think that dementia is a normal part of the ageing process and (iii) more worrying, 62% of physicians think the same. Thus, even if there are significant benefits to pursue the WHO's recommendations, the willingness to pursue them aggressively must be lower, given the conviction against them being successful. In the case of cancer, early detection remains the best bet for survival. In the case of dementia, much work is being done on bio-markers to identify this chronic illness early on, but success has been elusive thus far. Even if early detection is successful, the prospects for slowing the disease are still uncertain at best, and an outright cure is nowhere in sight.

The one gleam of cheer in the data is that the age-specific prevalence of dementia has been going down in USA, UK, Sweden and the Netherlands, and is forecast to continue doing so. China and Japan, however, have seen the opposite, an increase (Livingston et al., The Lancet Commission (2017). In the UK case, this decline is, however, almost entirely focussed on men in the 65–75 age range, see Kingston, et al. (op cit, p. e450). This is very likely due to the fact that the proportion of men giving up smoking has been higher than that of women.[3] Apart from that, prevalence remains much the same, except that high dependency is expected to increase far faster than medium dependency. Table 4.2, from Kingston et al. (2018b), gives definitions.

While it may be possible to care for dementia sufferers at home for those with medium dependency, or less, it would be difficult to do so for high dependency. The numbers, again from Kingston et al. (op. cit., Table 4.2), are projected to be as follows in 2035 for the UK, including percentage change from 2015 (Table 4.3).

---

[3] Also obesity is more common in women.

Table 4.2 Interval-of-need dependency categorisation

	CFAS II	ELSA
High dependency	MMSE score 0–9 or needs help using the toilet, or transferring from chair or bed, or incontinent and needs help putting on shoes and socks, or needs help to feed (from proxy interview) or is often incontinent and needs help to dress (from proxy interview)	Needs help using the toilet or chairfast or bedfast or has problems with continence and needs help putting on shoes and socks
Medium dependency	Needs help every, or most days, to put on shoes and socks, or cook a hot meal, or unable to dress without help (from proxy interview)	Needs help putting on shoes and socks, or to prepare a hot meal
Low dependency	Needs help to wash all over or bathe, or cut toenails, or considerable difficulty with household tasks (from proxy interview)	Needs help with bathing or showering, or difficulty pulling or pushing large objects, or difficulty doing work around house and garden
Independent	Not otherwise classified above and no missing items from other categories	Not otherwise classified above and no missing items from other categories

CFAS—Cognitive Function and Ageing Study; ELSA—English Longitudinal Study of Ageing; MMSE—Mini-Mental State Examination
Source Kingston et al. (2018)

Table 4.3 Dependency in UK expected in 2035, and change from 2015

(000s)								
	Total population		Dependency					
		%Δ	Low	%Δ	Medium	%Δ	High	%Δ
65–75	6908	+31	967	−15	98	−49	241	−15
75–84	2778	+51	1400	+29	171	+5.7	378	+42
85+	2815	+114	1537	+148	293	+73	446	+92

The number with high dependency is projected to go up from 783 to 1065, an increase of 36%. As noted earlier, the burden of dementia has risen primarily because of the increase in life expectancy, not because of an increase in prevalence. It is not just occurring in the high-income countries. The biggest increases in dementia are occurring in low- and middle-income countries (LMICs), see the World Alzheimer Report (WAR) (2018), Foreword.

In this report, the estimate for the number of people living with dementia rises from 50 million in 2015, to 82 million in 2030, to 152 million in 2050 (ibid., p. 34), tripling over these 35 years.

But there is no cure in sight, yet. As the WAR (2018, p. 7) notes,

> Since 1998, 100 drugs have been tested and only four have been authorized for use. And these are not magic pills. They can help manage some of the symptoms of dementia, for some people, but only for some people, and most people in the world don't get near them. But anyone who knows anything about the disease knows that there is not going to be a magic pill.

It was under strange circumstances, in October 2019, a new drug, Aducanumab, appeared which had failed its initial test, but on further review was thought to have some promise in slowing down the onset of Alzheimer's for a subset of sufferers. That this has been hailed by the British press as a major advance is either a sign of desperation or a highly premature celebration at best.

While we can hope for medical breakthroughs, it would be unwise to plan on the basis that they will be forthcoming. Meanwhile, the gap between the relative success in curing/replacing, even rejuvenating other parts of the body (below the brain), and the relative failure in mending brain damage becomes even wider. Yet there has been *far less* research and funding for neurodegenerative disorders than for cancer alone. Again, as stated in the Foreword to the WAR (2018, p. 4),

> Overall the report aims to clarify whether our call for increased research expenditure in dementia is still relevant and how much so. And indeed it is: compared with the number of people developing dementia – one every 3 seconds – the amounts devoted to research are tiny. For a start there isn't enough original research. The global ratio of publications on neurodegenerative disorders versus cancer is an astonishing 1:12. At the same time, not enough people are getting into research on dementia. While there are many reasons for this, it is not surprising, given that it has been 40 years since any significant breakthrough.

A recent *Financial Times* report on Alzheimer's, June 25, 2019, included the attached chart (Diagram 4.1).

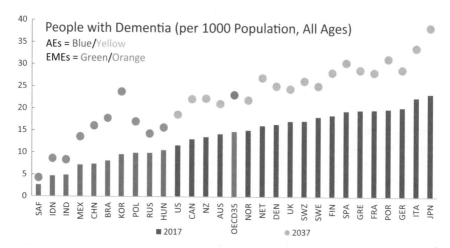

Diagram 4.1 As people live longer, the burden of dementia is bound to increase (*Source* OECD Health Statistics 2017)

4.3 The Costs of Dementia

The most widely quoted cost of dementia, from Prince et al. (2015), is that it will have amounted, as of 2018, to somewhere around $1 trillion. The World Dementia Council ("Defeating Dementia: The Road to 2025", December 2012) believes this cost is set to double to $2 trillion by 2030.

Many of the costs of dementia are hidden, in the sense that they do not enter into the calculation of GDP, representing neither measurable output, income nor expenditure. But they are real nevertheless. There are three types of costs associated with dementia: first, the cost to the patients themselves, second, the cost of the carers of patients and third, the cost of R&D 'including sunk costs' and successful and (thus far almost entirely) unsuccessful trials, the sum of which has been extremely low, compared to those for cancer treatment and compared to the gigantic cost of the problem.

The main costs, of course, fall on those suffering from dementia, in the explicit medical cost and in the guise of reduced quality of life. We are not aware of any attempt to measure the cost of the reduced quality of life explicitly, for example, in order to undertake a cost/benefit exercise on proposals to deploy greater resources towards research or care for dementia. For a brief discussion on 'measuring the economic value of healthy ageing', see Egglestone (2019). But it could, and probably should, be done, e.g. by survey methods; an example is given in the footnote below.[4]

---

[4]Approach a sample of adults. Explain how the probability of dementia rises with age. Then ask what proportion of their annual income (from now until retirement) they would be prepared to

The second heaviest burden falls on carers. When carers are not professionals, they are typically family members (occasionally friends), usually partners or children, who act as unpaid carers of those with dementia, at least until the dementia, and/or co-morbidity, becomes so extreme that the demented have to go for specialist treatment in a hospital, or care home. The Lancet Commissions on 'Dementia prevention, intervention, and care' (2017, p. 2710) argues that families prefer to have people with dementia living at home in order to protect the quality of life of the patient, even though it takes its toll on carers. Family carers of people with dementia tend to suffer from depression or anxiety, worse physical health and negative effects on their work-life.

In the UK, the way that such dementia costs are handled is, in our view, unacceptable.

Damian Green notes (June 2019),

> The [medical] system should also not discriminate between different conditions. Some long-term conditions, such as cancer, are treated medically by the NHS; treatment is therefore free at the point of use. Other conditions, such as dementia, are largely dealt with through the social care system, and can therefore end up costing individuals significant sums of money. A new social care system must end this "dementia lottery".

The dementia lottery can be even more difficult when mixed with changing social structures. Kingston et al. (2017, p. 1681) note that family fragmentation (divorces, more geographical dispersion within families, increases in female labour participation) makes it difficult for care to be provided at home. That may leave those deemed to have 'low dependency' significantly worse off. In England, the authors note, authorities have made eligibility criteria much harder for publicly funded care, which means those with low dependency are unlikely to qualify, leaving them without public funding or the attention of their stretched family unit.

Prince et al. (2015) pull together these direct (private and public) and indirect costs of dementia to estimate that it will have amounted, as of 2018, to somewhere around $1 trillion, 'around 1% of the aggregated world Gross Domestic Product' (ibid., Chapter 6.1, p. 56),

---

pay to reduce the probability of becoming subject to dementia by 10% throughout, e.g. from, say, 40% at age 82 to 30% at that age, assuming that could be done with certainty. The results of this hypothetical test would be subjective and indicative only, but better than nothing. Also on this, see Kydland and Pretnar (2018, 2019).

Apart from informal care, where the costs are large, but quantification extremely difficult and uncertain, the conclusion in our view is that the total expenditures are remarkably small, especially in LMICs, given the scale of the concern.

Thus, in the 2015 Estimate of Dementia Costs from Prince et al., World Alzheimer Report, 2015, Chapter 6, pp. 56–67, it was stated that:

> The per capita costs are divided into three cost sub-categories: direct medical costs, direct social care costs (paid and professional home care, and residential and nursing home care) and costs of informal care.

These costs are divided up as show below in (Tables 4.4 and 4.5):-

Such costs also vary greatly between countries, as the FT report (ibid.) showed in diagram 4.2:-

Table 4.4   Costs of dementia

Countries	Numbers with dementia (mn)	US$ bn	$ Per head
G7	12.9	508.7	3943
Rest of G20	24.6	245.5	998
Rest of world	9.3	63.6	683
World	46.8	817.9	

And it is made up of the following components (from Table 6.6, p. 60)

Table 4.5   Sub-category costs of dementia in 2010 and 2015 by country income level

	Direct medical costs		Direct social sector costs		Informal care costs	
	US$ (billions)	Per cent	US$ (billions)	Per cent	US$ (billions)	Per cent
2015 (WAR 2015)						
Low income	0.2	20.4	0.1	10.4	0.8	69.2
Lower middle income	3.7	23.9	2.0	13.2	9.6	62.9
Upper middle income	19.3	22.	17.7	20.5	49.3	57.1
High income	136.0	19.0	308.1	43.1	271.1	37.9
Total	**159.2**	**19.5**	**327.9**	**40.1**	**330.8**	**40.4**

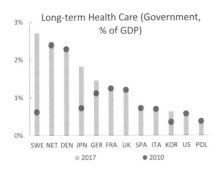
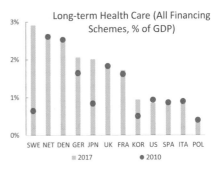

Diagram 4.2 Public spending on long-term care varies among rich nations (*Source* OECD)

The consequence is that, 'Dementia is currently under-detected, under-diagnosed, under-disclosed, under-treated and under-managed in primary care' (WAR 2016, Executive Survey, first page). The major studies of dementia that we have consulted, e.g. The Lancet Commission, 'The World Alzheimer Reports', are replete with examples of insufficiency.[5]

In the World Alzheimer Report (2016) on 'Improving healthcare for people living with Dementia', the authors tried to model the 'Cost implications of the dementia healthcare pathways' (Chapter 7, pp. 110–121). The pathways were constructed specifically to measure healthcare services consumed by those diagnosed with dementia.

The resultant estimated costs were tiny, relative to GDP, or as a percentage of total health expenditures (see, ibid., Table 7.4), ranging from a maximum of 0.04% of GDP and 0.5% of total health expenditure in South Korea, to a minimum of 0.0003% (GDP) and 0.01% (total health expenditure) in Mexico. The point of this example is to illustrate how little is being done, or is under consideration on this front, relative to the scale of perceived needs.

A question then is, why? Why have more resources (public or private) not been allocated towards preventing, arresting or reversing dementia?

---

[5]For example, on diagnosis, The Lancet Commissions, (2017, p. 2690), states,

> A timely diagnosis, meaning communicating a diagnosis at a time when the person with dementia and their carers will benefit from interventions and support, is a prerequisite for good dementia care. Many people with dementia are never given the diagnosis, only 20–50% of those with dementia have a diagnosis recorded in primary care notes, and this number is lower in lower-income countries than high-income countries. Many receive a diagnosis when it is too late for them to make decisions about their own and their family's future or to benefit from interventions.

The third category of costs, the R&D costs of dementia treatments, has been very low by all measures thus far.

The main reason is that, until recently, nothing has worked well, neither drugs nor simple support measures. There is more cautious optimism among specialists in the field because of the launch of Biogen's Aducanumab and (to a lesser extent) China's Oligomannate (also known as GV-971). Leaving aside the results that the use of these drugs will generate, the initial rejection and subsequent revival of Aducanumab have raised questions about its efficacy, while the opaqueness around the process of approval in China is a cause for concern for many. This is the only bit of success that the medical fight against dementia has had to date, and its cautious reception is both welcome and necessary. Part of the optimism is also that it might invite more financial and research participation.

Both drugs hope to slow down the onset of dementia, but the bio-markers that can identify the condition have not seen successful trials yet and there is no optimism yet about progress towards a reversal of the dementia.

The second reason is the lack of official support. As the prior discussion suggests, very little of the dementia-related treatment is supported by public spending. In turn, that implies a lack of steady financial flows from the public sector to private firms. Some changes can be seen in the system, too small relative to the problem at hand, and at a glacial pace. And, as with every other issue we highlight here, there is great variety among countries when it comes to official support.

In the USA, dementia is being considered a chronic disease equivalent to diabetes and hypertension. HCC51/52 risk adjustments will allow increased Medicare payments to dementia patients. As a result of this change, the Global Alzheimer's Platform estimates that 'approximately $2 billion will flow into the system in 2020 to detect, diagnose and treat dementia under these codes' (Dwyer 2019). That is double the estimated $1 billion of venture capital investment that US companies have seen in the last decade. But this is still but a pale shadow of the $16.5 billion of venture investment into cancer-related drugs over the last 10 years (Vradenburg 2019).

The changes in the recognition and the treatment of dementia are happening far too slowly to make a dent in the challenge that is increasing every day.

4.4   Implications for the Macro-Economy

While the failure to respond adequately to the growing needs of the elderly is a tragedy for those afflicted and their family carers, and a social scandal, we can still ask what are the quantifiable macroeconomic implications. The need for extra health expenditures is one such,[6] but this is discussed further in Chapters 11 and 13. Here, we focus, instead, on three issues: first, the redirection of an increasing portion of the labour force towards caring for an ageing population, and particularly for those suffering from dementia, Sect. 4.4.1; second, where is the supply of employed carers, e.g. in care homes and those supporting the aged, and their unpaid family carers, at home going to come from, Sect. 4.4.2; and, third, what is the combination of the deferred age of marriage/child rearing together with the increase of old-age dependency going to do to the personal life cycle, Sect. 4.4.3?

4.4.1   The Growing Redirection of the Labour Force into Health Care

The basic problem is that ageing is going to require increasing amounts of labour to be redirected towards elderly care at exactly the time that the labour force starts shrinking. There are two dynamics to consider here.

First, a portion of the labour force looking after the elderly will produce services for immediate use rather than durable consumption. These services, as we have argued earlier in the chapter, are unlikely to be replaced by automation. That means the rest of the labour force has to raise its productivity in order to generate a greater amount of future output. As we argue in Chapter 3, we need all the automation that we can get in the rest of the economy in order to raise productivity adequately, partly needed to compensate for that which will be lost to caring for the ageing population.

Second, these idiosyncratic services cannot be offshored the way the lowest value-added activities in manufacturing were offshored. The process of globalising the manufacturing supply chain has itself achieved most of its gains, which means there will be fewer tailwinds from globalisation just as ageing problems mount globally.

---

[6]In his paper on 'Fixing the Care Crisis', Damian Green (ibid) would introduce a tax-funded new Universal Care Entitlement, 'which guarantees everyone a decent standard of care', to be supplemented by a privately purchasable 'Care Supplement'. Also see Kydland and Pretnar (2018, 2019).

4.4.2 The Supply of Carers

As the ranks of the old grow, there will be a growing need for the relevant professionals, geriatricians, neurologists and psychiatrists. Subject to fiscal constraints and other competing resource requirements, there should be no barrier, *in principle*, to meeting such needs in high-income countries (HIC). But it will be more difficult to do so in LMIC, (i.e., low and middle-income countries) and coverage, in practice, remains insufficient in HIC.[7] Similarly, as the number and needs of the old expand, primary care providers, GPs and senior nurses in surgeries will become more aware and better trained in both diagnosis and potential treatment, again more so in HIC than in LMIC.

Whereas the available supply of qualified professionals in this field is and will remain higher in HIC than in LMIC, the reverse is likely to be, and to remain, the case for basic employed carers, i.e. excluding unpaid family (and friend) carers. The job of providing assistance for the activities of daily living (ADLs) that those with dementia can no longer do for themselves, e.g. dressing, bathing, going to the toilet,[8] walking, reading, etc., is neither glamorous, fulfilling (as teaching can be), nor well paid. Yet the job involves several key qualities, empathy, patience, kindness and communication.

As Camilla Cavendish wrote, *Extra Time* (2019, p. 97),

"One job where EQ [Emotional Quotient] is already paramount, or should be, is caring.[9] The demand for carers will increase sharply as populations age, and the skills most needed will be the ones that... robots cannot provide: emotional resilience, intuition and empathy. Yet people who do caring jobs are often looked down on, or described as 'unskilled', because they have talents which are not 'academic'.

I saw this for myself when I travelled around England in 2013, interviewing junior nurses and care workers for an independent review I was commissioned to carry out by the Department of Health. I met hundreds of these wonderful staff, working in hospitals or helping care for people at home, and was struck

---

[7]World Alzheimer Report (2016, p. 6),

Dementia specialist care is underdeveloped in LMIC. There are very few geriatricians, neurologists and psychiatrists, and few hospital or community-based services dedicated to diagnosis and continuing care. Coverage of continuing care services remains low in HIC, in part because of low diagnostic coverage, but also because specialist services struggle to provide continuous and responsive care to rapidly increasing numbers of people with dementia.

[8]In Japan apparently more old people's nappies are sold than for babies.

[9]Robots have an EQ of zero. While robots can play a limited role, see the Lex Column in the *Financial Times*, Monday, June 10 2019, p. 22, 'Robots/ageing Japan: I, carebot', the emphasis should be placed on the limitations of that role.

by the extraordinary maturity and resilience that is needed to walk into the home of an elderly stranger, establish a relationship and help them take a shower. I was surprised and upset by the patronising attitudes that some senior nurses and doctors had to the junior healthcare assistants in hospitals who were 'only' making tea, lifting patients out of bed or helping them eat. Yet these are the people who spend most time at the bedside, who are most likely to notice when something is wrong and can make all the difference to whether a patient feels secure or afraid."

In that earlier Review, *The Cavendish Review* (July 2013), Executive Summary, p. 7, she wrote,

"The phrase "basic care" dramatically understates the work of this group. Helping an elderly person to eat and swallow, bathing someone with dignity and without hurting them, communicating with someone with early onset dementia; doing these things with intelligent kindness, dignity, care and respect requires skill. Doing so alone in the home of a stranger, when the district nurse has left no notes, and you are only being paid to be there for 30 minutes, requires considerable maturity and resilience.

Like healthcare assistants, social care support workers are increasingly taking on more challenging tasks, having to look after more frail elderly people. Yet their training is hugely variable. Some employers are not meeting their basic duty to ensure their staff are competent. I have talked to staff who were given a DVD to watch at home before being sent straight out to the frontline. I have talked to others who were asked to pay for mandatory training out of their own pocket. This is why the Review proposes minimum standards of competence before staff can work unsupervised, in the form of the "Certificate of Fundamental Care" – and a code of conduct for employers (Recommendations 3, 15)."

From where are we going to get the paragons prepared to do a difficult job requiring high EQ that is poorly paid and regarded as unskilled and of low prestige? The continuing and growing need for carers in this field shows up the emptiness of the job guarantee programs that have been suggested in some quarters. There are continuing vacancies for carers,[10] but young uneducated males, for example, might neither want to do such work nor again be suited

---

[10]In the *Financial Times* (Lex, Monday, June 10 2019, p. 22), it was stated that

Japan has the most rapidly ageing population in the world. Low birth rates have continued for three decades. Almost a third of the population is over 65. To help look after them, Japan needs to increase the number of care workers almost sevenfold over the next decade from the current 1.5 m. Paid carers would constitute more than a 10th of the workforce.

to it. The Cavendish Review (op. cit.) has an excellent Chapter 6 on recruitment and training, but does not tackle the question of where the supply of appropriate trainees could come from.

Our view is that there will remain a chronic shortage of suitable candidates in the UK and probably in most other HIC. On this, also see the presentation by Mayda at the ECB Forum on Central Banking, at Sintra, Portugal, June 2019. The most feasible solution would, we think, be targeted immigration. There should be a visa category, giving preference to women over men, and to the mature over the young, where the entrant commits to working as a carer for, say, two years (and can stay in the UK only after successfully fulfilling his/her commitment) and in return is given preliminary training (including, if necessary, language training), and assisted housing initially (deported if failing to become certified) for free, and allowed to change jobs and stay in the UK after completing the required time period. In the FT Lex report on 'ageing Japan', it was stated that, 'Government moves to fill vacancies with foreign workers have not always succeeded. Cultural and language barriers are high. Immigration is controversial politically'.

4.4.3 The Changing Life Cycle

Besides the increase in life expectancy, and hence in the incidence of dementia, there has been another demographic shift, whose macroeconomic implications have also been insufficiently considered; this is the rise in the age of marriage and of the age when a woman has her first baby (Diagrams 4.3 and 4.4).

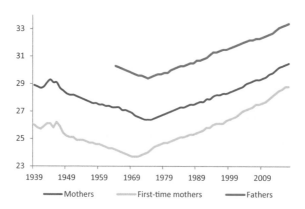

Diagram 4.3 UK: Average age of parents at the birth of their child (*Source* Office for National Statistics)

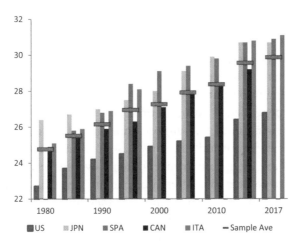

Diagram 4.4 Mean Age of Women at the Birth of their First Child (Age) (*Source* OECD)

Combining these two trends together means that the life cycle is now distinctly different from that, say, 40 or 50 years ago. In a simplified time line back then, we could divide life up into some four stages (Table 4.6):-

Because the prevalence of dementia increases exponentially with age, and social care is limited, children, now of age 50–67, will be more likely to be stuck with having to cope with dependent (and demented) parents than would have been the case some 40/50 years ago. Think of the one child policy

Table 4.6 The changing life cycle

Traditional life-cycle used to be				
0–20	20–40	40–60		60–70+
Young	Married (Work) with dependent children	Working No dependents		Retired
Nowadays the life cycle has five segments:				
0–20	20–30	30–50	50–67	67–80+
Young	Single (Working)	Married (Work) with dependent children	Working with dependent parents	Retired, often dependent

in China,[11] with one grandchild to four grandparents, two of whom could easily contract dementia at some stage!

In the old days, people were mostly free of dependency cares from around 40 until retirement, when their earnings were highest and the prospect of retirement coming into sight. That encouraged saving. Nowadays people will be most free of dependency caring in their 20s, when earnings are lower and the prospect of living until 90+ almost unimaginable. Not a good time for saving. Then from 30 onwards, in some cases continuously, until your own retirement, looking after your own children[12] would be followed in short order by the need to help look after your parents. See Bauer and Sousa-Poza (2015, 2019). Looking after dependents, whether children or elderly parents, takes time, effort and money. Given a combination of immediate emotional ties and time discount, we tend to believe that support for dependents will take precedence over saving for an uncertain future.

In other words, we see the changing life cycle as a force likely to reduce the personal sector savings ratio and to throw a yet higher fiscal burden on the public sector to provide acceptable standards of living and health care for the elderly.

---

[11]In the *Financial Times* report on 'Foreign operators take on Chinese elderly care', July 16 2019, p. 14, it was stated that

> About 90 per cent of Chinese seniors rely mainly on family support, 7 per cent on residential community-based care services and 3 per cent on nursing homes, according to the Qianzhan Industry Research Institute, a consultancy.

[12]The number of such child dependents per family has been falling, which reduces the time span of having dependent children by a few years. But offsetting this, the increase in take-up of higher education means that each child will probably stay at home with his/her parents for longer.

5

The Resurgence of Inflation

Inflation is the outcome of several interacting forces. These include underlying structural trends, demography and globalisation, and the macroeconomic balance between savings and investment, as well as purely monetary phenomena. Intuitively, the balance between workers, who normally produce more than they consume, and dependents (old and young), who do the opposite, matters. A more complex argument depends on how different sectors of the economy (households, corporates and the government) change their savings and investment behaviour in response to ageing.

If we are right in our political economy assumption that the social safety net will remain in place, then the age profile of consumption will continue to be flat or even upward sloping. The elderly will depend on (and vote for) government support and continue to save too little for the longer life they have inherited. The ineluctable conclusion is that tax rates on workers will have to rise markedly in order to generate transfers from workers to the elderly.

Workers, however, would not be helpless bystanders. Labour scarcity in AEs (and some EMEs) will put them in a stronger bargaining position, reversing decades of stagnation in AEs. They will use that position to bargain for higher wages. This is a recipe for recrudescence of inflationary pressures.

The world is still not ready to think about the inflation that is likely to rise structurally. Central banks will, soon enough, have to revert to their normal behaviour. The zero lower bound (ZLB) is largely the consequence of a combination of a China effect, an unprecedented demographic backdrop and the deepest cyclical shocks since the Great Depression, once during the financial crisis and more recently during the pandemic.

© The Author(s) 2020
C. Goodhart and M. Pradhan, *The Great Demographic Reversal*,
https://doi.org/10.1007/978-3-030-42657-6_5

The re-birth of inflation is our highest conviction view among the effects of demographics, and it is one that both financial markets and policy-makers are dismissing at their own peril. But what is the logic behind this deeply counter-conventional inference?

5.1   Inflation as the Product of the Outcome Between Savings and Spending

The renewal of upwards pressures on inflation stems from three interacting and interlocking viewpoints:

- An intuitive balance based on the dependency ratio;
- An exercise based on labour market demand and supply, otherwise known as the Phillips curve; and
- A consideration of the relative balance of savings and investment in the (non-financial) private sector, and the effects of this on the public sector, and its policies.

5.1.1   Inflation from Dependents Versus Deflation from Workers

In order to make hiring workers profitable, employers must plan to pay them less than the expected value of their production. Unless workers dissave from their past accumulated wealth, workers' compensation is necessarily less than their production. This is a deflationary impulse. Dependents who do not work, on the other hand, consume and do not produce. Dependents are inflationary.

Almost by definition, an improvement in the overall participation rate is deflationary, as workers outstrip those who do not work. As the dependency ratio falls, the disinflation from more workers overwhelms the inflationary impact of dependents. By the same token, a rise in the dependency ratio will be inflationary (too many mouths chasing too little food). Normally inflation is treated as a monetary phenomenon. Given the expansionary monetary policies in recent decades, trying to explain current disinflationary pressures in this way would be a struggle.[1]

---

[1] For an account of the relative weight of demographics and monetary factors in the earlier European inflation between 1500 and 1700, see Melitz and Edo (2019).

Of course, there is also the return to capital, profits. But again, relatively more workers will tend to raise profits. As consumption out of profits is less than consumption out of wages, see, e.g. Kalecki (1954), an improvement in participation rates is deflationary.

Ageing is inflationary empirically, too. Juselius and Takats (2016) uncover an empirical relationship—'a puzzling link between low-frequency inflation and population-age structure: the young and old (dependents) are inflationary whereas the working age population is disinflationary'. They use data from 22 countries between 1955 and 2014, breaking up that time period so they are not biased by periods of high or low inflation. Their analysis shows that 6.5% of the disinflation in the USA from 1975 to 2014 can be accounted for by age structure. The age structure, they argue, 'is forecastable and will increase inflationary pressures over the coming decades'.

The intuition behind this result is simple. An increase in consumption by itself creates an inflationary impulse for a given basket of goods and services. The act of production has the ability to expand the stock of goods and services for a given level of consumption and is therefore disinflationary. Dependents (the young and the old) are purely consumers and hence generate an inflationary impulse, whereas workers can offset this inflationary impulse through production. If the growth rate of workers in the economy outweighs that of dependents (as was the case during the demographic sweet spot), the world will go through a period of disinflation as it has for the last few decades. Over the next few decades, the rate of growth of dependents will outstrip that of workers. In levels terms, the level of workers will still be greater than that of dependents over the foreseeable future, but it is the rate of growth that is changing throughout, and that matters here.

5.1.2 The Phillips Curve and the Impending Rise of the NRU

Wage growth has shown a surprising tendency to remain low despite a sharp reduction in unemployment, which we discuss at much greater length in Chapter 8. Suffice it to state here that we believe that this has largely derived from a falling Natural Rate of Unemployment (NRU). The decline in the NRU resulted from the progressively weaker bargaining power of labour, combined with a shift of jobs towards the unskilled, who are both less productive and paid less.

These forces have combined to make the Phillips curve, relating wage (and price) growth to unemployment, seem more horizontal. But there is a limit to such trends. We have already suggested that it is likely to become increasingly difficult to raise participation rates among those retiring soon much further, since the participation among the 55–64 aged cohort of the population has already seen a substantial pickup. The combined effect of a cutback in globalisation, opposition to immigration, and the decline of new young entrants into the workforce, will lead to a shrinking of the labour force in demographically challenged countries. As this happens, the bargaining power of labour in such countries will rise again. The continuing downwards shifts both in the NRU and in the size and power of private sector trade unions will first stabilise and then start to reverse.

The NRU will once again start to rise invisibly behind the scenes. As usual, this will catch the authorities unawares. From the 1950s to 1970s, politicians and officialdom failed to appreciate that the NRU (or U*) was steadily rising, ushering in decades of rising inflationary pressures. From the late 1980s until very recently, they similarly failed to appreciate the reverse trends, leading to decades of deflationary pressure. We think it more than likely that, once again, the authorities will fail to see the underlying (demographic) trends and will attempt to keep growth up above, and unemployment below, its sustainable rate in coming decades.

5.2   Sectoral Balances: Private Sector Surplus Set to Erode, Can the Government Reduce Its Deficit?

If the non-financial private sector (households and the corporate sector) starts to move back into deficit, then macroeconomic balance requires that the government sector switches towards surpluses. However, switching from a deficit to a surplus when age-related expenditures are going to skyrocket will be extremely painful, and we think not politically feasible. Inflation then becomes a way that macroeconomic balance is restored.

5.2.1   The Household Sector Surplus Is Set to Erode

Ben Bernanke (2005) famously attributed the declining real rate of interest from the 1990s onwards to a 'savings glut'. This was down to two drivers: first, baby boomers saving for their future retirement and, second, by the ageing, but increasingly prosperous workers in Asia (especially in China) saving for their old age due to an inadequate social safety net. The result was that household savings ratios were high. But as the baby boomers retired, and the ratio of the old (individuals who were dissaving) to workers (who were saving) rose, the household saving ratio started declining. We plot the personal sector savings ratio against the dependency ratio for a selection of countries below, indicating that as the dependency ratio worsens (i.e. rises), the household savings rate falls (Diagram 5.1).

In steady state, with the dependency ratio constant, the personal sector savings ratio would be a positive function of the rate of growth, since working savers would put more aside for their old age than dissaving retirees. But dependency ratios are likely to worsen for decades to come and the growth rate of output to decline. Many of those who argue that personal sector savings will remain high enough to keep real interest rates and aggregate demand low (the secular stagnation camp) do so on the assumption that (i) the age of retirement will rise relative to the expected age of death, and/or (ii) that state benefits to the old will fall relative to the average income of workers. If either were to happen, the rate of increase of expenditure on the elderly would be less than the output generated by workers. Both are possible, but neither are likely, for social and political reasons.

There are two other factors to consider for the balance in the household sector: first, the often neglected role of housing and, second, the impact of postponing the age of marriage, having children and leaving home.

The sectoral surplus depends on the balance between investment and savings. Most personal sector investment is housing related. The demographic forecasts for most countries show total population still rising, comprising a falling share of under 65s and a rising proportion of over 65s. How will this affect personal sector housing investment? (Table 5.1 and Diagram 5.2).

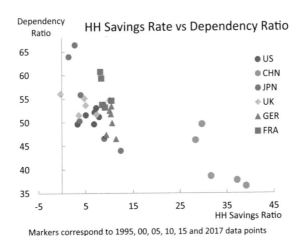

Markers correspond to 1995, 00, 05, 10, 15 and 2017 data points

Diagram 5.1 The household savings rate falls as the dependency ratio worsens (*Source* OECD)

Table 5.1 Total population of over-65s in six major economies

	USA	UK	Germany	France	Japan	China
1990	252,120	57,134	79,054	56,667	124,505	1,176,884
2000	281,711	58,923	81,401	59,015	127,524	1,290,551
2010	309,011	63,460	80,827	62,880	128,542	1,368,811
2020	331,003	67,886	83,784	65,274	126,476	1,439,324
2030	346,942	70,485	83,136	66,696	120,758	1,464,340
2040	366,572	72,487	82,004	67,571	113,356	1,449,031

Source UN Population Statistics

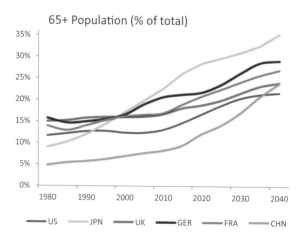

Diagram 5.2 Proportion of population aged over 65 (*Source* UN Population Statistics)

Moving home is stressful; some measures place it almost on par with the stress of divorce. The old have generally paid off their mortgages and have no need to move, until and unless they become incapacitated and cannot look after themselves. The frequency of housing moves therefore declines with age (see Diagrams 5.3 and 5.4). With the aged still living in houses that are becoming too big for them, the ratio of housing space to population is likely to rise. The result? Housing investment will not fall by as much as the decline in the working population.

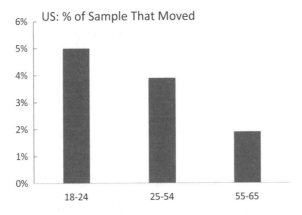

Diagram 5.3 Older people less likely to move in the United States (*Source* Hernandez-Murillo et al. 2011)

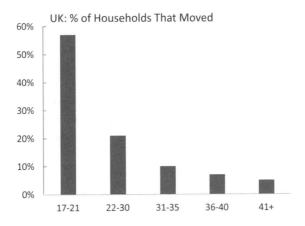

Diagram 5.4 And in the United Kingdom, too (*Source* Meen 2005)

From 'A home alone explosion', by L. Mayhew (2019) Cass Business School, in *Financial World*, June/July 2019, pp 13–15.[2]

Under-occupancy is identified as one of the key issues. Average household size has fallen from 2.48 in 1980 to 2.36 in 2018, largely because of the ageing population. If household size today were the same as in 1980, there would be 1.3m more dwellings available. If people lived in homes more suited to their needs, 50,000 fewer homes would need to be built each year. One of the main findings is that the number of people set to live alone will increase by 30 per cent by 2040 - a result primarily of population ageing...

Between 2020 and 2030, the number of households is set to rise by around 2m to 30.7m, but 35 per cent of the increase will comprise older households and, of these, 61 per cent will be one-person. The outlook is similar for 2030 to 2040, with further growth of 1.6m in the number of households to 32.3m, with 38 per cent of the additions forecast to be older households, of which 67 per cent will be one-person. Without any change, this spells a very inefficient use of the housing stock, not to mention the health and social care implications of so many older, often frail, people living alone.

The rising age of marriage/family creation and particularly the increasing age of having children (Diagrams 5.5 and 5.6) are bound to affect the investment/savings balance for households. Note the increasing number of women having children in their forties. Back in the 1970s and 1980s, most people would marry in their early twenties, have had most of their children by age 35 and have expected their children to have left home by their late forties. That left some twenty years, unencumbered by looking after children, to plan and save for retirement.

Nowadays, all those datings have shifted onwards by several years. We assume that young singles, below 30, tend to discount the probability of decades of aged retirement so much that they will not save adequately for it. Moreover, children are staying at home longer due to youth unemployment, the rising cost of housing and extended education. From the point of view of the young, staying at home means they can save on rent and other amenities. But they need to allocate those savings for the future use, e.g. for housing down payment, or indirectly by building up human capital. From the point of view of parents, these social changes will then be reducing the prime period of saving for retirement by a large chunk (reducing that period from, say, 45–65 to 52–67). And the rising cost of housing and of university education puts pressure on the bank of Mum and Dad. If that bank is

---

[2]Reproduced with permission from The London Institute of Banking and Finance.

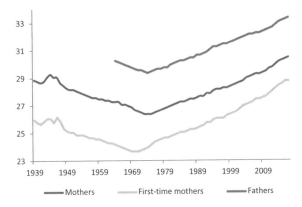

Diagram 5.5 UK: average age of parents at the birth of their child (age) (*Source* Office for National Statistics)

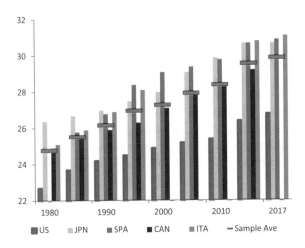

Diagram 5.6 Mean age of women at the birth of first child (age) has risen across the AEs (*Source* OECD)

providing more finance to their children, there can be less set aside for future retirement.

Some assume that forward-looking households will consume less with an eye on their pension plans. Papetti (2019) argues that:

[with] perfect foresight, the representative household realizes that the growth rate of the number of effective workers in support of the number of total consumers (the population size) is shrinking over time. Therefore, with the goal of smoothing consumption per capita into the future and depending on the pension scheme in place, the representative household anticipates this change

with a willingness of consuming less and saving more, i.e. becoming more patient thus decreasing the real interest rate, everything else being equal.[3]

This has patently *not* happened in most AEs in recent decades, for several obvious reasons, e.g. myopia and a failure of imagination. People do *not* save adequately to smooth out their consumption over their expected life cycle. In a paper for the World Economic Forum, Wood (2019) claims that,

> most male retirees in the six economies included in the study [USA, Netherlands, UK, Australia, Canada, Japan] can expect to live around a decade longer than their retirement funds can pay for. The savings deficit is even greater for women, who live on average two years longer than men.
>
> Significant differences also appear between economies. Japan's combination of longer lifespans and lower average savings – because they invest in safer assets, with fewer gains over time – is leaving retirees there particularly exposed.

Wood went on to ask,

> Why are people outliving their retirement savings? Poverty has decreased just as medical advances and improved healthcare provision have increased.
>
> Along with other factors like greater global awareness of the benefits of a healthy diet and regular exercise, this means people are living longer.
>
> By the middle of this century the proportion of over 60s in the world's population is set to reach 22%, almost double the 2015 figure, according to UN figures.
>
> Our aging population has placed unsustainable pressure on government and employer-sponsored pension systems, leading to a growing trend for individuals to take responsibility for financing their own retirement. But savings have failed to keep pace with the decline in traditional pension plans, leading to the current retirement savings deficit.

Nor does the World Economic Forum see the personal savings deficit declining in future. Instead, they argue that, in the eight countries that they cover, the six above plus China and India, it will grow significantly in all of them between 2015 and 2030, by an amount ranging from 2% per annum in Japan to 7% in China and 10% p.a. in India (see WEF, 2018, 'How we can save for the future', Figure 1). Even if we make some allowance for the wish of the WEF to highlight the dangers of insufficient retirement savings, the

---

[3]Also see Schön and Stähler (2019), who note, p. 24, that, 'Because savings increase sharply (and suddenly) on impact when people start realizing that they live in an ageing world the drop in the world interest rate is highest on impact'.

conclusion is starkly clear that, at least currently, people do not save enough to smooth their consumption over their longer expected lifetime.

To assume that this long-standing failure to save adequately for life-cycle consumption smoothing will suddenly change is, to say the least, implausible.[4] Also see McGovern (2019) and Button (2019, p. 10).

In summary, we expect the personal sector surplus to erode sharply over coming decades.

5.2.2 The Unusual Surplus of the (Non-financial) Corporate Sector Should Move into Deficit

Ever since the financial panic accompanying the GFC abated in 2009, conditions for the corporate sectors in most advanced economies have become extremely favourable. The share of corporate profits in national income over the years 2010–2017 has increased quite strongly in most countries, Italy being an exception, and has become much higher than during the years 1990–2005 (Diagram 5.7).

During these same recent years, interest rates, both real and nominal, have declined sharply, and equity valuations have increased in a continuing bull market, except in Japan.

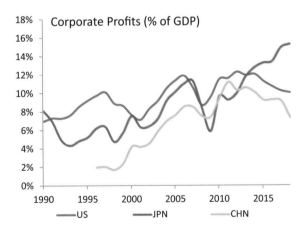

Diagram 5.7 The profit share of gross domestic product has been rising, particularly after the GFC (*Source* Bureau of Labor Statistics, China Ministry of Finance)

---

[4]Even over much shorter time periods, the theory that borrowing/saving is primarily done by households in order to smooth consumption is not fully supported by the facts. Thus, Hundtofte et al. (2019) state that 'on average – individuals do not use borrowing to smooth consumption when they experience a typical transitory income shock of unemployment. Instead, individuals smooth their credit card debt and overdrafts by adjusting consumption'. As a result, the demand for credit is procyclical, amplifying the business cycle.

Under these circumstances, one might have expected that fixed investment would have increased strongly. Instead, however, investment ratios in western economies have remained stagnant, although the investment ratio in China has remained elevated (Diagram 5.8).

The result is that the non-financial corporate sectors in several advanced western economies have been in surplus in recent decades. The main exception is China, where investment has continued apace, largely financed by higher debt (Diagram 5.9).

So, a key question is what has caused such investment ratios to be so low, despite the otherwise favourable circumstances that have seemed to have held during recent years? There are several competing explanations, none of which are mutually exclusive, and all of which may have played some role in this. There are, perhaps, four main candidates as explanations. These are:

1. Growing corporate concentration and monopolisation;
2. Technology;
3. Managerial incentives;
4. Cheap labour.

1. Growing corporate monopolisation
There is some evidence, mostly relating to the USA, that there has been an increasing degree of concentration and monopolisation in the corporate

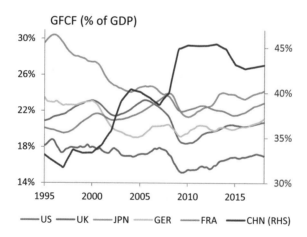

Diagram 5.8 Gross fixed capital formation (as a % of gross domestic product) has been stagnant in the AEs, but not in China (*Source* IMF)

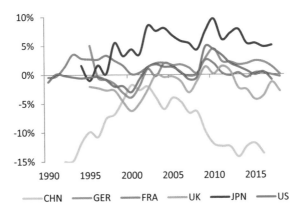

Diagram 5.9 Corporate sector net saving (% of gross domestic product) will move further into deficit (*Source* OECD)

sector, see, for example, Autor et al. (2017, 2019), Covarrubias et al. (2019), Crouzet and Eberly (2019) and Philippon (2019). If so, then that would lead to higher profit margins, a greater share of profits in national income than otherwise, and lower investment. In a recent NBER Working Paper, Liu et al. (January 2019) have argued that the continuation of very low interest rates has itself led to greater market concentration, reduced dynamism and slower productivity growth. Also, see the references to the earlier literature on the relationship between lower interest rates and the rise in industry concentration and higher corporate profit share, included in footnote 2 on page 5 of that paper.

2. Technology

The leading sector currently comprises technological companies, who rely much more on human capital than on fixed capital in the form of steel, buildings, heavy machinery, etc. The development of software, for example, requires a lot of human skills and effort, but relatively little fixed investment. Insofar as technology is shifting the balance towards human capital and away from fixed investment, the ratio of expenditures on fixed capital to total revenues and output is likely to decline, possibly quite sharply.

3. Managerial incentives

As will be discussed in much greater length in Chapters 11 and 12, the alignment of managerial incentives with those of shareholders enjoying limited liability is likely to lead to a focus by managers on maximising short-term equity values. This can be done most easily by buy-backs, i.e. using profits to increase leverage by substituting debt for equity; but short-term profitability can also be enhanced by cutting back on longer-term fixed investment and

R&D. This line of argument has been stressed by Smithers in several books (see Smithers, 2009, 2013, 2019).

4. Labour has become cheap

The combination of globalisation and the demographic sweet spot has led to an unprecedented jump in the available global supply of workers within the world trading system. Why invest in expensive equipment at home, in order to raise productivity, when one can increase output at lower cost by shifting production abroad, e.g. to China or Eastern Europe, or employ immigrants? Meanwhile, competition from such potential outsourcing, and inward migration, has reduced the power of private sector trade unions and held down real wages over the last few decades. Under these conditions, investment has migrated to those countries where labour has been particularly cheap and has taken the form of labour-using and capital-saving techniques.

What the balance might be between these four explanations is not easy to discern, and we make no attempt to do so here. But we think that all these potential explanations have merit, perhaps particularly the final two, that managerial incentives have been, from the point of view of society as a whole, misaligned, and that investment in most western economies has been held down by the shift of production to China and Eastern Europe.

The trends of globalisation and of demography are now beginning to reverse. Populism and protectionism have become powerful political influences in the context of economies where real wages have stagnated over the last 30 years. Meanwhile, the demographic sweet spot, leading to a massive increase in the workforce and fall in dependency ratios, is on the verge of reversing sharply, as has already happened in Japan. This will have the effect of raising real wages in most western economies, and that is likely to lead businessmen to invest more per unit of labour in order to raise productivity and to hold down unit labour costs.

But insofar as the low investment ratio has been due to the short-termism of managers, owing to the incentive structure under which they operate, this particular cause of low fixed investment will continue.

In Chapter 12, we shall argue that a key, perhaps necessary, way out of the accumulation of excessive debt, notably by non-financial corporates, will be to shift managerial incentives, and to encourage equity finance in place of debt. In any case, we claim that growing labour market tightness will raise wages and unit labour costs. For such reasons, we think it quite likely, though far from certain that, in future, investment per worker will rise. Whether this will be enough to offset the declining growth rate of workers, tending to reduce investment, is uncertain. So corporate investment may rise, or fall, but will not, we believe, fall by much.

On the other hand, rising unit labour costs, and the increasing relative bargaining power of labour, will curtail profitability, compared with the glory decades of 1980–2020, when globalisation, demography and easy money delivered a capitalist heaven. Those days are swiftly passing by, and the future for capitalist profitability will be becoming much harder earned.

Traditionally, and normally, the (non-financial) corporate sector has run deficits, with investment exceeding retained profits. Quite unusually, as demonstrated earlier in this section, this sector has in many countries moved into surplus. For the reasons set out above, we expect this to be a relatively short-lived feature, with such surpluses eroding, and, quite likely, returning to deficit in the coming decades.

5.2.3   Will the Public Sector Really Be Able to Reverse Its Deficits in a Time of Ageing?

In recent decades, the household/personal sector and the (non-financial) corporate sector have both been tending to move into sizeable surplus, for the reasons just explained. It is thus just a matter of arithmetic to show that, in order to maintain macro-economic equilibrium, the public sector *had* to move into a balancing deficit. For individual countries, however, such a deficit would be more, or less, dependent on whether they were running a current account deficit (i.e. the Rest of the World was also in surplus), or surplus. Countries with large current account surpluses, such as Germany, could achieve balance with a smaller public sector deficit, or even a surplus, as in the Netherlands; vice versa for countries with large current account deficits, such as the UK and USA.

You might think that the requirement that the public sector *has* to run a deficit to maintain macro-economic balance would be celebrated as a 'good thing', a chance for more public expenditures and less taxation. But this has not been so. Historically, continuing deficits on the scale of the last two decades (see Diagram 5.10) have only been observed in wartime and have often required a combination of both persistent austere fiscal surpluses and (unexpected) inflation to tame. For peacetime, the scale and level of public sector deficits and debt has now become unparalleled after the GFC. What is worse is that the extrapolation of current trends for income and for the support of the old, as evidenced by the longer-term projections of the Congressional Budget Office (CBO) in the USA and the Office for Budget Research (OBR) in the UK, show that the debt ratio is likely to rise at an exponential rate, as already demonstrated in Diagrams 1.8 and 1.9 in Introductory Chapter 1. This is further discussed in Chapter 13 below. In

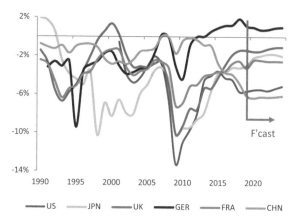

Diagram 5.10 General government budget balances (shown here as a % of GDP) have been in deficit persistently (*Source* IMF)

particular, this is due to the rising costs, under existing plans, of health care and pensions for the old. In one respect, such costs are currently largely underestimated; this relates to the massively increased incidence of dementia and other forms of morbidity among the aged, a subject already discussed in Chapter 4.

Against this worrisome background, the natural instinct of Ministers of Finance (other than populists) and of many prudent politicians has been to err on the side of caution in counter-cyclical policy, and to seize such opportunities as presented themselves to reduce the deficit to a more manageable size and to stabilise, and then to start gradually reducing, the level of debt. In short, the context has been such that fiscal policy has allowed macroeconomic deflationary pressures to persist. This has been especially so in the euro-zone, where a combination of conservative policies in Germany and constraints on the deficit euro-area countries has reinforced deflationary tendencies.

We have argued above that the prior combined surplus of the personal and corporate sectors will in coming decades switch back towards a deficit. If so, again by simple arithmetic, the public sector will *have* to shift in turn from deficit to surplus. That will need to involve politically painful decisions to cut back on public expenditures or to raise taxes. Because that is more immediately politically painful (than rising deficit and debt levels), it will tend not to get done, at least not sufficiently to provide macroeconomic balance. The result is almost certain to be consistent and persistent inflationary pressure. We discuss at greater length the implications of these various demographic and macroeconomic trends for both future fiscal and monetary policies in Chapter 13.

5.3   Overall Macroeconomic Effects

How do we pull together the overall macroeconomic conclusions? It would have been quite a task. Fortunately, a group of Birkbeck economists (Aksoy et al. 2015) have undertaken an econometric and theoretical study of the consequences of such demographic changes. Since we largely accept both the direction of travel, and rough magnitudes, of most of their results, we have simply reproduced their main table (Table 5.2).

Their main conclusions, with which we agree, are:

- overall growth and total hours worked will slow down as ageing advances (which we can see because β3—which represents the coefficient on the aged profile of the population—is negative for growth and even more so for total hours worked);
- both the proportion of young and old are inflationary for the economy—this can be seen clearly by the coefficients for inflation of β1 and β3; and
- both the investment and the personal savings ratios fall thanks to demographics—as seen by a negative value for β3 for both investment and the personal savings ratios.

These conclusions fit with our own thinking about the effects of demographics, in that:

- Growth is the first and most obvious casualty, with a decline in overall growth; and total hours worked will inevitably fall. However, human happiness depends on many other factors besides per capita gross domestic product. So, a slowdown in growth does not necessarily imply an equivalent reduction in overall happiness;
- Both higher proportions of young and old are inflationary, and it is only the working cohort that can be deflationary for the economy. Both of the former are net consumers and it is only the latter cohort that can offset the demand for goods and services by producing those goods and services; and

Table 5.2 Economic effects of demographic change

	B_1 (young 0–21)	B_2 (working 21–60)	B_3 (old 60+)
Growth rate	0.04	0.10	−0.14
Investment ratio	0.07	0.09	−0.16
Personal savings ratio	0.33	0.23	−0.56
Hours worked	−0.70	1.70	−1.00
Inflation	0.75	−0.87	0.12

Source Aksoy et al. (2015)

- Both the investment and personal savings ratio will decline, though we add (as we previously have) that we believe savings will fall faster than investment.

6

The Determination of (Real) Interest Rates During the Great Reversal

6.1 Introduction

A key and central conclusion of our work is that the Great Reversal of demography and globalisation will lead to more inflation. When this takes hold, though it may be a few years from now, and expectations adjust, then nominal interest rates will rise. Of that, we are confident. But the more difficult and interesting question is whether nominal interest rates will rise by more than inflation, i.e. whether real interest rates will rise, or whether the reverse will happen and real interest rates will fall.

Rather than looking for explanations of changing real rates in any one country at a time, the focus needs to be on global factors. Ex post, savings have to equal investment in a closed economy, i.e. the world. So, if one points to a particular country, say China, where savings have exceeded investment and there is a current account surplus, then by definition there is another country (or countries such as the UK or USA) where savings have been below investment and there is a current account deficit. What we need to look at is the ex ante desired savings versus investment dynamics on a global scale, and think of the equilibrating interest rate as a global price.

One of the great difficulties of trying to analyse the likely path of real interest rates is that there are so many factors involved. For example, in Heise's book (2019), on *Inflation Targeting and Financial Stability*, he lists eight driving factors in four categories, shown in Table 6.1.

Here, we shall review the likely future for real interest rates under six successive headings. First, in the next section we shall discuss the role of growth in determining the equilibrium real interest rate. Then, we shall review likely

© The Author(s) 2020
C. Goodhart and M. Pradhan, *The Great Demographic Reversal*,
https://doi.org/10.1007/978-3-030-42657-6_6

Table 6.1 Where are global real interest rates heading in the long-term?

Driving factors	Impact on real interest rate: slightly up
Shift in saving curve • Demography: rising population of older people • Lower savings in emerging markets	Upward
Shift in investment curve • Pressure from private sector deleveraging eases • Public sector investment rises slightly • Importance of intangible investment remains high	Slightly upward
Portfolio shifts • Little change of regulatory preference for government bonds • Preference for safe assets on the side of investors remains?	Unchanged?
Productivity growth • Positive impact of information and communication technology	Slightly upward

Source Heise (2019). Also see Brand, et al. (2018), and Rachel and Smith (2015)

trends in ex ante investment and saving in three sectors, starting with the personal (household) sector, then going on to the non-financial corporate sector, and then finally discussing what would need to be done in the public sector to equilibrate the economy. Following that, we shall have a short digression to discuss what, if anything, might happen to the effect of risk and illiquidity aversion on the return to riskless assets; in other words, is there likely to be a (continuing) shortage of 'safe assets'? Finally, in this chapter, we will discuss whether political pressures may get increasingly imposed on central banks to modify their adherence to a 2% inflation target.

6.2   Will Declining Growth Cause Real Interest Rates to Remain Low?

In some of our other work, we have focussed on the importance of the relationship between the rate of growth (g) and the real interest rate (r), and we take the view that macroeconomic management becomes much more difficult if r rises above g. Another of our main conclusions is that g, the rate of growth of real output, must decline, as the growth of the workforce slows, and in many countries absolutely declines.

Moreover, it is commonly assumed that an intrinsic relationship exists between potential output growth and the equilibrium real interest rate. Laubach and Williams' (2003) popular model uses the Ramsey framework to impose a long-term factor that is common to both potential output growth and the equilibrium real interest rate. That assumption, more than anything else, drives their estimates of the equilibrium real interest rate over their estimation period. However, this assumption does not find much support in the data.

In an empirical study designed to investigate the determinants of the equilibrium real interest rate in the USA, Hamilton et al. (2015) find that the only significant relationship of US real interest rates is that they are co-integrated with real interest rates in the rest of the world. Growth plays a part, as do many other factors, but shows no dominant relationship in determining the equilibrium real interest rate, using data from 1858–2014. Also see Rachel and Summers (2019, pp. 11/12), and Rachel and Smith (2015).

Cyclically too, much of the perceived link between growth and interest rates, we suspect, comes from observing a decline in both growth and interest rates during economic slowdowns and connecting the two. The decline in real interest rates cyclically also has more to do with the behaviour of ex ante investment relative to ex ante savings and, in particular, to the greater amplitude of the swings in investment relative to those of savings. As desired investment falls sharply (while desired savings tend to remain more steady) towards the trough of the cycle, so do interest rates. Similarly, an increase in desired investment relative to savings during expansions leads to higher interest rates. These relationships are then (mistakenly) assumed to hold over the structural horizon.

6.3 Sectoral Changes in ex ante Savings and Investment

Rather than use growth as the determinant of the equilibrium real interest rate, we use the standard classical theory that in the medium and long run (after the temporary effect of central bank policy on local real short-term rates dissipates), real interest rates move to adjust differences in ex ante savings and ex ante investment, falling when desired savings are greater than desired investment, and vice versa. The declining trend in real interest rates over recent decades, from 1980–2015, is prima facie evidence that ex ante savings have exceeded ex ante investment over this period—but that is likely to reverse.

6.3.1 The Personal Sector: The Life Expectancy-Retirement Age Gap, and China

The main problem is that demographic changes normally have the same directional effect both on ex ante savings and on ex ante investment. Slower population growth will lower savings (assuming a constant dependency ratio), but will equally lessen the need for more capital, houses, equipment, etc. However, this doesn't tell us whether the capital/labour ratio will fall or rise, thereby raising or lowering the marginal productivity of capital. With both ex ante S and ex ante I moving in the same direction, assessing the likely balance between the two becomes problematic. The behaviour of household savings according to the life-cycle hypothesis in the presence of a social safety net and the impact of ageing on China's savings explain why savings will fall.

If all retirement consumption was provided by prior savings, then the age-related profile of consumption should be downwards sloping, since younger generations benefit from higher life-long earnings. The life-cycle hypothesis suggests that the consumption of an individual should be constant over time. Myopia, and an underestimation of longevity, would cause an even greater downwards slope to age-related consumption. But, actually, the data (Diagram 6.1) show that age-related consumption is flat, or even rising, with age. This must, and does, imply a considerable transfer from workers to the old.

We argue there are two reasons for this. First, spending on medical services increasingly dominates the spending patterns of the elderly, especially in the final years of life (Diagram 6.1 shows a sharp upward spike in consumption at

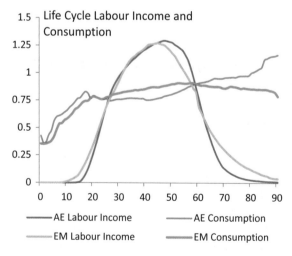

Diagram 6.1 Consumption rises over the life cycle (*Source* National Transfer Accounts)

life's end in AEs). Much of this is provided for free by the public sector (NHS in the UK; and Medicaid and Medicare in the USA). Second, most AEs have a safety net to prevent those elderly who do have not the personal resources to afford medical attention from falling into destitution. See French, et al. (2019).

Our key political economy assumption is that the safety net will remain in place, keeping savings from rising proportionally with longevity. While there is bound to be some scaling back on commitments, the pension and healthcare safety net will more or less remain in place. This will be incorporated into the savings habits of individuals, keeping them from saving more in anticipation of retirement.

Almost inevitably, health expenditures will rise further (Diagram 6.2), while the retirement age simply hasn't kept up with longevity. Both health expenditures and expenditures on public pension transfers (Diagram 6.3) will continue to rise along with the ageing of AE societies. So far, measures to enforce participation in the labour force by raising the retirement age have not materialised, except in a handful of places which have enforced a modest increase in retirement age. Longevity, on the other hand, has gone up significantly thanks to medical advances and might go up further if the science of ageing makes rapid advances. As a result, the gap between longevity and the retirement age has been increasing in line with increases in longevity, see Diagram 6.4.

And then there's China. Everything about China is enormous; its demographic dynamics have been and remain remarkable, as already stated in Chapter 2, and the consequential movements in its savings and investment

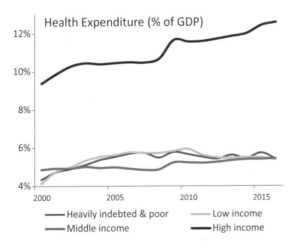

Diagram 6.2 Health expenditure rising globally, mostly due to high income economies (*Source* World Bank)

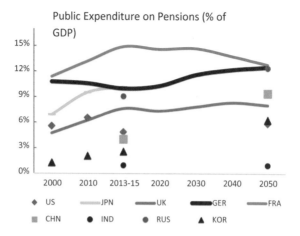

Diagram 6.3 Public expenditures on pensions will continue to rise (*Source* OECD)

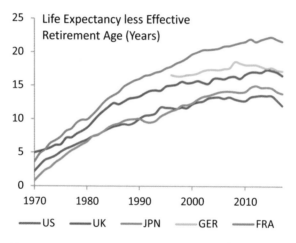

Diagram 6.4 Life expectancy less effective retirement age is rising across the AEs (*Source* OECD)

ratios have been extraordinary. As China's labour force dynamics change direction, the savings-investment balance within and even outside China will change as a result.

Demographics will ensure that China's extraordinary savings will fall. Prior to modern times, the (relatively few) old in China were cared for in the extended family.[1] But the one-child policy, extended for too long, has meant

---

[1] 'About 90 per cent of Chinese seniors rely mainly on family support, 7 per cent on residential community-based care services and 3 per cent on nursing homes, according to the Qianzhan Industry Research Institute, a consultancy'.

that support has gotten more and more scarce for the aged. With an insufficient social safety net, personal savings rose to plan for retirement. Add to this the incentive on the managers of state-owned enterprises to retain, rather than pay out, profits, and the explanation of these extraordinary savings ratios becomes clearer.

What will happen in the future? Although a higher proportion of the old work in Asia than in Europe or North America, increasing longevity will increase the dependency ratio, in China and elsewhere. The result will be a decline in the personal sector savings ratio and in China's current account balance; indeed, this has already begun, as already noted in Chapter 2.

China's ageing will also reduce excess savings among oil exporters. The economic impact of China on the world economy has been great. One dimension of this has been to impart upward pressure on the price of raw materials including, notably, oil. Much oil has been produced in relatively sparsely populated countries (Saudi Arabia and the Gulf and Norway). With China's growth declining, and with the need to shift from fossil fuels to renewables, the net savings and current account surpluses of the petro-currency countries are likely to erode.

Indeed, all those countries which have had current account surpluses (large net savings) are either ageing rapidly (China and Germany), or are likely to see their relative advantage reduce (the petro-currency countries).

A large proportion of overall capital, and of personal wealth, is tied up in housing and housing-related infrastructure. Many expect that as population growth slows down, the demand for housing will decline sharply. However, that does not take into account the elderly's preferences. As nations become richer, the old stay in their existing homes rather than relocate to their adult children's homes. Moving is stressful, and those among the old who are homeowners have little incentive to relocate, as already described in Chapter 5. As the young come of age and gain financial independence, they will not move into existing housing vacated by the elderly, but will move into new homes that have to be built. In our view, a shift in the balance of the population of a given size towards more old and fewer workers will raise, not lower, the desired stock of housing. That will support residential and housing-related investment.

Could social behaviour change? Could the elderly sell their homes and live together with their extended family? This could of course happen. But we think it is more likely to happen in EMEs than in AEs. In the latter, breaking long-standing social mores would require that pressures from demographics become substantially worse before any such changes become widespread.

6.3.2 How Will the Non-financial Corporate Sector Respond? a Tricky Story

One aspect of the demographic impact that does not suggest a ready answer is the behaviour of the corporate sector. There are two polar arguments. The popular argument is that the corporate sector will respond to demographic headwinds by slowing down the rate at which it accumulates capital so much that the capital/labour ratio falls. Our view is that the corporate sector is likely to respond by raising the capital/labour ratio, i.e. by adding capital to compensate for labour, which is the factor of production that will be getting scarcer and more expensive.

There will be a rising cost of labour and a falling cost of capital. We cannot think of any other time in history when the prices of the two main factors of production will be moving as clearly in opposite directions. Even before demographics start pushing wage growth up, the price of capital goods has already been falling. As wages begin to rise, compensating for more expensive labour will be easier thanks to a lower cost of capital goods. The resulting increase in productivity will somewhat temper the increase in wages and inflation. The savings and investment lens gives us another way to view this response. Given significantly cheaper capital goods, the cost of accumulating a given stock of capital uses up a smaller amount of the economy's stock of savings. To some extent, this can counter the savings deficit created by ageing demographics and somewhat temper the rise in both the interest rate and wages.

Historical experience after the oil shock provides evidence of such substitution. Manufacturing in many economies that faced favourable/unfavourable shocks to the price of an input of production underwent a change in the capital/labour ratio in a significant way. Data from 1972–88 from manufacturing plants in the USA (Davis et al. 1996) show that the 1970s oil price shock led to the demise of energy-intensive manufacturing. Plants, employment and wages all shrank as the US economy reacted strongly to protect itself against the then-current and future fluctuations in the price of oil. The opposite effect can be seen in economies that were net producers of energy. The hollowing out of Russia's knowledge-intensive manufacturing sector within an oil-dependent economy showcases this transformation all too well.

We fully expect technology to have a significant beneficial impact on productivity and hence on restraining inflation and nominal interest rates. But we prefer to take an agnostic view because we have no particular expertise in predicting the pace of innovations. Indeed, it is difficult to tell whether much of the debate around technology is about the pace of innovations or whether it is properly recorded in the statistics. Gordon (2012), for example, argues that productivity in the USA has fallen since 1973 and is unlikely to pick up from here. But Mokyr et al. (2015) argue that statistics do not adequately capture technology and hence are misleading. Given that this issue is unlikely to be resolved any time soon, we prefer to remain agnostic on this topic.

Structurally, it is still early days and perhaps until recently the relocation of production abroad remained an alternative and attractive option. The demographic headwind and the associated increase in wages have not yet affected large parts of AEs. Even in Japan, China and Korea, where these demographic pressures are already starting to show, they are still in relatively early stages, with some wage pressure beginning to be evident in Japan's labour market and the labour force in all three economies shrinking already.

Even at this early stage, signs of a new capital expenditure cycle are already being seen in Japan. The economies of China and Korea, with excess capacity still a problem, are naturally not showing the same response. Most of the advanced world resembles Japan in two ways: (i) labour will shortly become more costly and will become even more costly in an absolute and relative sense and (ii) the manufacturing sectors have seen neither the large capital expenditure growth nor an increase in private sector debt of their EME counterparts. AEs, therefore, are more likely to show a response to demographics that resembles Japan's more recent experience rather than China's or Korea's (and Japan's previous experience too).

Cyclically, it is somewhat of a puzzle why corporates are saving rather than investing (particularly in the advanced economies and China). It is quite possible that global excess capacity that was closing only slowly and demand that was rising equally slowly kept corporates from investing in physical capital. There are some early signs of change in EMEs where capital goods imports (a reasonable leading indicator for investment) have picked up for the first time in half a decade. But the key remains the unlocking of the US investment cycle. The corporate sector of the USA has thus far preferred to increase ROE, i.e., the return on equity, by leveraged buy-backs of shares and to increase output by employing more. If wage growth eats into corporate profits as it has recently begun to, then there should develop a greater willingness to invest in order to raise labour productivity and protect corporate profitability. Whether that bit of economic logic will be enough to kick-start investment remains to be seen.

On the other hand, non-financial corporate debt ratios have now climbed so high that any rise in interest rates, or fall in profitability, could put the solvency of many highly leveraged companies under pressure. Should this happen, they would have to cut back new investment severely for short-term self-protection, thereby worsening the macro-economy still further. On this, see Chapter 11 below on the Debt Trap, and Kalemli-Özcan, et al. (2019).

Overall there are so many cross-currents to charting the future of the non-financial corporate investment/savings balance that it makes one's head spin.

6.3.3   And What About the Public Sector?

In the previous two sections, and in Chapter 5, we have argued that the savings ratio will fall by more than investment in both the personal and non-financial corporate sectors. The personal sector will therefore move from the surplus of the past towards a deficit. It follows, almost by definition, that in order to equilibrate the economy, the public sector should move out of deficit towards greater surplus.

But this will be extraordinarily difficult, particularly because of the pressure of the need to increase payments for medical care and pensions, as noted on several occasions throughout this book. Cutting expenditures and raising taxation are always going to be politically hard to do.

One of the reasons for the declining trend in interest rates up till now has been that this longer-term prospect has made Ministers of Finance unwilling to allow deficits to rise sufficiently to balance the economy at a time when the world's savings ratio, notably in China, exceeded ex ante investment, Ben Bernanke's 'savings glut'. By the same token, we think it highly likely that the fiscal position will not move sufficiently strongly into surplus to offset the larger deficits that we expect to see within the private sector.

Because fiscal deficits were not sufficient to equilibrate the economy over the last 30 years, central banks were forced to do so by lowering interest rates, 'the only game in town'.[2] In the same way in future, we expect real interest rates to have to rise in order to play the same equilibrating role because the public sector will not save enough.

6.4   Risk Aversion and a Shortage of Safe Assets?

In many of the studies surveying the reasons for declining real rates of interest over recent decades, considerable weight has been put on risk aversion and the flight to safety; indeed, there is a sizeable literature connected with the work of Caballero, e.g. Caballero et al. (2017), suggesting that there has developed

---

[2]Rachel and Summers (2019) see recent fiscal deficits as raising the neutral real rate. Yes, in the sense that, if the fiscal deficit had been even less, interest rates would have had to be *even lower*, but no, in the sense that fiscal deficits have been too low to prevent the need for sharply declining interest rates.

a shortage of 'safe assets'. For example, the ECB study on 'The Natural Rate of Interest: Estimates, Drivers and Challenges to Monetary Policy' (Brand et al. 2018), states that 'Risk aversion and flight to safety are shown to have contributed to a further decline in the wake of the global financial crisis', p. 5; also see their Box 2, pp. 16–20.

During this period, central banks have hoovered up much of the available outstanding stock of riskless government debt in their QE policies, and the potential for default or redenomination has made the existing debt of several European and Latin American countries apparently more risky. An argument that has been put forward, e.g. by these authors, and also Marx, Mojon and Velde, 'Why Have Interest Rates Fallen Far Below the Return on Capital?' (2019), has been that aversion to risk and illiquidity has driven an increasing wedge between the return on capital and riskless interest rates. Because the required return on capital remained high, thereby deterring investment, riskless interest rates had to be lower in order to equilibrate the macroeconomy.

We are not convinced by these arguments. If there was concern about illiquidity, then the wedge between relatively riskless bonds and riskier bonds ought to have expanded, i.e. the wedge between AAA and BBB corporate bonds ought to have increased. Diagram 6.5 shows the path of this wedge from 2006 to 2018. As shown by the chart, the wedge increased very sharply during the Great Financial Crisis, but has since declined steadily to its current low level. Indeed, one of the key purposes and features of recent monetary policy has been to try to encourage agents to take on more risk by reaching

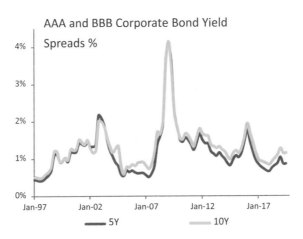

Diagram 6.5 Wedge (spread) between yields on corporate AAA bonds and on BBB bonds (*Source* FRED)

for yield, and the evidence is that they have achieved this objective. Rachel and Summers (2019, p. 2) came to the same conclusion.

That still leaves the question of why the return on capital has remained so high relative to the riskless rate. In our view, the rise in equity valuations is a natural consequence of the decline in riskless rates since, as rates fall, equity prices have to rise to a level at which the future return on holding such equities falls to the point at which the future expected return, adjusted for risk, is in line with the riskless rate. So, you cannot point to the path of equities to show a wedge resulting from enhanced risk aversion. What does remain a serious question is why conditions in which profitability has been so high, and both equity prices extremely high and interest rates so low, has not led to a much greater demand for corporate investment. In our view, the answer to this has nothing to do with risk aversion, but rather the incentive on corporate managers to maximise the short-run return on equity (RoE), which we shall discuss further in Chapter 11, also see Smithers (2009, 2013, 2019).

6.5   Political Pressures

Another of our continuing themes has been that the comfortable relationship between politicians and independent central banks over the last 30 years will become much more adversarial. During these last 30 years, central bankers have remained the best friends of Ministers of Finance. By bringing interest rates steadily downwards, they have enabled the debt burden of sharply rising debt ratios to be completely offset. In future, this is going to change, and in a way that will make life for both those parties more difficult. Rising nominal interest rates, at a time when the prospect is for continuing, and, in some cases, worsening fiscal deficits, and still sharply rising debt ratios, is going to make the life of Ministers of Finance, and Prime Ministers, considerably more problematical. Moreover, the rise in debt ratios in the corporate sector, outside of the banks, is going to mean that the attempt to maintain the inflation target may leave the corporate sector, and the macroeconomy, at greater risk of default and recession.

Under these circumstances, the pressure from politicians, primarily, but not only, those described as populist, will increase. We touch on this same theme again further in Chapter 13. As described further in that chapter, the independence of central banks is actually quite restricted, with the exception of the European Central Bank. Inevitably, therefore, central banks have to be politically agile, and their ability to offset political pressure is limited.

6.6   Conclusion

Short-term interest rates are determined by official fiat, at least in the short and medium run, whereas longer-term interest rates depend more on market forces. Largely because of the political context which we see unfolding, we think it highly likely that short rates will be held below the increase in inflation which we see developing over the next few decades. In contrast, however, as this new, uncomfortable, world emerges into clearer sight, long rates will start rising and very likely rise above the current rate of inflation. So, one of our conclusions is that the yield curve, which is currently flattened to an unusual degree, will probably steepen sharply.

So, we are, in a sense, hedging our bets, suggesting that short rates may continue to run at low real levels, but that longer, e.g. ten-year rates, are likely to show rising real rates.

7

Inequality and the Rise of Populism

7.1 Introduction

The advent of China into the world's trading system and its subsequent dramatic growth have been the outstanding features of the last three decades. This allied a densely populated country, where the workforce was poor, but reasonably well educated and relatively efficiently governed and organised,[1] with the Western advanced economies with much higher technical skills, wealth and capital. The result was, in a sense, a triumph for macroeconomics. The West exported know-how, management and capital to China, and China exported cheap goods to the rest of the world.

Global inequality began to *fall*, from about 2000 onwards, as the rise of real incomes and real wages in much of Asia, led by China, greatly outpaced that in the West. For the previous two centuries, global inequality had risen steadily, not because inequality was rising within countries, but because income inequality was growing between countries, Milanovic (2016, Chapter 3). During that earlier period, real incomes in Europe, North America and Australia/NZ were bounding ahead, whereas they stagnated at near subsistence levels in Asia and Africa. Your position on the global income scale depended as much or more on where (which country) you were born, rather than who your parents were.

Besides the peasants and working classes in China, and neighbouring Asian countries, S. Korea, Taiwan, Vietnam, Thailand, Malaysia, Singapore,

---

[1] Pace Desmet et al. (2018), we do not think that density of population is sufficient, or necessary, *by itself* to stimulate innovation and rising productivity. We pursue this topic further in Chapter 10 on India and Africa.

© The Author(s) 2020
C. Goodhart and M. Pradhan, *The Great Demographic Reversal*,
https://doi.org/10.1007/978-3-030-42657-6_7

Indonesia, etc., the other main winners over the last three decades have been those with good technical skills and qualifications, the managerial class and those with wealth for capital investment. As we showed earlier in Chapters 2 and 3, the combination of globalisation (essentially the China effect) plus the highly favourable trends in demography led to an unprecedented surge in the effective labour supply during these recent decades, more than doubling in the space of some 30 years. In that context those with the ability to provide that hugely expanded labour supply with the relevant managerial oversight, skills and equipment were bound to prosper.

But there were losers also. These were the lower middle classes in the Western advanced economies. They suffered, as we will show in Sects. 7.2 and 7.3, not only from globalised competition, cheaper production in China, but also from technological developments. Milanovic's famous elephant diagram (Figure 1.1, p. 11) relates to such factors.

In this section, we shall show in more detail how, and why, the lower middle class in advanced Western countries lost out so comprehensively during recent decades. Considering how beneficial the overall effects of globalisation/demography has been to the World's economy—the two decades, 1988–2008, were the best ever as ranked by growth, rising employment and low and steady inflation—the winners could have compensated the losers (the Kaldor/Scitovsky welfare criterion). But, of course, they did no such thing. A rust belt of decay formed in AEs, extending to towns, types of job and categories of workers.

There are many more workers than there are owners of capital. If large swathes of the working class become disaffected with the current economic and political set-up, they can vote for a change. In Sect. 7.4 we go on to suggest why such disaffection has largely taken the form of growing support for right-wing Populist leaders, rather than (more traditional) left-wing Socialists. To preview our main answer, a key element has been the differing attitudes of left-wing leaders—as contrasted with their traditional supporters—to immigration. Left-wing political leaders are mainly idealistic believers in the 'brotherhood of man'. Their party usually has the support of past, current and future immigrants; they tend to be soft on inward migration controls. In contrast, the typical blue-collar worker sees immigrants as competitors, partly responsible for holding back wage increases and bringing with them unwelcome cultural and societal changes. Right-wing politicians stress national patriotic values (Make America Great Again; Take Back Control) and oppose large-scale inward migration, positions that resonate with many blue-collar workers and their families.

7.2   Inequality

Although global inequality has started to fall, as inequality *between* countries has declined quite sharply, inequality *within* countries has in the vast majority of cases risen, in many cases rather strongly, reversing the decline that took place from about 1914 until about 1980. Thus, the earlier hypothesis, embodied in the Kuznets[2] curve, whereby economic development would initially cause inequality to rise, but peak and then fall continuously, appears to have become refuted. First, we shall document what has happened in this respect. Then in Sect. 7.3 we shall discuss the mixture of reasons that have been advanced to try to explain such an outcome.

There are two main databases, the World Bank's PovcalNet database and the World Inequality Database. Out of the many potential measures of inequality we initially select four, (but they all tend in the same directions), to wit (i) the Gini coefficient,[3] Diagram 7.1, for a number of OECD countries, (ii) for a few selected countries the share of income of the top 10 and 1% of the distribution, Tables 7.1 and 7.2, and (iii) the share of wealth for the top 10%, Table 7.3. We show these latter data points for the income inequality data at five-year intervals for the USA, UK, Germany, France, Sweden, Italy Japan, China, Brazil, Egypt and India, and the wealth inequality data for four countries, USA, China, France and UK.

These tables show that among these countries income inequality was least marked, at the end of our period, in Sweden and Italy, but most extreme in Brazil and India. By the same token, such income inequality appears to have increased most in China, Germany and India, and least in Japan.

A saving grace to this dismal outcome is that the post-tax and transfer incomes of the poorest two deciles of the populations (households) in most countries continue to be protected, largely by policy measures, such as welfare benefits, minimum wage laws and medical support. This has been less so in the USA and developing countries, and more so in Europe and Japan.

---

[2]Kuznets was a Nobel Prize-winning, empirical economist working at Harvard, with whom Goodhart worked temporarily as a Research Assistant in 1960/1961.

[3]The Gini index is a measure of statistical dispersion intended to represent income or wealth distribution of a nation's residents and is the most commonly used measure of inequality. The data for the Gini index (World Bank estimate) are based on primary household survey data obtained from government statistical agencies and World Bank country departments. For more information and methodology, please see PovcalNet. Zero would represent absolute equality and 1 absolute inequality, so an increase implies rising inequality.

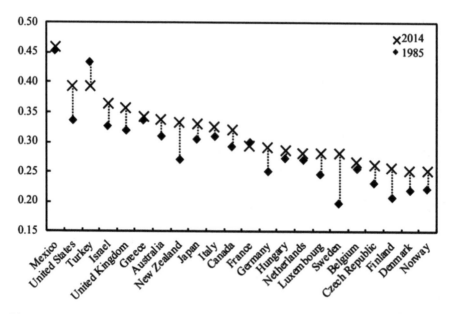

Diagram 7.1 Gini coefficient of disposable household income across the OECD (*Source* Rachel and Summers (2019))

Table 7.1 Top 10% income share

	1990	1995	2000	2005	2010	2015
USA	0.39	0.41	0.44	0.45	0.46	
China	0.30	0.34	0.36	0.42	0.43	0.41
Germany		0.32		0.39	0.40	
UK	0.37	0.39	0.41	0.42	0.38	
France	0.32	0.32	0.33	0.33	0.33	
Japan	0.39	0.36	0.38	0.42	0.42	
Sweden	0.22	0.26	0.26	0.27	0.27	0.28
Brazil				0.55	0.55	0.56
India	0.33	0.38	0.40	0.45	0.52	0.56
Egypt	0.51	0.51	0.51	0.49	0.46	0.49
Italy	0.26	0.28	0.29	0.29	0.29	0.29

Source World Inequality Database

In their paper 'The Great Divide'; 'Regional Inequality and Fiscal Policy', the authors, Gbohoui et al., state that:

Redistributive fiscal policies have helped reduce, but not fully offset, rising nationwide income inequality (IMF 2017; Immervoll and Richardson 2011). For advanced OECD countries, the average redistributive effect of fiscal policy—measured by the difference in Gini coefficients on household income

Table 7.2 Top 1% income share

	1990	1995	2000	2005	2010	2015
USA	0.15	0.15	0.18	0.19	0.20	
China	0.08	0.09	0.10	0.14	0.15	0.14
Germany		0.08		0.13	0.13	
UK	0.10	0.11	0.14	0.14	0.13	
France	0.09	0.09	0.11	0.11	0.11	
Japan	0.13	0.09	0.09	0.11	0.10	
Sweden	0.05	0.08	0.07	0.08	0.08	0.09
Brazil				0.28	0.28	0.28
India	0.10	0.13	0.15	0.19	0.21	0.21
Egypt	0.19	0.19	0.19	0.18	0.17	0.19
Italy	0.06	0.07	0.08	0.08	0.07	0.07

Source World Inequality Database

Table 7.3 Top 10% wealth share

	1990	1995	2000	2005	2010	2015
USA	0.64	0.66	0.69	0.67	0.73	
China	0.41	0.41	0.48	0.52	0.63	0.67
UK	0.46	0.47	0.51	0.51		
France	0.50	0.51	0.57	0.52	0.56	

Source World Inequality Database

before and after taxes and transfers—is about one-third (from 0.49 Gini points from market income inequality to 0.31 Gini points for disposable income inequality in 2015) (Figure 6 top left panel). About three-quarters of the fiscal redistribution was achieved on the transfer side, while progressive taxation contributed the remaining one quarter. Across household income classes, benefits and transfers have helped reduce inequality more so than tax and social contributions.

The redistributive impact of fiscal policy, while still large nationwide, has declined since the mid-1990s in some OECD countries. Progressive fiscal policies provide an automatic mechanism to counter the rise of income inequality, even without active policy measures. The redistributive effects of fiscal policies seem to have flattened (in many European countries) or diminished (such as in the United States). The average redistributive effects (the change of Gini coefficients between before and after tax and transfer) have declined from 53 percent to about 50 percent in the group of selected OECD countries over the last decade (Figure 6 top right panel). This reinforces earlier findings that the fiscal redistributive role has declined over the mid-1990s to mid-2000s (Immervoll and Richardson 2011) (Diagram 7.2).

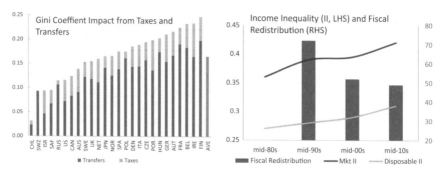

Diagram 7.2 Fiscal redistributive impact is still large but declining in some OECD countries (*Source* OECD, Income Distribution Database, Immervoll and Richardson (2011))

There are two main constituent reasons for such trends in inequality. The first, already discussed in Chapter 3, is that trend growth in the returns to capital have been much stronger than the increase in real wages over this same, three-decade, period. The second main constituent reason for the increase in inequality is that the return to human capital, as proxied by educational attainment, has risen alongside the return to fixed and financial capital. In contrast, the return to muscle-power and simpler repetitive tasks has stagnated. The US data are taken from Autor (2019, p. 2) (Diagram 7.3).

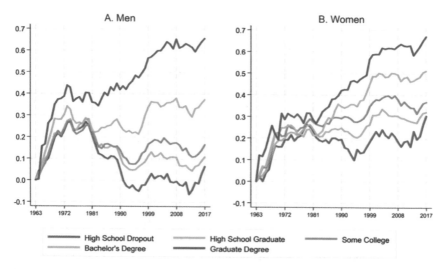

Diagram 7.3 Cumulative change in real weekly earnings of working age adults aged 18–64, 1963–2017 (*Source* American Economic Association)

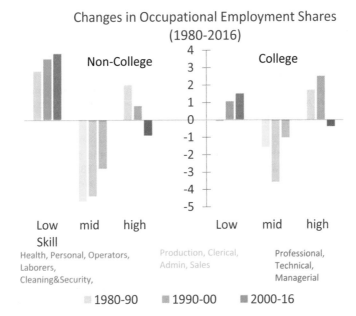

Changes in Occupational Employment Shares
(1980-2016)

Diagram 7.4 Changes in occupational employment shares among working age adults, 1980–2016

The implication of all this, i.e. that the very poorest have been protected, whereas the return to human and fixed capital has soared relative to the return to the unskilled and semi-skilled, has been that the lower middle class, say between the 20th and 70th income percentile, has come out the worst. Another aspect of this same phenomenon has been that mid-skilled jobs have fallen relative to both low- and high-skilled jobs, see Diagram 7.4, so that those in the lower middle class who could not raise their human capital were forced back into lower skilled jobs,[4] see Autor (ibid., Figure 5, p. 10), also see Borella et al. (2019). This is best documented for the USA, but we believe it to be also the case in most other advanced economies.

---

[4]Autor also shows that the loss of mid-skilled jobs was the greater the higher the density of the population, op. cit., pp. 13–15 and Figure 6, i.e. that the proportionate rate of mid-skill job loss has been greatest in urban and metropolitan areas. Why this has been so, and whether this is also the case in other advanced countries is less clear. Bayoumi and Barkema (2019) argue that greater inequality, and higher housing prices, have reduced internal migration in the USA and thereby made the situation of those trapped in decaying areas even worse.

Minimum Wages

Concerns about the transition from semi-skilled to low-skilled jobs, the

resulting loss of bargaining power in the gig economy, and rising income inequality, may well have been factors in recent hikes to minimum wage rates both in AEs and EMEs. Among the advanced economies, the following countries have raised or introduced minimum wages recently:

UK:
From April 1, 2019, the National Living Wage (NLW), the statutory minimum for workers aged 25 and over, was increased by 4.9% to £8.21 per hour. Rates for younger workers also increased above inflation and average earnings.

Canada:
Raised by 13% in 2017. The increase had averaged 3 ½ p.a. over previous decades; never previously raised by so much.

Germany:
Recently introduced a minimum wage.
And among EMEs, the following have been notable:

Poland: the ruling party proposed a hike of nearly 80%! over the next five years kicking off the cycle with a 15.6% hike in 2020. On average minimum wages have been rising by about 6% (since 2010).
Hungary/Czech Republic: robust minimum wage growth over the past couple of years (11% on average in both).

Mexico: After a 10% rise last year, minimum wages were hiked by 16% in 2019. More so, in municipalities located within 25 km from the border with US, where minimum wages will rise by 95%!

Russia: 31% hike on average over the past two years vs 5% on average during the previous seven.

South Korea: a hike of 11% in 2017 and 16% in 2018. Also, limitations on how many hours an individual can work legally during a week (from about 60 to 50).

7.3   Explanations of Rising Inequality

There are, at least, four sets of explanations for such worsening trends in within-country inequality. These are:

  i. Ineluctable Trends
 ii. Technological Changes
iii. Growing Monopoly Power and Concentrations
iv. Globalisation and Demography

We shall consider each in turn.

7.3.1 Ineluctable Trends

For authors in this camp the aberration was the period 1914–1979 when inequality generally declined within many, perhaps most, countries. They see this as primarily the result of a series of special factors, two World Wars, the Great Depression, post-war inflation, Communism/Socialism/price/rent controls, all temporarily depressing the natural condition of rising inequality. For Piketty (2014), this is because the return to capital (i) is assumed, normally and naturally, to exceed the growth rate (g) of the rest of the economy. For Scheidel (2017), this is because the strong will always bully the weak unless restrained by one of the four horsemen of the Apocalypse, war, pestilence or rebellion. Also see Durant (1968), Chapter VIII.

While we cannot disprove such pessimistic fundamentalism, we do not believe it. We see no reason for Piketty's inequality necessarily, or naturally, to hold, and we do not have as bleak a view of the nature, character and future of humankind as Scheidel professes. In contrast, we do think that there is more merit in each of the following three explanations.

7.3.2 Technological Changes

As already indicated by Autor's work, there is no doubt that technology has eliminated (or greatly reduced), the demand for some categories of (semi-skilled) workers. Stenographers and law clerks have gone; secretaries a vanishing breed; welders replaced by robots. Before the arrival of GPS (SatNav in the UK), taxi drivers in a city with such a complicated street map as London had to learn it by heart, and take a test (called 'The Knowledge') before being licensed. Now anyone can drive for Uber without any such qualification. Indeed, the ability to use and read maps is being eroded by the availability of Google maps on your mobile.

The wider question, however, is whether, and how far, the patent effect on *individual* categories of work spills over into explaining the relative stagnation of real wages, and of labour's share of income, as a *whole*? Superficially one might think that, if labour-saving technology was largely responsible, productivity should have grown faster than has been the case in the last two decades. But what if public policy to maintain aggregate demand and full employment has its main practical domestic effect on low productivity service industries, and the 'gig economy'? A plausible hypothesis.

Let us put the question another way; why would such technological developments change the slope and/or position of the Phillips curve? With the same level of overall unemployment, why would the associated aggregate wage/price outcome be less? Here the suggestion is that workers in the unskilled (gig) economy may have less relative bargaining power, and are less unionised, than those who previously worked in semi-skilled areas. Perhaps; but this leads on to the next two issues which relate more directly to the comparative bargaining power of employees and employers, of workers and capitalists.

7.3.3 Concentration and Monopoly Power

There is considerable evidence that concentration and monopoly power have been increasing in private sector industries in the USA in recent decades, see Stiglitz (2019, especially Chapter 3 and the footnotes relating to the prior literature) and Philippon (2019). Such concentration tends to bring with it monopsony in the associated labour market (Stiglitz, footnote 20, for a listing of prior literature on this topic). As is often the case, there is less evidence whether the same has been happening in other advanced economies, but the presumption is that it has.

While such additional concentration/monopoly power may well have been largely responsible for the combination of high profitability and low fixed investment (in the USA at least), it is less clear why and how it might have changed the slope and position of the Phillips curve. But 'again' the suggestion is that the more powerful is the employer relative to the employees, the tighter must the labour market become, the lower must be the Natural Rate of Unemployment (NRU), to get the same real wage increase. See Krueger's luncheon address at the FRB Kansas City (Jackson Hole) (2018), Symposium on *Changing Market Structures and Implications for Monetary Policy.* But, while the direction of effect seems clear enough, once again trying to estimate the overall aggregate impact on real wages and the labour share of income is horribly difficult.

7.3.4 Globalisation and Demography

We can be brief here, since we have already covered this subject in our earlier Chapters on the economic effects of globalisation and demographic change. But for our purposes here it is enough to restate that the unprecedented surge in the availability of labour to employers, both at home, partly met by immigrants, and by out-sourcing abroad, see Boehm et al. (2019), has greatly weakened the relative bargaining power of labour, and of its Trade Unions, and hence played a significant role in reducing real wage growth, and the Natural Rate of Unemployment. Again, see Krueger (2018).

Thus, we have three different forces, technological change, concentration/monopolisation, globalisation/demography, all together tending to reduce the bargaining power of labour. It would be extraordinarily difficult to give any quantitative estimate of their relative effect, and we do not have the skills to attempt this here. But trying to give some, even subjective, weighting matters. If the main cause of the weakness in wage growth/labour share is primarily globalisation/demography, as we think, then it will reverse over coming decades. If it is primarily a technological matter, then it may well continue, as artificial intelligence (AI), for example, kicks in. And whether concentration/monopoly in private industry grows, or lessens, in future is largely a matter for public policy, and could go either way.

So our view is that the growing inequality within countries has been mainly caused by the unprecedented surge in labour availability, caused by globalisation and demography (Chapters 1 and 3), leading to a dramatic decline in labour's bargaining strength (Chapter 5). If so, Piketty is history. But we could, of course, be wrong.

7.4 The Rise of Populism

Whereas highly skilled and well-educated workers have prospered mightily in the last three decades, alongside the capitalist class, there are far fewer of them than there are of the lower middle classes. Even though we suggested that the poorest members of society have been reasonably well looked after by policy measures, the greater bulk of the workforce and of society has had a rough time, seeing little progress in real living standards. And all this was happening while their bosses were receiving eye-watering, well-publicised, multi-million pay packets. The ratio between the pay of CEOs and their average worker has sky-rocketed in most advanced countries, with the partial exception of Japan, in recent decades towards unprecedented levels, see Diagrams 7.5 and 7.6. Our capitalist system has hardly seemed fair, especially when even those presiding over failing firms could walk away not only with vast accumulated wealth but also super-generous future pension pay-outs.

Pay packages typically include an annual bonus and 'long-term incentive plan' (LTIP) on top of base salary. While salary increases have been steady since the late 1990s, performance-related payments have increased dramatically, driving a rapid increase in total pay over the same period.

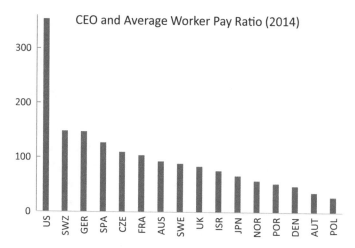

Diagram 7.5 Ratio of remuneration between CEOs and average workers in world in 2014, by country (*Source* Washington Post, September 25, 2014)

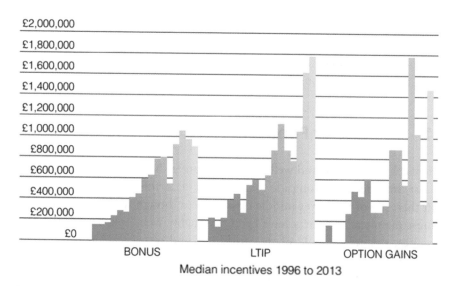

Diagram 7.6 Median cash incentive payments for FTSE 100 lead executives 1996–2013 (*Source* High Pay Centre)

In such circumstances, one might have expected the voting support of those who have lost out relatively during the last three decades to go to left-wing parties in their own countries. After all, these parties were usually founded to foster the interests, and to look after the welfare, within the political scene of the working classes. Yet this has not generally happened in Europe and the USA, though it did in Latin America. Instead, the support of those left behind has gone in Europe mainly to radical, populist, right-wing parties. Examples are easily available; Trump in America, Brexit in the UK, the League of the North in Italy, Rassemblement National in France, AFD in Germany, Orban in Hungary, Law and Justice in Poland, True Finns, etc. For an excellent discussion of such trends, see Rodrik (2018).

Why has this been so? One simple answer is 'attitudes towards immigration'. The politicians and activists in left-wing parties are usually idealists, and they are idealists who support the brotherhood of man, without discrimination relating to nationality, race, sex or anything else. Note that, as we stated earlier, globalisation has actually led to higher world equality despite its adverse effects on inequality within individual countries. As emphasised in Desmet et al. (2018), the authors there claim that their 'results indicate that fully liberalising migration would increase welfare about three-fold…'. Moreover, the left-wing parties are usually the parties which migrants, once on the electoral roll, generally support. Thus, it is much more difficult for left-wing parties to propose tight controls on inward migration, than for right-wing parties to do so. The latter emphasise much more the virtues of patriotic nationalism and the maintenance of local cultures. Although we tend to believe that globalisation has adversely affected the lower middle classes more through the outsourcing of jobs and work to countries abroad, what workers tend to see with their own eyes is the effect of inwards migration on economic development at home. Although the question of whether inward migration has had *any* significant deleterious effect on the jobs and wages of domestic, local workers, remains a contentious issue in the professional literature (Mayda 2019, for example, points to its beneficial effects), an ounce of personal experience is worth several pounds of abstract expert advice. Moreover, it is the fear of what enhanced migration might do, rather than its actuality, that tends to drive opinion. Thus, in the Brexit referendum, there was a negative relationship between the *level* of prior migrants in each constituency and the vote to leave, but a positive relationship between the percentage *change* in recent migration and the vote to leave. So, while people in practice tend to adapt relatively smoothly to different cultural and ethnic differences in due course, it is the fear of cultural and social and economic change that drives opinion, especially among the elderly, though Comertpay et al. (2019) state that in the European Union attitudes towards immigration are a U shaped function of age.

Public Opposition to Immigration

For a few examples, see Rolfe (2019, p. R1) (also see Bratsberg, et al. (2019)),

Because of the ease with which EU migrants can be recruited under the EU's freedom of movement, it is often assumed that employers prefer to recruit migrants and that they do so to undercut the pay of locals and as an alternative to training. Research consistently shows that these assumptions are not supported by evidence. (George et al. 2012; Rolfe et al. 2018; MAC 2018)

And Rolfe et al. (2019, p. R5),

The debates played out in the media and public debate are reflected in opinion polls which show consistently high levels of concern [on immigration] about economic impacts, alongside those on public services. Yet these concerns are not supported by evidence which was recently reviewed by the Migration Advisory Committee (2018). It found no evidence that immigration has reduced natives' job prospects or wages on average, though there are some, very small, effects on employment and wages of lower-paid and lower-skilled natives. Impacts on public finances have been found to be positive through increased tax revenues, and broader concerns about potential negative impacts on public services appear to be largely unsubstantiated (ibid.). At the same time, immigration has led to higher productivity including by increasing innovation. Other, 'cultural' factors are also believed to be responsible for public opposition to immigration (Hainmueller and Hiscox, 2007, 2010; Kaufmann, 2017). Whether separately or combined, and whether evidence based or not, these factors result in support for free movement from the EU to end.

And (ibid., R10 and 11),

The available data show that public opposition to immigration has been widespread in the UK. Historically, people have perceived the economic and cultural impacts overwhelmingly negatively, and polling has consistently found that the British public would like to see immigration to the UK reduced. (Ipsos MORI 2018; Duffy and Frere-Smith 2014)
    Indeed, survey studies show that people vastly overestimate the proportion of refugees and asylum seekers in the migration population. (Blinder 2015)

So, the right-wing populist position on migration, and on reinforcing nationalism, were far more in harmony with the underlying views of those left behind, than the more widely inclusive position of left-wing parties. It is not clear whether and how this realignment of political views might change. In a sense, those voting for populist right-wing parties are correct. Among the factors that have made their lives more difficult in recent decades, globalisation has been one of the more significant. The coming to power of much more nationalist populist parties is likely to put a major spoke in the wheel of globalisation and turn back the clock of history. But while this, combined with the demographic effects already described, will tend to relatively benefit the left behind in each country, it will, as the same time, have strongly adverse effects on world growth and equality, and exacerbate national and regional political tensions.

It is easy enough to see what went wrong. It is much more difficult to see how we can get out of this mess, which is currently plaguing the political systems of the USA and Europe.

8

The Phillips Curve

8.1   Introduction: The Historical Development

The Phillips curve traces out the relationship between unemployment and wages (or prices). When unemployment is low, the demand for labour is high relative to the available supply, and wages will rise faster. When unemployment is much higher, supply outstrips demand and wages/prices may start to fall. See Phillips (1958), especially Figure 1, page 285, for the years 1861–1913, and Figure 9, page 294, for the years 1913–1948.

Exactly the same relationship can also be expressed in terms of the interaction between percentage employment, in somewhat simplified terms the available workforce less those unemployed, and wages/prices. In early Keynesian analysis, this had been thought to be shaped like a reverse L, as depicted in the example below, with wages/prices constant at their existing level until everyone in the workforce was employed. Once that happened, extra demand *had* to be reflected in higher prices so the relationship, previously horizontal, would become vertical at that point (Diagram 8.1).

That approach was not as naïve/simplistic as it may now seem. Wages/prices had remained roughly constant in the UK between 1815 and 1914. Such temporary fluctuations as had occurred had been mainly due to the vagaries of the harvest, while longer-term trends could be ascribed to global phenomena such as opening up North America (lowering the cost of foodstuffs) and gold discoveries. Once World War I was over, once again the tendency was deflation, not inflation, in the inter-war period. Inflation then seemed to be primarily a consequence of wars and other major political disturbances. The over-riding concern, when Keynes was writing the General

© The Author(s) 2020   **117**
C. Goodhart and M. Pradhan, *The Great Demographic Reversal*,
https://doi.org/10.1007/978-3-030-42657-6_8

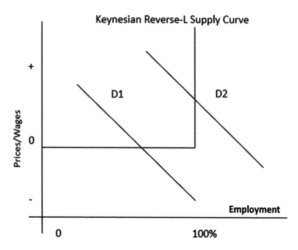

Diagram 8.1   Keynesian reverse-L supply curve

Theory, was to restore and to maintain reasonably full employment, not to control inflation.

It is in some ways a measure of the success of Keynesian economics that since World War II, at least until the twenty-first century, the main problem that faced us was to combine reasonably full employment with price stability. Of course, the initial recovery to full employment at the end of the 1930s and early 1940s owed more to rearmament and World War II than to Keynesian economics. But after World War II and into the early 1950s, the initial major concern/expectation was that the advanced economies might fall back into a further bout of stagnation/deflation. It was not until the later 1950s and 1960s that full confidence in Keynesian demand management to maintain reasonably full employment became widespread.

Once there, the reverse L Keynesian curve came to appear obviously oversimplified. Industries and labour differed in their characteristics, heterogeneity, with bottlenecks occurring at differing pressures of aggregate demand. The overall, macroeconomic relationship between unemployment/employment and wage rate growth/inflation should obviously be curvilinear, rather than constant/kinked. So, the Phillips curve analysis arrived in a welcoming context. Quite quickly economists working in the Civil Service, especially Ministries of Finance, saw their function as to help their political masters to set demand, mainly via fiscal policy, to achieve that point on the Phillips curve that would minimise the political disutility of unemployment on the one hand and inflation on the other (Diagram 8.2).

That period, perhaps running from the Korean War until about 1973, was a transient golden age for macroeconomics. Mainframe computers (IBM)

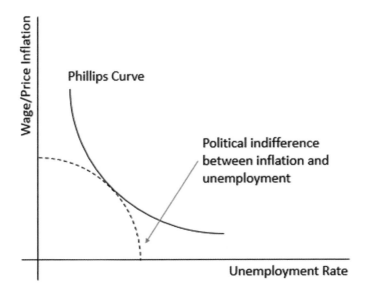

Diagram 8.2 Achieving the political optimum on the Phillips curve

could now allow us to develop quantifiable models of the economy. Growth was good, employment high, and inflation not too high, and (we thought) it could be fixed, more or less, via the Phillips curve analysis. At that juncture, macroeconomists began to feel that they could use an engineering-type blueprint to steer our economies along an optimal path.

It all then went horribly wrong in the 1970s, just as the second golden period for macroeconomics (1992–2008) went horribly wrong after the Great Financial Crisis (GFC). What then occurred, starting in the 1960s, but worsening dramatically in the 1970s, was that the combinations of unemployment and inflation that arose began to move outwards, towards the North–East, so we had simultaneously more inflation and, at the same time, more unemployment, 'stagflation' as it was termed (Diagram 8.3).

Prior to the 1940s, expectations of prices, outside of wartime, would normally have been of stability, but Keynesian demand management, mainly aiming to maintain high employment levels, mindful of the horrors of the Depression in the 1930s, began to lead to regular inflation. Thus inflation in the five year periods from 1955 to 1970 averaged as follows (Table 8.1).

Workers and employers were, of course, mostly concerned with the 'real' outcomes of their contracts, i.e. after adjustment for expected price inflation. So, as (initially low-level) inflation became endemic, built into the system, so did those involved in wage negotiation begin to adjust their demands/offers for real wage increases to take account of such expected inflation. With politicians/civil servants/economists being loathe to give ground on their objectives

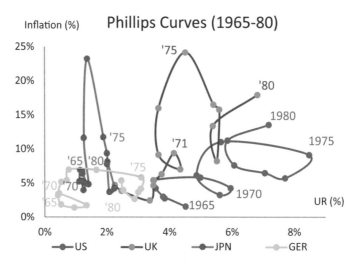

Diagram 8.3 Stagflation in advanced economies (*Source* FRED)

Table 8.1 Worsening inflation, 1956–1970

	USA (%)	UK (%)	France (%)	Japan (%)
1956–1960	2.1	2.8	6.7	1.6
1961–1965	1.3	3.8	4.0	6.6
1966–1970	4.6	5.0	4.6	5.9

Source IMF

for full employment, that led to yet faster inflation. Indeed, there were times when people almost began to expect accelerating inflation, a positive second derivative, see Flemming (1976).

Once the importance of inflation expectations became factored into the analysis, by Phelps (1968) and Friedman (1968), this led on to the concept of the Natural (or Non-Accelerating Inflation) Rate of Unemployment (NAIRU or NRU).[1] This is the level of unemployment at which, in the longer term once expectations have fully adjusted to outcomes, the rate of inflation would remain constant. The assessment was that the long-term Phillips curve would be roughly vertical[2] at the NRU. In the short-run, with expectations largely fixed, the Phillips curve would remain downwards sloping. But if the authorities tried to take persistent advantage of that, in order to lower unemployment

---

[1]There are some technical distinctions between the NAIRU and NRU, but only the cognoscenti are concerned with them.

[2]Or somewhat back-bending, owing to the use of effort and resources to escape the ravages of higher-level inflation, e.g. on taxation.

below the NRU, the result could only be to cause an ever-increasing rate of inflation.

This concept, of a vertical long-run Phillips curve, was an important buttress for the subsequent move to Central Bank independence, with a mandate to concentrate on price stability via an inflation target. With such a Phillips curve, Central Bank measures to maintain price stability would not of themselves affect longer-run employment, growth or productivity, which were (in the long term) determined by supply-side factors, not by monetary, short-term demand-side policies.[3] Thus, concentration on the control of inflation, via monetary policies, would be of itself beneficial, with no offsetting disadvantages.

This term, the Natural Rate of Unemployment, suggests that this would be constant. Friedman defined it, as the rate that would occur when everything has settled down in equilibrium. While there is continuous discussion about the potentially changing levels of the equilibrating (neutral) level of the real interest rate (r^*) and of the underlying, sustainable, rate of growth (g^*), the common assumption is that the NRU (u^*) is fixed and constant.

But the evidence is contrary. u^* appears to have been *more* variable over time than either r^* or g^*. Apart from the Asian countries (China and Japan), the sustainable rate of growth in advanced economies has seemed to vary in recent decades between about 3.5 and 1.5% per annum, and the equilibrating real interest rate between 2 and 0% per annum. In contrast, u^* has varied between about 5 and 2%. After the unhappy experience of the 1930s, economists such as Beveridge and Keynes initially thought that achieving a level of 4–5% would be a good outcome. But the success of full employment policies bringing UE down to around 1.5% after World War II, initially with relatively little inflation, led to the aim of holding UE below 2%.[4]

Demand management, and full employment policies, greatly strengthened the bargaining power of workers and trade unions. The alternative to not agreeing to the employer's wage offer would be another job elsewhere, rather than unemployment. Also, as noted in Chapters 3 and 5, demography led to an improving dependency ratio. Union membership generally rose until about 1980 (Diagram 8.4).

---

[3]As always, there are qualifications, for example hysteresis, whereby the short-run can affect the long-run equilibrium.

[4]Economists such as Dennis Robertson and Paish were then widely excoriated for suggesting that equilibrium might require an average unemployment rate above 2%, e.g. Robertson (1959).

N.B. The idea that there could be an equilibrium rate of unemployment, and that expectations mattered, had been voiced long before Friedman/Phelps. But the narrative seemed less compelling then.

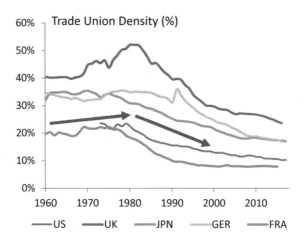

Diagram 8.4 Trade union density has been falling since around 1980 (*Source* 1980)

Another way of describing the NRU is that it marks that level of UE that makes workers content with the real wage growth that their enhanced productivity makes possible. The growing bargaining power (relative to employers) of labour between 1945 and 1980 meant that the underlying NRU was increasing commensurately, perhaps to as much as 5.5%. It is deeply ironic that Keynesian demand management led inexorably to a much higher NRU.

There has been recently, in the period 2007–2020, yet another twist in this tale. Whereas the focus in the (unhappy) 1970s was on a (vertical) Phillips curve, the opposite has occurred in the (equally unhappy) years of the GFC and its aftermath. Over the last decade, or so, the Phillips curve, rather than being vertical, has appeared to become almost horizontal, see Diagram 8.5. Unemployment has varied quite a lot, from a peak in 2009 to a low point in 2019, whereas inflation has remained quite low and stable. First, inflation failed to fall (as much as predicted, given the high and rising UE in 2009/2010), and then, after the recovery to much lower levels of UE, it failed to rise from the prior doldrums. The Phillips curve combinations of UE and price inflation are shown, over the years 2006–2018, separately for the USA, UK, Germany and Japan.

This outcome has surprised, indeed baffled, economists, inside and outside government, with forecasts for inflation systematically overstating subsequent outcomes as unemployment fell back. Understanding, and explaining, this is crucial to the general longer-term outlook for our economies.

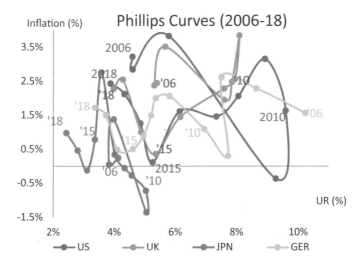

Diagram 8.5 The horizontal Phillips curve, 2006–2018 (*Source* FRED)

In the next section, we review no less than six different sets of explanations:

   i. The Phillips curve is defunct;
  ii. Expectations are all that matter;
 iii. Successful monetary policies;
 iv. A changing structure of employment;
  v. Growing weight on global factors;
 vi. A shifting NRU.

8.2 A Horizontal Phillips Curve?

8.2.1 The Phillips Curve Is Dead

It is now quite common to hear it stated that the Phillips curve is dead, and that our economies are settled into a rut with nominal wages growth of around 2–3%, real output growing at about 1% and inflation at 1–2%; in other words extrapolating the recent past into the indefinite future.

Such extrapolation is without any theoretical basis. Moreover, the Phillips curve *cannot* have disappeared, since it just reflects the balance of the demand and supply of labour. At the limit that balance could, in theory, revert to the (reverse) L curve of early Keynesian analysis, but in practice that is highly unlikely. The Phillips curve may change its slope and shape, for reasons that need to be assessed and appreciated, but it cannot just disappear.

8.2.2 Expectations Dominate?

It was the (partial) failure to take the role of expectations into account that led the initial short-run Phillips curve to become unstable. By contrast it is now sometimes asserted that expectations are *all* that matters. Thus it is sometimes implied that, so long as expectations of future inflation remain 'well anchored', at the Central Bank's target, wages growth and actual inflation will also remain stable at roughly current levels.

But as a matter of principle/theory, that cannot be true. Once every potential worker is employed a further increase in demand *has* to be reflected in higher inflation. And, because of the heterogeneity of industries/labour, bottlenecks and inflation are almost bound to start rising well before total full employment is achieved.

What 'well anchored' inflationary expectations *do* cause is to make people assume that deviations from target inflation will be *temporary*, not permanent. Thus, when prices fell in 2009/2010, people did not expect this to persist, and vice versa when inflation rose above target, as it did in the UK for a few years after the depreciation of sterling in 2008/2009. This does have the effect of making the slope of the *short-term* Phillips curve somewhat more horizontal, but, of itself, should not change either the position, or the verticality, of the *long-run* Phillips curve. If the position of the long-run Phillips curve had remained constant, the steady fall in unemployment that has occurred over the last decade would have *had* to have resulted in an acceleration in inflation, which has not happened.

Lindé and Trabandt (2019) argue that a non-linear Phillips curve could explain both the 'missing deflation' in 2008–2010 and the slow recovery subsequently. 'Put differently, even though economic growth may resume after a deep recession, price and wage inflation will only increase modestly until economic slack has subsided sufficiently', p. 3. But, given the current historically low levels of unemployment in the USA, UK and Japan, this cannot be a satisfactory explanation, unless the NRU had previously shifted, which takes us to the explanation in Sect. 8.2.6 below.

8.2.3 Successful Monetary Policies

McLeay and Tenreyro (2018) have reminded us, in their paper on 'Optimal Inflation and the Identification of the Phillips Curve', that the purpose of monetary policy is to stabilise inflation at its target level. If all shocks were to demand, so that inflation and output co-vary, and policy was perfectly successful in stabilising inflation, then, by definition inflation would be constant. Under those conditions, the correlation between unemployment, also affected by other structural factors, and wage, or price, inflation would be zero. This would be so even though the structural underlying relationship (the Phillips curve) between slack in the labour market and inflation may have remained strong, stable and constant. If the shocks affecting the economy were supply shocks, such as oil price variations and changes in indirect taxes, tariffs and (externally driven) exchange rate changes, then policy would have to balance the loss from disequilibrium output against the loss from failing to hit the inflation target. In order to identify the Phillips curve in such conditions of simultaneity, one would need to be able to assess and quantify occasions of supply shocks and/or monetary policy errors.[5]

That is not easy. What we do know, however, is that supply shocks were far more prevalent between 1970 and 1990, e.g. oil shocks in 1973/1974, 1979, 1986 and commodity price shocks and monetary policy errors more obvious, than in the subsequent years, especially during the Great Moderation, 1992–2005, when everything macroeconomic seemed to remain stable. Thus the fact that the slope of the calculated relationship between unemployment (or the output gap) and wage (price) inflation appeared to become more horizontal in these later decades may be just an artefact of better monetary policies and fewer supply shocks, rather than representing any change to the underlying structural relationship. If this was so, then calculations of Phillips curve relationships for separate segments of a single monetary area, e.g. where monetary policy could not offset regional diversities, should show a greater (negative) slope.[6] This does seem to be so, as evidenced in some current empirical work, e.g. not only McLeay and Tenreyro (ibid.), but also Hooper, Mishkin and Sufi, 'Prospects for Inflation in a High Pressure Economy: Is the Phillips Curve Dead or is it just Hibernating?' (May 2019).

8.2.4 A Changing Structure of Employment

Karl Marx opined that wages would be held down by 'the reserve army of the unemployed'.[7] Perhaps nowadays it might be more accurate to suggest that it is the reserve army of the elderly that has played a major role in limiting

---

[5]Owing to lags in the transmission mechanism between policy measures and their effect on wage/price inflation, unforeseen deviations between (official) forecasts of unemployment and inflation and actual, ex post, inflation might help to identify the underlying structural relationship.

[6]While this does seem to hold for the wage/unemployment version of the Phillips curve, attempts to resurrect the price/output gap formulation of this relationship have been rather less successful. What has caused this divergence, e.g. time varying profit mark-ups, is beyond the scope of this work.

[7]From Wikipedia, https://en.wikipedia.org/wiki/Reserve_army_of_labour,

wage growth. There are two separate margins for transmission into, and out of, employment, to wit unemployment, and participation. Whereas workers in the prime age range, 20–55 years old, mainly move between employment and unemployment, the elderly, 55–75 years old, tend to switch between employment and non-participation in the work force, e.g. in the guise of (early) retirement.

As already demonstrated in Chapter 3, participation rates in many countries have been increasing rapidly in recent years, especially elderly women, as job availability rises; (though the rise has been more limited in the USA). It appears that they can be tempted back to work quite elastically in response to reasonable opportunities regarding openings and pay. Indeed, as Mojon and Ragot, (2019), show, if you strip out the elderly from the calculated relationship, then the adjusted Phillips curve tends to fit much better.

This finding has several implications. First, as long as there remains a sizeable buffer of elderly still prepared to switch elastically between work and retirement, then the Phillips curve will appear to be more horizontal, since employers can fill job vacancies from that source (as well as from migrants) rather than having to raise wages. Second, the existence of a reserve army of elderly has meant that the NRU will have fallen, since one can run the economy at a higher pressure of demand so long as that reserve army acts as a safety valve.

But there is a limit to this. Not all the elderly can be tempted back to work; some cannot, and others do not want to do so. Further increases in participation rates may become less elastic and harder to achieve. When the available reserve army has all been conscripted, the pressure of demand may have to be moderated again.

8.2.5   A Greater Role for Global Factors

Kristin Forbes (2019) has done a detailed study, 'Has globalization changed the inflation process?', though it focusses more on price than wage inflation. One of her conclusions is as follows, p. 30,

---

Although the idea of the industrial reserve army of labour is closely associated with Marx, it was already in circulation in the British labour movement by the 1830s. Engels discussed the reserve army of labour before Marx did in Engels famous book (2018), *The Condition of the Working Class in England* (1845). The first mention of the reserve army of labour in Marx's writing occurs in a manuscript [on 'Wages'] he wrote in 1847, but did not publish....

The idea of the labour force as an "army" occurs also in Part 1 of *The Communist Manifesto*, written by Marx and Engels in 1848. (see Engels and Marx 2018)

The impact of global factors has also changed significantly over time – especially for CPI inflation and the cyclical component of inflation. For example, in both the Phillips curve and trend-cycle frameworks, changes in the world output gap and commodity prices have had a greater impact on CPI inflation and the cyclical component of inflation over the last decade. Inflation models should not only more carefully control for changes in the global economy, but also allow coefficients in the models to be dynamic and evolve over time.

Somewhat similarly, Stock and Watson (2019), advocate using a Cyclically Sensitive Inflation index (CSI), which lowers the weights on products whose prices are set internationally, or are poorly measured. Thus, they conclude, p. 90, that,

> the CSI index provides a new window on movements in the rate of inflation. Because the CSI index tends to focus its weights on sectors with locally determined prices, it provides a way to separate out prices that are domestically determined from prices that are heavily influenced by international conditions.

> By using both inflation components and filters that eliminate trends and focus on cyclical variation, a different picture of the stability of the Phillips curve emerges. Whereas the standard accelerationist relationship between changes in inflation and gaps has flattened, the relationship between the weighted cyclical components and cyclical activity is substantially more stable.

8.2.6 A Shifting NRU

Successful Keynesian demand management, and rising dependency ratios, before the baby boomers came of working age, strengthened the relative bargaining power of labour in the years 1945–1980. Both an effect, and then also a supplementary cause, was the increasing membership, militancy and power of (private sector) trade unions. As a measure of such militancy, see the time path of days lost to strikes and number of workers stopping work in the USA and UK, Diagram 8.6.

What was not so easily perceived was that such trends caused the NRU to rise steadily. Even though average UE tended to rise slightly in the 1960s and more in the 1970s, politicians and the voting public consistently underestimated the NRU, and inflation accelerated. It was not until Volcker, Reagan, Mrs Thatcher and Lawson/Howe temporarily abandoned targeting aggregate demand, replacing that with versions of monetary targetry, that the inflationary spiral was broken.

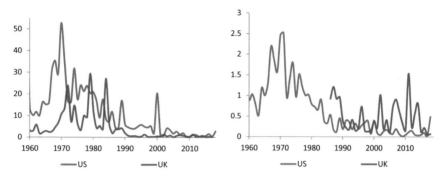

Diagram 8.6 Working days lost to strikes (Mil.); Work stoppage workers involved (Mil.) (*Source* BLS, ONS)

It is the thesis of the first half of this book that from about the early 1990s, a combination of demographic factors, e.g. improved dependency ratios, and globalisation, especially the advent of China into the world's trading system, dramatically switched the underlying context from inflation to deflation. Again, both an effect, and a supplementary cause, was a reduction in the membership and militancy of (private sector) Trades Unions. Just like the earlier period (1945–1980), but now in reverse, the authorities, and the macroeconomists advising them, have recently failed to realise that u* (NRU) was driving ever lower, in line with the declining bargaining power of labour.

But now labour has retaliated, not at the wage bargaining table, but in the voting booth. Globalisation has been checked by populism, just at the time that demographic factors are swinging back to labour's advantage. Meanwhile, those who extrapolate the recent past into the future, ignoring longer-run forces, are asserting that we will remain in secular stagnation.

The slow-moving pendulum is about to swing back again. It may be that, for a year or two, we could combine even lower unemployment with price stability, but that will not last. The message of this chapter is that, not only is the long-run Phillips curve vertical at the NRU (u*), but also the position of u* is continuously and systematically shifting owing to longer-run demographic, political and economic forces. You ignore such trends at your peril. Forecasts which ignore them will be subject to systematic and one-sided errors.

9

'Why Didn't It Happen in Japan?' A Revisionist History of Japan's Evolution

9.1 Introduction: Flaws in the Conventional Analysis

"Why didn't it happen in Japan?" is often the simple but powerful counter-argument to our economic predictions that ageing will raise inflation and possibly real interest rates too. After all, Japan is the tip of the spear of demographic change, with a population that is both ageing and shrinking. For many, Japan is therefore the experimental cauldron that provides an authoritative economic blueprint for an ageing world.

At first blush, what happened in Japan appears to be a contradiction of our thesis. The bursting of Japan's asset bubble in the early 1990s, whereby the values of land, housing and equities then collapsed, which had all skyrocketed during the 1980s, and the rapidly dwindling supply of its labour force was accompanied by corporate deleveraging, a collapse in investment and growth, and stagnation, even deflation, in wages and prices. Almost exactly the opposite of what we are arguing an ageing world has in store for us.

Japan's lessons, however, when read as above, are tainted by two shortcomings.

First, if you read the conventional analysis of Japan's evolution closely (see the box below), it is an analysis of an economy in autarky—one in which the rest of the world doesn't exist. The local drivers (the asset bust, local demographics) are therefore almost *forced* into explaining the local outcomes (deflation, weak investment and growth, etc.).

Perhaps an analogy will help. Let's say there's construction on 6th Avenue in New York that causes complete traffic gridlock. This is a local shock, but

© The Author(s) 2020
C. Goodhart and M. Pradhan, *The Great Demographic Reversal*,
https://doi.org/10.1007/978-3-030-42657-6_9

there should be no impediment to driving along other paths uptown or on the cross-town streets—implying relief is available outside the local epicentre. Traffic would quickly move on to these alternate routes—in a steady state, there would be very little congestion on 6th Avenue. Rush hour, however, is a very different animal. Every route uptown is equally busy. This is a global shock with no relief. The first scenario is where Japan was over the last few decades. Faced with labour headwinds at home but an abundance of labour in the rest of the world, Japan sought relief outside its borders and imported global trends. The second and more frustrating scenario is where most of the world will find itself now, without an obvious way to get out of the demographic gridlock. The reader with the morning coffee might point to the subway, but New Yorkers will know that traffic is as bad as it is during rush hour despite the subway network. Even this overextension of our analogy has parallels to the points we make in Chapter 10 about the ability of technology to offset demographic pressures.

The conventional interpretation of Japan's evolution

The conventional view paints Japan's demography driving growth, inflation and interest rates lower. The argument is simple enough to be compelling. A declining supply of labour could only be offset by a faster accumulation of capital that led to a surge in productivity. However, the combination of bursting of the housing bubble and the deleveraging of the massive stock of debt built up during the ascent of Japan paralysed the corporate sector. Declining investment lowered the demand for loanable funds and interest rates fell. The decline in economic growth created persistent deflationary pressure that complemented the decline in nominal and real interest rates.

The decline in growth, the deflation and falling interest rates in Japan are all facts. However, the rationale behind why these happened is seriously flawed because the narrative fails to account for the significant influence of global forces. Equally, it fails to account for other facts that stand at odds with this desultory narrative, namely an impressive record of productivity and fairly good wage growth under the circumstances.

This chapter aims to rectify those shortcomings and provide a revisionist history of Japan's economic evolution after the bursting of the asset bubble in the early 1990s.

Yet it is inconceivable to think that any economy, particularly such an open economy as Japan, could escape the inexorable global forces that we have seen unleashed upon the world. If global factors are explicitly included in an era when they were so dominant, surely the interpretation itself must be transformed.

In the simplest of terms, how could China's ascent since the 1990s change everything in the world but have no role in explaining the evolution of Japan?

Our line of investigation to answering this simple question will be to pursue clues to a global footprint in Japan's trail. In a nutshell, we proceed under the null hypothesis that Japan evolved the way it did precisely because the rest of the world was overflowing with labour exactly as Japan's labour supply was ebbing. Japan's corporates acted to take advantage of this global tailwind to offset local headwinds. Their rational response to these conflicting forces has helped us to formulate a truly global, revisionist history of Japan.

Second, Japan's evolution over the last 30 years is tainted by the decade following the asset bust. The years 1991–1999 were indeed a lost decade. The response to the asset crash in 1991 involved several serious policy mistakes, with the result that the crisis dragged on, and had a second peak around 1995 when several banks failed. That was followed shortly afterwards by the Asian Crisis in 1997/1998. So, during these years, unemployment rose, wages fell and output stagnated.

But it is a mistake to treat Japan from the early 1990s to the present as a single period.

From 2000 onwards, the situation recovered and has remained far more benign.

Total output has growth at around 1% annually even as the workforce has shrunk by 1% a year. The difference between the two is productivity. Output per worker has grown by 2% annually on average—almost every other advanced economy in the world would bite your hand off if you offered it 2% productivity growth per worker for the last two decades. As the workforce has shrunk, wage growth has mostly stagnated while inflation has averaged 0.5%. All this while unemployment has stayed very low. Considering the local decline in workforce, the outcome for Japan since 2000 is really rather good.

What then is the problem about Japan? There are three main issues:

First, output growth was and remains poor. Japan does look rather poor when it comes to the growth of total output compared to other nations. However, where output per capita has been low, productivity as measured by output per worker has done better than in almost every advanced economy since 2000.

Second, inflation remains low. Although it is arguable that there is nothing inherently wrong with having inflation at about 0.5% p.a., the BoJ's target has consistently been 2%, and it has failed to reach that.

Third, perhaps the main problem for our thesis is that the unemployment in Japan, though never high, fell to levels that, by Western standards, were remarkably low and yet that did not raise wages. So, the Phillips curve does seem to have been extremely flat in Japan for nearly two decades now. And that is what the standard analysis now expects for the West; so how do we explain the Phillips curve? And why would the West not follow Japan in this respect?

We address the last two issues in the discussion on the Phillips curve in Japan further below. The key question there is whether the Phillips curve has indeed remained flat or has there simply been much more slack in the Japanese labour market than the unemployment rate would suggest? Incorporating the singular characteristics of Japan's labour market into our analysis suggests that the robust headline unemployment rate did hide a considerable amount of slack in Japan.

But first we turn to the first issue, Japan's productivity profile, not just for its own sake but also en route to understanding the nature of Japan's Phillips curve.

I. Japan's Productivity Surge and the Global Clues Embedded in its Outbound FDI

The wedge between the 1% growth rate of Japan's total output and the 1% average decline in its workforce is the contribution of productivity. Diagram 9.1 shows Japan's outperformance over almost every advanced economy when it comes to output per worker.

Rising firm productivity, as a matter of fact, is one of two competing hypotheses to explain Japan's exit from its lost decade. A surge of exports in 2000 and its contribution to GDP growth for the rest of the decade is the other. Ogawa et al. (IMF 2012) decompose the export function into two parts—one that depends on the income stream of Japan's trading partners and the other that is a function of the 'total factor productivity' of firms as well as input costs. Total factor productivity, they find, accounts for around 50% of the variation in export growth whereas incomes among trading partners

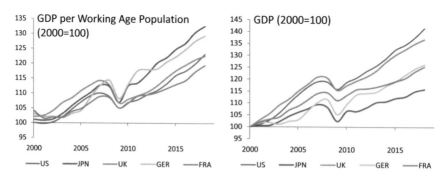

Diagram 9.1 Japan's GDP per worker has outperformed that of its peers handsomely (*Source* IMF)

account only for about 20%. The strenuous efforts in restructuring shown by firms during the 1990s, they argue, might account for this dynamic.

This *is* what we should be seeing from profit-maximising firms faced with structural headwinds, but how they did it is where the evidence of a global footprint on Japan's productivity trail can be seen.

The first clue to the global footprint in Japan's story is the considerable investment by Japan's companies not within, but outside, its borders—outbound FDI (O-FDI hereafter). Japan's corporates showed a dynamism in overseas investment that was in sharp contrast to the desultory performance at home. O-FDI appears to be a safety valve designed to escape headwinds from local demand and expensive labour in favour of the dual tailwinds of strong overseas growth and cheap labour delivered by global demographic tailwinds. O-FDI was strong even during the 'lost decade' and has continued its rich form since.

9.2   Domestic Investment—The Boom and the Bust

The story of domestic investment in Japan breaks neatly into two eras. The corporate expansion during the heady years of expansion of the 1960s, 1970s and 1980s was very different to the multi-decade anaemia seen during and even after the lost decade.

9.2.1   Corporate Expansion—The Heady Years

There are two distinct regimes which incentivised Japan's firms to rapidly accumulate capital.

First, Japan accumulated capital rapidly during the 'miracle' of the 1960s and 1970s during a period of demographic outperformance during which MITI orchestrated Japan's rapid ascent from the shadows. Johnson (1982) argues that the miracle actually began only in 1962. By 1975, the manufacturing industry had increased threefold. And by 1978? By 400%. In fact, the bulk of the increase during that period came only after 1966. That astonishing period of growth had much to do with not only with MITI's industrial policy, quietly shepherding the expansion of corporate Japan from the wings, but also with a then-benign demographic profile within Japan compared to other economies. MITI—Japan's powerful Ministry of International Trade and Industry—provided specific incentives and helped direct the flow of capital during Japan's rise. Johnson and others attribute a significant chunk of Japan's single-minded improvement to MITI's efforts. It was later transformed to the Ministry of Economy, Trade and Industry and remains influential but far less proactive than its former self.

That such a surge occurred as Japan's dependency ratio fell below 50 after falling for decades helps explain why output grew so rapidly. Japan's dependency ratio (the number of dependents for every 100 workers) fell from around 70 in the 1940s to just over 40 by the end of the 1970s. Around the same time (specifically from 1946 to 1976), Johnson shows that industrial output grew an astonishing 55-fold. The combination of rapid capital accumulation, an increase in the labour force (demographically and via internal migration), combined extremely well with MITI's drive to help import capital goods embedded with manufacturing technology. By 1976, Japan accounted for 10% of global output despite occupying only 0.3% of its land mass and being home to only 3% of the world's population.

Second, capital accumulation surged after the Plaza Accord of 1985. If the 1960s and 1970s were economic miracles, then the period after the Accord was the classic stuff of bubbles. As the Yen appreciated rapidly after the Accord, policymakers moved to counter the move via domestic policy measures. The massive monetary and fiscal easing to offset the rapid appreciation of the Yen led to funds being ploughed into real estate, but also into corporate Japan. The result was excess capacity and excess leverage in the corporate sector in addition to all the ills of a well-documented housing bubble.

9.2.2   From a Multi-Decade Boom to a Multi-Decade Investment Recession

The bubble burst in 1991/1992 with equity, land and housing values collapsing. The Nikkei fell from its peak of around 40,000 to a low of 10,000. After the bursting of the asset bubble, both the economy and the corporate sector were battered into reversing the excesses present in the economy.

Corporate Japan aggressively reduced the leverage it had built up at home. The domestic debt/GDP ratio for non-financial companies fell from a peak of 147% of GDP in 1994 to 97% of GDP in 2015, offset by public sector leverage that rose throughout that period. From the point of view of the corporate sector, however, leverage had to be reduced. Basic math says reducing the pace of borrowing or paying back debt when revenues are not growing means that other spending has to be pared back. That is what domestic corporate investment in Japan shows (Diagram 9.2).

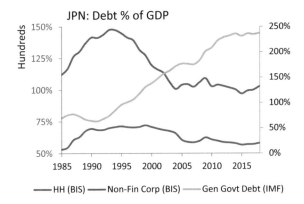

Diagram 9.2 Japan's corporate sector delevered, public sector leverage rose (*Source* BIS, IMF)

To get a clearer picture of that change, look at a smoothed measure of investment. A five-year rolling average of investment shows that investment growth in the two decades leading up to the asset bubble averaged 4.4% with a peak at nearly 10%. After the bubble, that average was 0%, with investment growth below zero for the most part, punctuated by brief bursts in the post-crisis period and more recently (Diagram 9.3).

Over much of the lost decade, investment growth was lower than consumption growth. Reflecting this rotation, the composition of the corporate sector has also changed over time. Manufacturing has been far more sensitive to economic conditions than services. Manufacturing firms thus participated to a greater extent in the investment downturn, with the share of manufacturing in total investment falling from 45% in the early 1980s

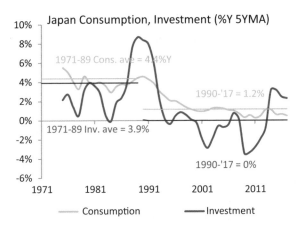

Diagram 9.3 Japan's consumption fell after the decline in investment (*Source* IMF)

to around 30% by 2002. Manufacturing employment has not been immune either. The share of manufacturing employment fell from around 28% in the late 1970s and 25% on the eve of the asset bust to just over 16% in 2017.

On the evidence thus far, the conventional description of a corporate sector weighed down by the need to shed excess leverage and capacity paints a gloomy picture of corporate Japan.

However, the picture of a Japanese corporate sector that succumbed to these excesses without a fight belies a mostly overlooked, but vibrant and globally savvy strategy to raise corporate productivity.

We argue below that Japanese corporates were actively expanding their footprint in a profit-maximising manner. They did so by reducing their dependence on Japan's struggling economy and its shrinking and expensive labour force, and relocating activity strategically to cheaper foreign labour markets where the outlook for growth was more promising.

9.2.3   Outbound FDI: The Investment Boom Outside Japan's Borders

The share of manufacturing in the domestic economy fell from 45% in the pre-bubble period to about 30% in the early 2000s. As above, that has happened against a backdrop of falling and very weak investment growth. Those declines painted a picture of a corporate sector in disarray, debilitated by the burden of debt. However, outbound foreign direct investment (henceforth O-FDI) and the dynamics of production abroad suggest otherwise. Over time, O-FDI has shown a similar trend for the non-manufacturing sector as well, with services O-FDI dominating recent increases.

The Yen's dramatic appreciation in 1985 was the trigger for something new to Japan's corporates—O-FDI. There is, however, much more to the story than such a simplistic explanation. The multi-decade persistence of this trend suggests a strong, structural driver beneath the surface (Diagram 9.4).

IMF estimates (IMF 2011, Japan Spillover Report) suggest that labour costs are the prime motivation when looking at the shifting patterns of location and production, while growth in the destination country comes in second. METI's survey suggests the opposite order as a rationale, by a wide margin. Firms' responses suggest that 70% think demand in the destination market is the key motivation, while the importance of qualified and inexpensive labour has fallen in recent years. Both studies may not be inconsistent with each other given the rise in unit labour costs (i.e. labour compensation adjusted for productivity) in China and the productivity-driven stability in unit labour costs at home in Japan. Japan's outbound FDI was just short of

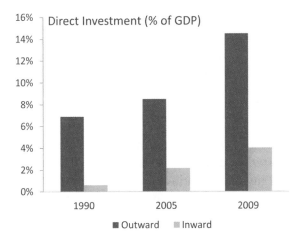

Diagram 9.4 Outbound Direct Investment has outstripped Inward Investment (*Source* METI, Japan)

20 trillion Yen in 2017, more than a sixfold increase in its value from the mid-1990s.

O-FDI's dramatic rise: Twenty years of rich information from METI's surveys on overseas business activities of Japanese companies give us a rich view of the evolution of O-FDI (Japan's Ministry of International Trade and Industry was reorganised into the Ministry of Economy, Trade and Industry in 2001). Tracking those surveys—the latest survey from 2018 being the 49th annual survey—provides a wealth of information and a sense of the dramatic changes in O-FDI:

- *Investment*: the Yen value of outbound FDI increased threefold between 1996 and 2012, while the ratio of investment made in foreign affiliates, as compared to investment at home by domestic firms, increased 10-fold between 1985 and 2013.
- *Number of affiliates*: Japanese companies owned around 4000 overseas affiliates in 1987. That rose rather quickly to around 12,600 by 1998 and stands at 25,000 in METI's 2018 survey.
- *Employment*: Overseas affiliates employment stood at 2.3 million in 1996. That number was 5.6 million in 2016.

While the absolute numbers are impressive and interesting by themselves, they are fascinating for our purposes when compared against domestic trends in Japan, particularly for the manufacturing sector, which saw big declines at home.

O-FDI compared to domestic trends within Japan

In the mid-1990s, O-FDI was growing at 7%, right around the time domestic investment growth was falling sharply (Kang and Piao 2015). By contrast, over 1990–2002, the average decline in Japan's domestic investment was 4% a year on average while non-manufacturing firms averaged around 2%.

The overseas capital investment ratio (the ratio of capital investment made in foreign affiliates vs domestic companies) stood at 3% in 1985, quadrupled to 12% by 1997 and reached 30% by 2013. The recent decline in the overseas-domestic investment ratio is one of the rare occasions that domestic investment has risen and overseas investment has fallen. Over the critical period when Japan's corporate sector was written off, overseas investment has handsomely outperformed domestic investment (see Diagram 9.5)

Japanese companies with overseas operations produced nearly 40% of their output abroad, while the overseas production ratio (manufacturing sector production by overseas affiliates compared to production within Japan) stood at 25% in 2017 (Diagram 9.6). For the key transportation sector, that ratio stands just below 50%.

The share of manufacturing has fallen in overseas investment too, but only because non-manufacturing companies have ramped up investment increasingly over time. The overall backdrop couldn't be more different from the domestic one—overall overseas FDI has seen a sixfold increase since 1990

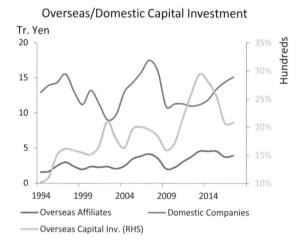

Diagram 9.5 The Overseas/Domestic Investment Ratio (Manufacturing) indicates a strategy to invest abroad rather than at home (*Source* METI)

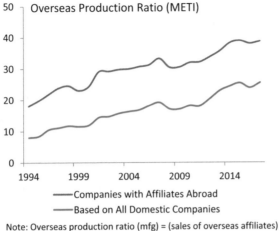

Note: Overseas production ratio (mfg) = (sales of overseas affiliates) / [(sales of domestic companies + sales of overseas affiliates)]

Diagram 9.6 The Overseas Production Ratio shows that Japan Inc. produced more through its overseas affiliates (*Source* METI)

while the ratio of overseas to domestic investment as well as production have increased dramatically.

Manufacturing employment within and outside Japan followed a similarly divergent trend as we document further below.

9.2.4 Why Has Outbound FDI Not Received Greater Attention?

Despite being a powerful narrative, the story of outbound FDI has been treated as an isolated trend, at least when it comes to analysing Japan from a demographic perspective. Why? These are simply guesses, but it might be in some part due to two reasons.

First, the domestic data appear to fit seamlessly into a consistent narrative of deleveraging and demographics that few have sought to question.

Second, overseas operations do not appear to contribute to the accounting profits of the Japanese corporate sector in a meaningful way. 'Only a fraction of the profits generated from overseas operations are repatriated to Japan and a significant portion is reinvested abroad for further expansion of overseas operations' according to Kang and Piao (2015). Why were profits not repatriated? If the objective of Japanese firms was partly to exploit lower labour costs and an expanding market overseas, then an external expansion would almost require profits generated abroad to be retained there for further expansion. The dramatic increase in capacity and employment abroad seems to suggest this is, indeed, what happened. Moreover, Japan's 'dividend exemption policy' meant that firms were disincentivised from repatriating profits back home (METI white paper 2011). Japan's overseas operations remained attractive enough to be pursued aggressively over decades, but Japan's corporates have not sought to bring those earnings back home.

Inside Japan though, it has attracted a lot of attention, mostly as an unwelcome trend. Overseas FDI has been worrisome enough for many to view it with concern because of the 'hollowing out' effect, that production overseas would lead to lower employment within Japan. There is some evidence of that correlation with METI estimating a negative impact from the 1990s and recent research reinforcing that message too—see Kiyota 2015.

Correlation is one thing, but could it not be that the causality runs both ways? The 'hollowing out' hypothesis is often tested as if Japan's outbound FDI was an exogenous trend that caused lower employment at home. Sakura and Kondo (2014) argue that it was the most innovative firms in Japan that often ventured overseas. If that is indeed the case, then one could argue that expanding overseas employment was merely a function of the desire of these dynamic firms to tap new markets and exploit further cost advantages abroad, while reducing expensive employment at home. The economic causality thus flows from lower employment at home to greater employment overseas.

9.3   The Changing Composition of Domestic Production and Employment

Reallocation of jobs within Japan

The percentage of Japan's workforce employed in manufacturing and agriculture has fallen in a straight line, from 22% and 5% in 1996, to 16% and 3% in 2018. The increasing share, naturally, has been going to the services sector.

The manufacturing sector has very little protection if it cannot maintain its profitability, which is usually tied intrinsically to productivity. The services sector, on the other hand, has enough local protection to protect itself by using inflation to drive a wedge between its revenues and costs (in other words, raising product prices relative to wages, for example). Unlike manufacturing, many services cannot be offshored or imported, which makes it very hard for competition to prevent companies in the services sector from using price increases to protect themselves.

One reason behind the downward pressure on wages in Japan can be traced back to the receding footprint of manufacturing and the expanding role of services, and hence in turn to the importance of the global factors that led to this reallocation. The local dynamics behind that reallocation are relatively straightforward:

- The aftermath of the asset bust and the two headwinds, tepid growth and an expensive and shrinking pool of labour, led to an investment recession.
- The manufacturing sector, least able to protect itself at home, begins to raise its productivity in three ways. First, it freezes any further increases in the capital stock and then slowly reduces its labour input. In doing so, the capital available per worker (a basic measure of productivity) slowly starts to rise. Second, manufacturing production slowly starts to get offshored. Third, selecting which activities to offshore completes the process—corporate Japan keeps the design and very high technology parts of the production at home and moves the more mechanical parts of the production line overseas.
- The manufacturing sector was unwilling to absorb its historical share of workers, and the share of manufacturing employment to total employment fell. The services sector (whose role in the economy was kept steady by the steady nature of consumption) began to face an increasing supply of workers. The share of services in total employment then rose.
- In order to protect its profitability, the services sector then drove a wedge between prices and wages, but by pushing wage growth lower. This was in part due to the dynamics we have described just above, but also partly due to the changing nature of Japan's labour market as it sought out ways to escape its institutional customs.

Bottom line: activity and jobs were reallocated both outside Japan's borders and within Japan as the corporate sector strategically and purposefully raised productivity to protect itself. Those efforts need to better recognised not only for delivering Japan's exit from the lost decade, but also with delivering productivity per worker that outperformed almost every other advanced economy in the world.

To do so, corporate Japan had to work within the constraints of Japan's singular labour market norms. The result was a shrinking labour force that didn't result in wage inflation.

The Phillips Curve: Why didn't a shrinking labour force lead to wage inflation in Japan?

'Unlike in the United States and Europe, where unemployment tends to increase during a recession, in Japan unemployment did not increase substantially, but instead wages declined considerably'.

—Bank of Japan Governor Kuroda, 2014 speech

There is much complexity behind this matter-of-fact simple statement. That complexity gives us clues about an economic fact that most analysis finds difficult to reconcile—why the shrinking supply of a factor should not raise its price.

There are three reasons we think ageing and a shrinking labour force did not lead to inflation in Japan:

9.3.1 Globalisation

As noted earlier, Japan's labour force was shrinking just as the world became overflowing with cheaper but efficient labour. So, Japan's tradeable goods sectors, primarily manufacturing, moved production abroad, notably to China. This meant that employment in manufacturing, which was largely well-paid, insider jobs, fell and that produced a strong shift of labour towards lower-paying outsider jobs.

9.3.2 'Insiders' vs 'Outsiders'

In Japan, the loyalty of insider workers is mostly to their company, rather than to a trade union, and the counterpart commitment from the employers is to maintain employment during downturns. So, the Phillips curve in this respect is very flat, with more of the adjustment to cyclical forces being felt in hours worked than in either unemployment or wages. Japan's local customs of long-term employment make mass layoffs and job destruction unviable options.

Outsiders had remarkably little bargaining power and bore most of the burden of the disinflationary pressure from the services sector to drive a wedge between prices and wages by pushing wage growth lower.

One simple episode is sometimes quite revealing. At the worst point of Japan's asset value collapse in 1993 as well as the lows of the Great Financial Crisis, Japan's unemployment rate rose to 5.5%, no more. In no other episode did Japan's unemployment rate ever rise above 3%. The speed at which the labour market adjusted is also striking. GDP growth fell from 6% in 1989 to −2% in 1994. The unemployment rate rose from around 2% in 1990 to 3% by 1995. It is only by 2003 that the unemployment rate peaked at just 5.4%. By contrast, the unemployment rate infamously rose to 10% in the USA during its own housing crisis. The unambiguous message from the labour market is that if there is one part of Japan's economy that does not participate in economic adjustment, it is employment, i.e. the Phillips curve has *always* been flat in Japan, more so than in other advanced countries.

The origins of Japan's labour customs: World War II changed Japan's labour market. Prior to that, only some senior employees had the benefits of long-term employment contracts. That practice was extended during the war to secure employment and encourage loyalty. After the war, employers were quick to see the advantages of the effects of these practices on employee morale and loyalty and they soon became the norm. Over time, these customs expanded to include not only long-term employment but on-the-job training, promotions in internal labour markets, and wage and promotion benefits based on seniority.

Over time, Japan's society as a whole came to prioritise job security above all else. Ahmadjian and Robinson (2001) wrote 'job security enjoys a high priority among Japanese social values. Termination of employment by the employer, for whatever reason, except under very rare and genuinely exceptional circumstances, is an act which is frowned upon and which is considered disgraceful and objectionable'. Under such severe social norms, it is not surprising that growth recessions in the Japanese economy were not accompanied by a rising unemployment rate as is the case in most economies.

Adjustment without layoffs: Since employment in Japan could not adjust rapidly by laying off workers in large numbers, labour market adjustment happened by a change in the structure of employment and inexorable downward pressure on hours and wages (see Diagram 9.7). Japan's customs of long-term employment, internal labour markets and seniority-based wages collectively skewed the outcome in this direction.

'Internal labour markets' allowed for the movement of workers within an organisation. The presence of the Keiretsu (huge conglomerates held together by a complex system of cross-shareholding) made extensive movements of personnel within these huge structures possible. Because long-term contracts

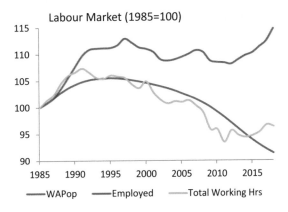

Diagram 9.7 Hours have adjusted because employment could not, mostly due to Japan's labour market norms (*Source* Ministry of Internal Affairs and Communication, United Nations)

came with seniority-based wage increases, a dual system emerged to benefit those working on the 'inside' but hurt those on the 'outside'.

During stressful times, a skew in employment in favour of the 'insiders' raised labour costs for firms, and the response of firms to rising costs, just as demand was falling, changed the structure of Japan's labour market as well as its wage dynamics.

Though he does not explicitly factor in the role of Japan's customs, Bank of Japan Governor Kuroda's previously referenced speech from 2014 is a good summary of some of these changes. In an effort to reduce costs to fight the pressure of low growth on revenues, firms increasingly sought to reduce wage costs. In the face of dimming prospects for growth, employees accepted wage cuts rather than risk unemployment. Wage costs were easier to control for non-regular employees, i.e. those who were not on long-term contracts (Diagram 9.8).

The role of part-time, i.e. non-regular, employees grew as cost pressures increased. Their share in total employment rose from about 13% in 1990 to just under 30% by 2018. From the firm's perspective, a fall in the ratio of insiders to outsiders was important very simply because 'outsiders' were not given long-term contracts which made their wages easier to suppress. So strong was the incentive to change this ratio that even in periods when full-time employees were actually being laid off, employment growth for part-time employees remained positive and even rose.

In a nutshell, dimming prospects for growth required that firms reduce costs to protect themselves. The customs in the labour market, however, would not allow for a rapid, Western-type adjustment in which layoffs pushed the unemployment rate higher rapidly. Instead, firms employed a far more

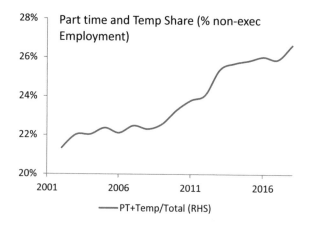

Diagram 9.8 The share of part-time workers in the workforce has grown dramatically (*Source* Ministry of Internal Affairs and Communication)

complex strategy that changed the structure of employment and forced wages and hours to do most of the adjustment.

9.3.3 Participation

As noted separately in the chapter on the Phillips curve, when the labour force ages, and the proportion of people over 55 rises, the key margin is that between employment and non-participation in the workforce, rather than between employment and unemployment. In this respect, Japan has been a world leader, increasing the proportion of those aged between 55 and 65 in recent decades in the labour force more than in any other country. The 'reserve army of the elderly' has been mobilised more efficiently in Japan than anywhere else (Diagram 9.9).

The participation rate among the 55–65-year-olds in Japan has been rising faster over the last few years and now stands at 75%—only New Zealand, Sweden and Iceland can top that.

Japan is not alone in seeing higher participation rates among the pre-retirement cohort. There are at least two reasons for this general trend. First, many have realised that they will live longer so that their planned savings look inadequate. Second, there has been a general degradation of pension benefits (designed to reduce the government's fiscal burden). In the next chapter, we deal in greater detail with this specific issue, detailing in a mini-case study how Germany's pre-retirees reacted sharply to a series of adverse changes in pension benefits that started in 2003.

Even among the over-65s, Japan's participation rate is just short of 25% and in the top quartile of its OECD peers (Diagram 9.10).

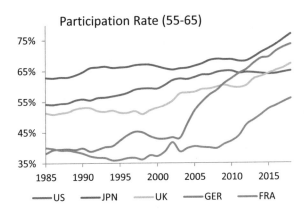

Diagram 9.9 Participation among Japan's 55–65 year olds has risen significantly (Source: OECD)

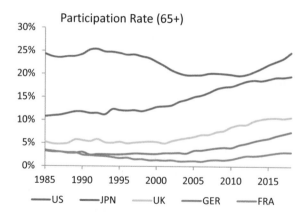

Diagram 9.10 Japan's 65–75 participation rate is joint-highest in the OECD (*Source* OECD)

Much greater slack and an uniquely Japanese Phillips Curve

So, for all the above reasons, the degree of potential slack in Japan at the beginning of 2000 was vastly greater than suggested by the comparative level of Japanese unemployment. Moreover, given the particular features of the Japanese labour market, with insiders having a largely guaranteed job, while outsiders have little bargaining power, not only was the Phillips curve inherently much flatter than elsewhere, but also the natural rate of unemployment is probably considerably lower in Japan than elsewhere.

9.3.4   Why the West Won't Follow Japan

In a nutshell, almost nothing from Japan's story is going to be applicable to most of the West as it ages.

First, the global backdrop over the next thirty years is going to be nothing like the last thirty. The world was swimming in labour thanks to the demographic tailwinds over the last thirty, but will struggle with the demographic headwinds over the next thirty. Put simply, while Japan had a global escape valve while its local workforce was shrinking, these options simply will not be available as the entire global manufacturing complex ages together.

Second, Japan-style labour market customs are not applicable to the West. There are serious economic costs to layoffs in the euro area, for example, but no western economy faces the kind of social constraint that Japan does. As a result, employment in other western countries is able to be the primary conduit for adjustment in the labour market, alleviating the pressure on wages and hours to do more than their fair share.

Third, participation rates have already been rising for the last twenty years in the advanced economies. Yet participation rates are well below Japan's levels and will take some time before they come close. Participation in most advanced economies varies inversely with the generosity of the pension system. Economies with generous systems have low participation rates and pension benefits will have to fall rapidly to push participation rates higher there. Varying combinations of pension benefits and participation rates will allow some AEs more flexibility in the future than Japan now enjoys.

10

What Could Offset Global Ageing?
India/Africa, Participation and Automation

Is the world really running out of workers? Automation and artificial intelligence, higher participation among the elderly and the promise of the demography-friendly economies of India and Africa are the arguments we hear most often as factors that could offset ageing. In one form or another, each of the factors above suggests that the existing stock and future flow of labour will be adequate, or at least far less of a concern than we make it out to be. Robotics, artificial intelligence and automation are changing the nature of capital and making labour redundant in many sectors. Participation among the elderly is rising as people are living longer and working until later in their lives. Finally, both India and Africa seem set to enjoy a regime of strong growth with an abundant supply of labour and their role in the global economy is rising.

Everything stated above is true—we have no reason to disagree with the direction. What we find difficult to agree with is the magnitude of change many take for granted.

Ageing economies can try to offset demography at home and abroad. At home, ageing economies have three options. First, use technology to offset the negative shock from labour to the production function. Second, raise the participation rate so that people work longer as well. Third, advanced economies can use some labour from abroad, particularly from emerging economies. If importing labour from abroad looks politically unrealistic, then perhaps capital can be exported abroad. There it can be converted into goods and services and repatriated to the advanced economies, the ones exporting the capital. The role of India and Africa—the demographically endowed parts

© The Author(s) 2020
C. Goodhart and M. Pradhan, *The Great Demographic Reversal*,
https://doi.org/10.1007/978-3-030-42657-6_10

of the world—has been advanced in this regard, most recently in a compelling paper by Desmet et al. (2018).

We argue below that none of these avenues has enough firepower to offset the demographic headwinds, and hence their effects, as we have described thus far in the book.

10.1 At Home: Automation, Participation, Migration

All three are attempts to protect the domestic production function from the coming contraction of the labour force. Automation seeks to do so by replacing the role of labour in the production function, while greater participation by elderly residents or enhancing migration are attempts to improve the flow of labour directly.

Automation is a global complement for labour, not a substitute.

Automation is a substitute for labour only in a very narrow sense. From a global, demographic perspective, automation is a vital complement. In other words, we will need all the automation we can get. For every job that automation may or may not make redundant, there is a job that is almost guaranteed to arise in age-related care. Without automation, demography would have a far more adverse economic effect than we have described.

Dementia, Alzheimer's and Parkinson's are diseases that cause a deterioration in the quality of life—Chapter 4 will have made that clear. The incidence of these ailments increases dramatically into the very late stages of life. What's more, none of these age-related diseases leads to an early loss of life. In fact, as life expectancy continues to increase, many of the oldest-elderly will live with these ailments for a long time. Elderly care in its broadest sense is a labour-intensive process, but it doesn't necessarily add to future national output growth in a way that other services sector employment does. Put differently, much of patient care is a consumption good rather than a capital good that creates value even in the future.

Job flows are likely to ebb in the manufacturing sector and flow towards the services sector. Some of this will happen thanks to automation, but the trend of reallocation of labour from manufacturing to services is not a new phenomenon. The manufacturing sector of most advanced economies has shrunk as a share of GDP since the 1950s. For all the disruption that manufacturing in the advanced economies has already faced, these employment trends have remained stable (apart from cyclical fluctuations) through the period of rapid expansion of the global supply of labour. Unless technology creates severe job losses across even the services sector, the demands of looking after the elderly in the services sector will offset the effects of automation. According to the Association of American Medical Colleges, the USA stands to see a shortage of 120,000 physicians by 2032, suggesting that automation has not yet made enough of an impact in the medical profession.

We prefer to be agnostic about the final impact of automation. That means adopting a balanced view, one that recognises the disruptive force of automation, but also the many arguments against an aggressive extrapolation of the promise of automation either over time or across all activities. Since the disruptive dimension of automation is (a little too) well known, the arguments below try to produce a more balanced view by pointing out shortcomings and extensions of the now-conventional view of automation. Rather than make any predictions about the final outcome, we try to present a balanced view about what it would take for the world to run out of jobs rather than workers.

Automation is widely considered to be the vehicle of the 'fourth industrial revolution'—a term that has been used over past decades on many occasions to herald a technology-driven transformation. The pace and extent of progress in automation make it difficult if not impossible to foresee its future progress. The realisation of the fourth industrial revolution depends on AI being able to continue the progress from its early days and translate that into widespread applications.

Ironically, where we *do* think automation will be unambiguously beneficial and widely applicable is in a part of the world that doesn't need it as much from a demographic point of view, i.e. in EMEs where the capital stock and the capital-labour ratios are both low. In such economies, the disruption caused by automation is very low. Instead, by helping these economies bypass an entire generation of capital that is becoming redundant in the AEs, automation can raise productivity in the EMEs much faster and at a much lower cost. We expect many of the innovations in the future to come from EMEs who first adapt existing technologies to their own purposes and then innovate from thereon. The most advanced EMEs naturally have a relatively higher capital-labour ratio, but they are located mostly in North Asia and have rapidly ageing populations. The poorer economies that would benefit most from widespread adoption of automation are the ones where demographic headwinds are far from severe.

On a global scale, the benefits of automation are not yet clear and large enough to offset the ageing of the global economy. Nor is it realistic at this point to think that the complex needs of elderly care can be delegated to robots.

Won't the over-65s simply work until later in their lives? The simple answer is yes. The harder part is actually raising the participation rate from where it already is.

Back in earlier decades from the 1950s until the 1970s, participation rates of the over 65s in most advanced economies were higher than they are today. In those days, the proportion of the elderly in the population was much smaller and life expectancy was lower, so there were very many fewer of the really old. In some large part as life expectancy rose, participation among old-aged workers trended steadily downwards from the 1960s until the end of the 1980s. But since then, it has been rising equally steadily over the last 30, or so, years. As one might expect, participation rates are higher for the 65-year-olds than for the 80-year-olds. As life expectancy rose, there were more of the oldest-elderly in the population and their participation rates were lower. However, life expectancy has kept rising and that should mean the participation rate should have kept falling as the impact of the oldest-elderly on participation rates of the over-65s rose (Diagram 10.1).

Why then did participation rates among the elderly rise when the compositional change above means they should have fallen? We suspect it was the result of two related forces. First, the increase in life expectancy will have been appreciated by those approaching retirement age. Second, as the gap between life expectancy and retirement age began to raise the burden on governments and pension systems, administrators clearly saw the same trend too. Many

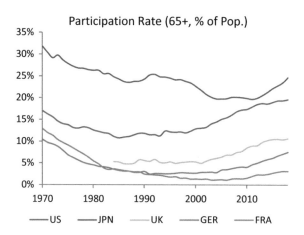

Diagram 10.1 Why has labour participation among the over-65s been rising? (*Source* OECD)

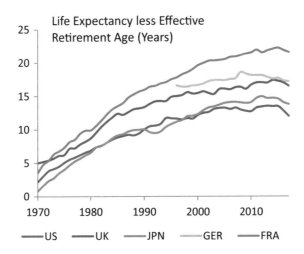

Diagram 10.2 Life expectancy has risen, but retirement ages have not (*Source* OECD, United Nations)

pension benefits were curtailed or downgraded in order to raise the sustainability of these systems. The combination of living longer with lower pension benefits is likely to have led to a rise in the participation rates. See Button (2019) for a discussion of these factors in the case of the USA (Diagram 10.2).

Pension systems are certainly not sustainable at the moment and life expectancy continues to rise, though more slowly nowadays. That's precisely why the argument is that the participation rate among the elderly will have to continue to rise, at least among the younger members of the elderly.

Unfortunately, there are limits to how much participation rates can rise in the future. The reasons we list below are not exhaustive, but the list is long and (we think) made up of compelling reasons to expect only modest improvements in future.

First, participation rates of the workforce have already gone up considerably, thanks to greater participation of the 55–64 cohort and especially women. How much further can this rise in the future? In other words, if much of the increase in participation needed has already been realised today, there is less room for improvement for the future when the size of the demographic problem becomes more severe (Diagram 10.3).

Second, the generosity of a country's pension system is inversely related to the participation rate, and our key assumption is that pension/retirement benefits can be reduced, but not by drastic amounts.

Diagram 10.4 suggests that the greater generosity of an economy's pension system generates lower rates of participation, and Germany's experience with pension reform explored in a mini case study below is highly suggestive of such a relationship too.

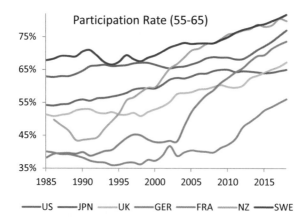

Diagram 10.3 Pre-retirement participation rates have already risen significantly (*Source* OECD)

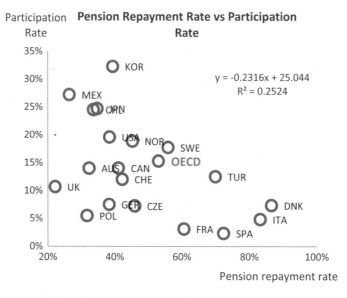

Diagram 10.4 Participation rates tend to be lower when pension benefits are higher (*Source* OECD)

A mini case study: Why did Germany's pre-retirement participation rise so rapidly from 2003?

Germany's experience with pension reform and the response of the participation rate serves to illustrate this relationship in a robust manner. While the participation rate has generally risen for the 55–64-year-olds across most G10 economies, Germany's participation rate had a distinct turning point in response to the pension reform proposed in mid-2003 and passed into law in 2004.

Borsche-Supan and Wilke (2004) show how earlier changes in regulations in 1958 and 1972 then made the German pension system unsustainable as it entered the era of ageing. The change in 1958 converted a fully funded system into a pay-as-you-go structure. The revision in 1972 not only guaranteed a high post-retirement allowance, but also allowed workers to retire at any time between ages 63 and 65 with no penalties for early retirement. Also see Börsch-Supan et al. (2014).

The first reform of 1992 tried to reduce some of the pension burden (by indexing to net rather than gross wages, and abolishing the 'window of retirement' for most), but it was too little and the adjustments were set with too much of a delay to create any meaningful change. Subsequently, in 2001, the pay-as-you-go system was converted into a multi-pillar system with a small but growing pre-funded pillar. Unfortunately, the pension budget went through another crisis, not even two years after this 'reform for a century' was passed. As a response, the Rurup Commission tabled concrete proposals in August 2003 which were passed into law in 2004. Its two most significant contributions were to convert the pay-as-you-go pillar (from the 2001 system) into a defined contribution system that was identical notionally to the previous one through the introduction of a sustainability factor into the indexation formula. Second, it recommended an increase in the retirement age.

As a result, the participation rate of the 55–64-year-old cohort increased dramatically from around 45% before the Rurup Commission proposals to almost the same level as Japan recently. The sharp break higher in the participation rate can be seen in Diagram 10.3. Participation rates started rising sharply around the time that the reform proposals were submitted in 2003 and carried on rising (like most of the rest of Germany's G10 peers), as further reforms reducing the burden on the administration and raising the responsibility of the individual were pursued.

The German experience above suggests that one (seemingly) simple way to ensure higher participation could be to simply raise the retirement age to track life expectancy better. However, Germany's own history, and the experience of Greece, suggests that it takes a debt sustainability crisis and considerable market pressure to get governments to take this deeply unpopular step. Brazil has finally passed its own pension reforms after several attempts, following severe market pressure. Raising the retirement age is a deeply unpopular step and no administration has managed to raise it by more than a couple of years.

Could migration offset demographic headwinds?

Could labour flows (i.e. migration from labour-abundant to labour-deficient economies) offset demographic headwinds? Not if current migration trends continue. Net migration flows into the AEs and out of EMEs peaked in 2007 at about 24 million each. When normalised against the size of the population, however, these flows are far too small to make a difference (Diagram 10.5).

Net migration has already turned. Inward immigration into the AEs and outward migration from the EMEs have receded. With demographic headwinds intensifying, more migration is necessary, but this remains a politically charged issue. If the current political tension surrounding immigration persists, as we fully expect it to, importing labour to offset ageing of the local labour force is not a viable strategy. Also see Börsch-Supan, paper presented at ECB Forum on Central Banking, at Sintra, Portugal, June 2019.

With the populist administrations and the popularity of right-wing, anti-immigration political parties in the advanced economies, it seems highly unlikely that any large transfer of labour to ageing economies will be possible.

If labour can't move across borders easily, why not export capital instead to economies with growing populations, produce there and import finished goods from there?

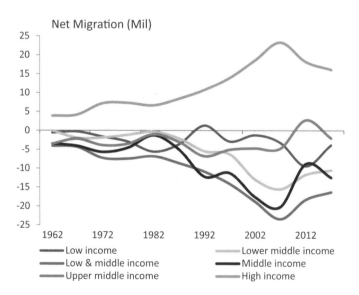

Diagram 10.5 Net migration is receding just when it needs to accelerate (*Source* World Development Indicators, World Bank)

10.2   Can India and Africa Offset Demographic Headwinds in the Ageing Economies?

Numerically, yes. Economically, highly unlikely. The demographic headwind in economies that are ageing very quickly could be offset to quite an extent numerically by demographic tailwinds in economies where the labour force is likely to grow for the next decade or more. The incremental additions to the global labour force are likely to come from India, some sub-Saharan economies and some other emerging economies (Diagram 10.6).

The world can access the abundant labour in these economies in two ways. First, immigration from these economies into labour-deficient ones can directly offset the shrinking labour force there. Second, if this more direct route of transferring labour between economies is unavailable, then capital can flow to the labour abundant economies. These flows of capital can be combined with the local supply of labour in the labour-abundant economies to produce goods and services which, in turn, can be exported back to labour-deficient economies.

Can India drive global growth like China did?

Like China did a few decades ago, India has quite a few advantages thanks to its attractive starting point.

First, it has an abundant supply of labour that will keep growing beyond 2050, a capital-labour ratio that desperately needs to be raised, and a level of human capital that can absorb new technologies much faster than its

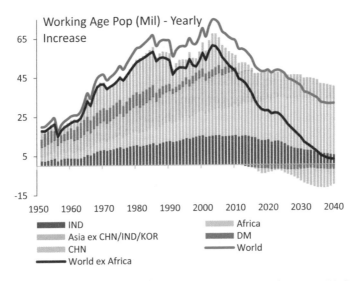

Diagram 10.6   India and Africa will defy global ageing (*Source* UN Population Statistics)

peers. Second, capital is therefore likely to continue to flow to India as this contrast becomes even more clear. Given the extremely poor capital-labour ratio, any such accumulation of capital will be transformative. Third, the inflow of new capital will bring with it the latest technology that is embedded in this capital. The incremental stock of capital will thus not only improve the capital-labour ratio, it will transform the quality of that interaction manifold. Anyone who has used India's old and new airports or metropolitan subway systems will attest to that. Fourth, elections are increasingly being dictated by the ability or failure of incumbents to convince aspirational voters of a decent economic future. Prime Minister Modi has been voted in with an even stronger mandate, and many state elections have been won or lost in keeping with this simple theme. Finally, regulators are using technology to upgrade an overwhelmed compliance network. The central bank, for example, has a digitised database of bank and corporate entities that are delinquent. The national 'Aadhar' card system means that money is sent directly to the intended recipient's bank account rather than being 'lost' somewhere along the way.

If all of that is true, then why has India's growth suffered so much over 2018 and 2019? Both India and China have gone through a significant slowdown over 2018–2019, and investors have attributed too much of that slowdown to political hubris and the trade war (respectively) and too little to the shock to the shadow banking sector. India's banking sector is going through a massive consolidation in its public sector banks and a clean-up of bad debts in the aftermath of aggressive lending by its non-bank financial companies over the last few years. While the constraints on lending are creating significant dislocations at the moment, cleaner banks are vital if India is to embark on a period of capital accumulation.

India's new bankruptcy code (the IBC) is a vital ingredient for the present and the future. The IBC has already been applied to a large number of firms in the manufacturing sector and it is also being applied to delinquent lenders in the non-banking financial company complex. Its resolution mechanism has helped lenders recover 60 cents on the dollar (compared to the historical norms of a 20% recovery). At the same time, the costs it imposes on delinquent borrowers will help future financial stability by disincentivising excess debt accumulation.

We think India will beat China in global growth over the next decade, and perhaps even the one after that. However, it will not be able to lift world growth the way China did for three reasons:

First, the global environment is materially different in two ways. The decline in nominal and real interest rates during (and caused to no small extent by) China's ascent created benign conditions at home in the AEs so that the ascent of China was not seen as a zero-sum game. That advanced the cause of globalisation in terms of social opinions. Now, India has to face a declining labour supply not just in the advanced economies, but in the manufacturing powerhouse economies of North Asia and Eastern Europe as well. If that means real wage growth, inflation and nominal interest rates are going to rise, then improving growth in ageing economies is going to be quite difficult, and so the political opposition to the transfer of production to India would be greater.

Second, the demographic goalposts have shifted. There won't be another 'China' for a long time, if ever. It is not just China's mobilisation but its grand history of dominating the global economy for most of the last few millennia that were an instrumental part of the equation. Over time, such global dominance inevitably creates at grass-roots level a system of entrepreneurship, production and efficiency. Economies like those in Africa that have had less sophisticated and highly disaggregated systems of small firms will have to build such systems as they progress. India has had a rich history of trading over the centuries, aided by empires that stretched over the bulk of its mass, but its disjointed social structure has often been a hindrance in creating a solid economic foundation.

And given the size of the demographic challenge, we might need not one but three Chinas.

Third and most important, India will be able to attract global capital to its shores, but the lack of administrative capital and its system of democratic checks and balances will not allow a single-minded, China-esque model of growth to materialise.

India's administrative capital is starting off from an extremely weak level and internal collisions within its multi-party system as well as between the states and the federal government make a coordinated policy of growth difficult to manage. India's rank in the World Bank Ease of Doing Business index has improved 73 places over the last 4 years but still stands at 67—it was ranked 140th out of 190 economies in 2015. Among certain measures (permits and access across borders), India has scored extremely well. However, on measures such as infrastructure quality and enforcement of contracts, which require greater coordination and effort, India continues to rank very poorly (e.g. 163rd in terms of enforcing contracts). Improvements are naturally easier to make in the earlier stages of development. It is entirely possible that India can build on its successes and use of technology to sustain momentum, but we think this will remain harder to achieve when it comes to change that requires broad participation.

The democratic hurdle rises a rung higher because of the internal political friction among states and between the states and the federal government. The political friction on even mundane issues suggests a very low probability of devising and abiding by a national strategy to direct financial and physical resources towards a China-esque mobilisation.

Inevitably, that means the private sector is to be the vehicle that drives India's growth. In turn, it is the extent to which the private sector is able and willing to grow that will determine the path of India's growth. Unlike the growth of SOEs under state patronage, the private sector needs an effective and level playing field to thrive. Thus, a lot depends on how quickly and efficiently India's administration can reform and deregulate the economy.

If it is to offset the headwinds from global demography, India will need help from Africa. However, mobilising Africa across its varied geographic, economic and political landscape is likely to be significantly more difficult than fostering growth in India.

Some African economies do score better than India on the 'ease of doing business' statistics, and a few even better than China. However, there are two key problems in Africa that also hamper their ability to attract and deploy capital in a big enough way to offset demographic headwinds in the advanced economies. First, they are a fragmented set of economies which implies a very low probability of a coordinated approach to creating a manufacturing complex that can rival China. Second, and more importantly, they lack the quantum of human capital that India enjoys as well as the deep-rooted and widespread system of apprenticeships, guilds and efficiency that has been honed over the centuries in China.

Africa's population in 2019 stands at approximately 1.32 billion, almost identical to India's 1.37 billion residents, but it hosts that population over an area that is almost ten times the size of India's 3.2 million square kilometres of territory. Over that area, Africa is made up of 54 countries. A key problem that Africa faces, therefore, is its fragmentation. Fifty-four national policies, each with their own domestic frictions like India's, will mean a much greater problem when it comes to coordinating policies for growth. It also means that migration within Africa is far more difficult because of national borders than it is within India's state borders.

The geographical fragmentation interacts with demography in a meaningful way. India's demography can be looked upon as unitary thanks to the freedom of movement inside its borders. Labour can move to areas of rapid growth fairly rapidly and hence be a meaningful complement to capital wherever it is deployed. However, Africa's borders are less porous than open

India's state lines, and its economies are at very different stages of demographic transformation. Labour in economies with abundant capital and low economic efficiency cannot thus move as seamlessly across national borders to areas where labour productivity and economic growth are improving. Sub-Saharan Africa (SSA) is only just embarking on its period of demographic tailwinds, but many parts of Africa that are quite advanced in terms of the demographic dividend are the ones that are also advanced in terms of administrative efficiency (IMF 2015).

Unfortunately, governance scores in the demographically rich SSA and in Africa as a region have generally deteriorated over the last two decades despite significant economic growth in many places and some solid progress in others. In Africa, political stability and lower violence are only evident among economies that are already on a relatively stable path, but it has deteriorated further in the ones that were politically fragile at the start. In the SSA region, governance scores have fallen across the board.

This doesn't mean that there cannot be improvements. The abundance of labour is likely to attract capital, which in turn could force the economies to take steps to stay ahead of their local competitors in order to attract these flows. Like India, though, Africa is unlikely to use their labour force to the extent that it offsets the demographic headwinds in the rest of the world.

Besides governance, the second key hurdle to rapid growth in Africa is its human capital. On the World Bank's Human Capital Index for 2019, India ranks in the third quartile. Only half a dozen or so economies in Africa share this ranking. Most of Africa ranks in the lowest quartile for Human Capital.

One could argue that country-level data can be misleading when it comes to beginnings. At the early stages of the build-up of a manufacturing base, the most talented pool of labour is usually attracted to the most profitable and rewarding activities. This is where the fragmentation of Africa creates a problem. While India's massive population in an area the tenth of the size of Africa makes it an attractive market for goods aided by a mobile population, Africa will find it hard to marshall either of the two. The population density is obviously much lower than India's so that choosing a manufacturing base still means exporting across over 50 countries and large distances. Human capital availability is limited to a few economies that do have the ability to attract capital. Others will have to import it from others or build it up slowly in their own economies by developing education systems. That will remain a serious impediment to the ability to transform incoming capital into goods and services on a big-enough scale.

In summary, neither India nor Africa have the ability to replicate China's ascent despite their vast and relatively untapped labour resources. Their own progress is likely to be solid, and at times spectacular, but it will most likely fall short of the kind of momentum that an ageing global economy needs. Kotlikoff's Global Gaidar model captures the benign dynamic but disappointing magnitude very well, describing 'catch-up growth, albeit at a very slow pace, in Africa, the Middle East, India and other historically slow-growing regions (Kotlikoff 2019; Benzell et al. 2018).

An influential and impressive paper by Desmet et al. (2018) argues forcefully in favour of a third conduit for such a convergence. The transfer of technology, they argue, to today's low-productivity, high-population density regions will lead to a 'productivity reversal' that favours parts of Asia and Africa, unless international and internal migration is stepped up. The intuition in the model stems from the high correlation between population density and GDP per capita that the authors find across different regions of the world, and even within economies thanks to the extraordinarily detailed geographical model they use. Under today's status quo, their model suggests that 'many of today's high-density, low-productivity regions in sub-Saharan Africa, South Asia, and East Asia becoming high-density, high-productivity regions, and North America and Europe falling behind in terms of both population and productivity'.

Their model, however, suffers from one key shortcoming—the absence of a role for administrative infrastructure. The main hindrance to development among emerging economies lies in their ability to execute a complex, coordinated and long-term economic strategy. We would go so far as to say that emerging economies that cannot transform themselves into advanced economies fail not because of the so-called middle-income trap but because of an administrative trap. The predictions of Desmet et al., while inspiring, are conditional on the development of the stock of administrative capital which these economies lack.

11

The Debt Trap: Can We Avoid It?

11.1 Introduction

Policymakers are caught in a box. Long periods of low interest rates have encouraged an increase in leverage and frequently a misallocation of capital. Improvements in growth and concerns about financial stability would prompt central banks to hike rates, only for those rising interest rates to hurt growth, and so then cyclically push inflation and interest rates lower again. How can we escape it? In this chapter and the next, we delve deeper into the debt trap and ways that the global economy can avoid or overcome it.

The extended leverage in the global economy is the biggest impediment to the normalisation of interest rates, and of the economy more widely, that demographics will ultimately deliver. We start by explaining how we came to be confronted by the debt trap, and proceed to explore the details of the problem and its possible solutions.

For the reasons set out earlier in Chapter 6, fiscal policy was never sufficiently expansionary, even before the Great Financial Crisis in 2007–2009, to offset the persistent deflationary pressures that had taken hold after the early 1990s. So, in order to maintain macroeconomic balance and the inflation target, monetary policy became steadily more expansionary, reinforcing the financial cycle, see Borio et al. (2019). The resulting falling nominal (and real) interest rates led to a housing, and construction, boom in the USA and on the periphery of Europe (UK, Ireland, Iceland, Spain, Portugal and Greece), financed not only by domestic banks, but also by capital inflows (with rising current account deficits) largely from foreign banks. The leverage ratios of banks in many of the main countries, and the debt to income ratios of many

© The Author(s) 2020
C. Goodhart and M. Pradhan, *The Great Demographic Reversal,*
https://doi.org/10.1007/978-3-030-42657-6_11

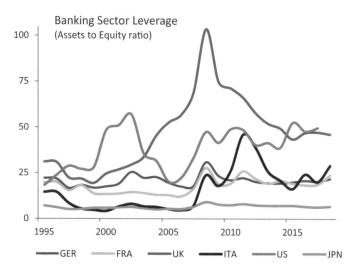

Diagram 11.1 Banking sector leverage ratios saw sharp rises during booms (*Source* OECD)

households where such booms took hold, increased, in some cases sharply, see Diagram 11.1. The dangers of this were not foreseen until too late to stop the GFC emerging in full fury in September 2008 with the collapse of Lehman Bros and AIG.

The authorities, mainly the monetary authorities, were then stung into action, introducing a successful combination of fiscal and monetary responses, which we do not need to list here. For the longer term, however, their main prudential response has been to require banks to maintain enhanced capital adequacy ratios (CARs), a program carried out much more successfully in the USA than in Europe. As a result capital adequacy, credit and deposit growth and bank equity values have all recovered more strongly in the USA than in Europe.

Why the USA did so much better than Europe in restoring its banking sector

Because Tim Geithner could use TARP (Troubled Asset Recovery Program) moneys to recapitalise banks, as necessary, he could establish credible stress tests, and require bank equity to be brought up to levels consistent with the desired ratios applied to deposit levels as at the date of the stress test. The application of such public (TARP) moneys to the relatively few banks falling below the desired levels was then protected by constraints on such banks' dividends, buy-backs and enhanced executive remuneration until all such moneys had been repaid; which it soon was.

In Europe, in contrast, there was no equivalent pool of public moneys available to recapitalise banks with insufficient capital. As a result, the stress tests were not deemed credible, since there was no immediate way of recapitalising banks shown as coming in below the desired level; as a result, virtually no banks would be, it was thought, shown as failing the test. Banks were still required to meet higher capital ratios, but given freedom to do so whether by raising new equity, or by delevering, i.e. running down assets and (deposit) liabilities. Given the weak condition of equity markets, and bankers' focus on their return on equity (RoE), they naturally chose to delever. With the authorities putting pressure on their own domestically headquartered banks, explicitly or implicitly, to maintain lending to local borrowers, such deleveraging naturally involved a massive cutback in European banks' cross-border lending.

But the authorities brought about a more securely capitalised banking system by regulatory diktat, rather than by trying to reform the institutional and structural features of the capitalist system of governance, which had led executives to prioritise short-term equity value maximisation over longer-term investment and growth. Partly as a result, the general deflationary pressures which had already been in evidence before the GFC became even more intense afterwards. With fiscal policies constrained for the reasons set out in Chapter 6, this brought continuing pressure on monetary policies to be even more expansionary, with quantitative easing (QE) and negative official interest rates; 'the only game in town'.

Whereas the first round of QE in 2009 was massively beneficial and successful in quelling the panic search for liquidity that the GFC caused, it is arguable whether the subsequent steps had much, if any, strong positive effects, partly because of the potential adverse effects on bank profitability; for a discussion on all this see Altavilla et al. (2018); Borio et al. (2017); Brunnermeier and Koby (2018); Eggertsson et al. (2019); Goodhart and Kabiri (2019); Heider et al. (2019); and Xu et al. (2019). But the conditions of extraordinarily low interest rates were conducive not only to the continuation but even to a faster pace of debt accumulation among non-financial corporates.

So, in Sect. 11.2, below, we start by demonstrating how, despite the GFC being widely blamed on excessive debt, its aftermath has brought even greater accumulation of debt, among non-financial corporates, the household sector in those countries previously unaffected by the earlier splurge and crisis in the run up to the GFC, and in the public sector. But as we also show, debt service ratios, the ratio of payments of interest and repayment of principal to income, have remained almost constant in most cases, since the rise in debt *levels* has been matched, almost exactly, by the fall in interest rates.

Not only have interest rates already reached the effective lower bound (we discount the likelihood of getting policies to abolish cash), but also we argue that inflation, and with that nominal interest rates, will most likely rise again. The problem is that the key macroeconomic sectors now carry such elevated debt ratios that any sizeable or sharp increases in interest rates would put large chunks of the private sector into solvency problems and add to the fiscal difficulties of Ministers of Finance. Also to protect themselves from such insolvency risks, the more indebted companies would feel the need to cut back sharply on new investment, thereby worsening any subsequent recession; on this see Kalemli-Özcan et al. (2019). Thus, the debt trap, which we discuss in Sect. 11.2, occurs, since to prevent future recessions interest rates will have to be kept at such low levels that there is little discouragement to further accumulation of debt.

So, we ask whether there is any practicable escape route from this debt trap in Sect. 11.3. As is already clear from prior chapters, we see little hope of any acceleration in growth, rather the opposite; deceleration is much more likely. Instead, we see more chance of an (as yet unexpected) surge in inflation; but what about Central Banks' inflation targets? If debtors cannot inflate their debt away, but find it almost impossible to repay, can such debts be renegotiated, or in the last resort defaulted (or forgiven)?

In an important sense we view the past and future macroeconomic maladies not only as a reflection of dramatic demographic trends, but also as a consequence of failures of corporate governance and in the structure of capitalism. Debt has been made too easy to adopt, and equity finance too unattractive. Equity finance is not attractive to corporate executives, so long as the focus on RoE remains, and such executives continue to share in the limited liability of all shareholders. There is more to be said for Islamic financing requirements than is commonly appreciated. There is so much to be said about all this that in the next Chapter 12 we discuss ways of trying to shift the whole structure of finance from a, primarily, debt basis, mainly for corporates, but also in some part for households and the public sector to a predominantly equity basis.

11.2   The Build-Up of Debt

Tables 11.1 and 11.2 show the ratio of debt to GDP for households, non-financial corporates and the public sector in 2007 and 2018, respectively, and the percentage change over this decade. The following points are notable:-

Table 11.1 Debt ratios in advanced economies

Dec-07	HH	NFC	PSC	Gov't	Total
US	99	70	169	65	233
EA	60	92	151	65	216
GER	61	57	118	64	181
FRA	47	111	157	65	221
SPA	81	124	206	36	241
ITA	38	75	113	100	213
UK	92	94	187	42	228
SWE	65	126	191	39	230
JPN	59	103	161	175	337
AUS	108	80	188	10	198
CAN	79	83	162	67	229

Dec-18	HH	NFC	PSC	Gov't	Total
US	76	74	151	106	256
EA	58	105	163	85	248
GER	53	57	110	60	169
FRA	60	141	201	99	300
SPA	59	93	152	97	249
ITA	40	70	110	132	242
UK	87	84	171	87	258
SWE	89	156	244	39	283
JPN	58	103	161	237	398
AUS	120	75	195	41	236
CAN	101	117	218	91	308

Change since Dec-07	HH	NFC	PSC	Gov't	Total
US	-22	4	-18	41	23
EA	-2	13	11	20	31
GER	-8	0	-8	-4	-12
FRA	14	30	44	34	78
SPA	-23	-31	-54	62	8
ITA	2	-5	-3	32	30
UK	-5	-11	-16	45	29
SWE	23	30	53	0	53
JPN	-1	0	-1	62	61
AUS	12	-5	7	31	38
CAN	22	34	56	24	80

Source BIS, IMF
Colour coded to help reader easier visualisation of debt levels and changes across the sectors and countries. Darker red colour stands for higher leverage or change in it within a sector of the economy and across our sample of countries, e.g. Australia displays the highest level in HH debt as % of GDP within our 10 country sample of advanced economies, and the lowest ratio on the public sector side.
HH—Households
NFC—Non-financial corporations
PSC—Private sector (HH + NFC)

11.2.1 Households

The household debt ratio has in general increased least, or even declined, in those countries most exposed to the prior housing bust, USA and the European periphery (including the UK). Those countries not then affected, such as Australia, Canada, Norway and Sweden, have taken over the housing boom vanguard, mostly concentrated in a few city centres, such as Stockholm, Toronto and Vancouver.

Emerging markets show a similar trend. Housing leverage has risen the most in the more advanced EMEs, all of which generally have had low and stable levels of inflation and interest rates to begin with. Most have participated in, and even outstripped, the disinflation in the global economy. As

Table 11.2 Debt ratios in emerging market economies

Dec-07	HH	NFC	PSC	Gov't	Total
CHN	19	98	117	29	146
KOR	72	89	161	29	189
IND	11	42	53	74	127
IDN	12	15	26	32	59
MAL	52	58	111	40	150
THL	45	46	91	36	127
HKG	51	126	177	1	178
BRA	18	30	48	64	111
MEX	14	15	28	37	65
CHL	29	66	95	4	99
COL	17	27	44	33	76
ARG	5	17	22	62	84
RUS	11	39	50	8	58
POL	23	34	57	44	101
CZE	23	46	69	27	97
HUN	30	78	108	65	174
TUR	11	30	41	38	79
SAF	44	35	79	27	106

Dec-18	HH	NFC	PSC	Gov't	Total
CHN	53	152	204	50	255
KOR	98	102	199	41	240
IND	11	45	56	70	126
IDN	17	23	40	29	70
MAL	66	68	134	56	190
THL	69	48	117	42	159
HKG	72	219	292	0	292
BRA	28	42	71	88	158
MEX	16	26	42	54	95
CHL	45	99	144	26	170
COL	27	35	62	50	113
ARG	7	16	22	86	109
RUS	17	46	64	14	77
POL	35	46	81	48	129
CZE	32	57	89	33	122
HUN	18	67	85	69	154
TUR	15	70	85	29	114
SAF	34	39	72	57	129

Change since Dec-07	HH	NFC	PSC	Gov't	Total
CHN	34	54	88	21	109
KOR	25	13	39	12	51
IND	1	3	3	-4	-1
IDN	5	9	14	-3	11
MAL	14	10	24	16	40
THL	24	2	26	6	32
HKG	21	94	115	-1	114
BRA	11	12	23	24	47
MEX	3	11	14	16	30
CHL	17	33	50	22	71
COL	11	8	19	18	37
ARG	2	-1	1	24	25
RUS	7	7	14	6	20
POL	13	11	24	4	28
CZE	9	11	20	5	26
HUN	-12	-11	-24	4	-19
TUR	4	40	44	-9	34
SAF	-10	4	-7	30	23

a result, in countries like Canada, Australia and Sweden, households across North Asia, Poland and Chile have seen double-digit increases in household debt. Household debt in China, Korea, Malaysia and Thailand has risen around 20–25%. Household debt to GDP ratios in Malaysia and Thailand now are closer to levels seen in advanced economies, while the household leverage in Korea is not far from that in the USA on the eve of the housing crisis.

With the personal sector in sizeable surplus, and asset markets very strong, the wealth of the household sector increased in the post-GFC decade far faster than its liabilities (n.b. the same was true in the previous decade 1997–2007).

The problem, both then and now, is not with the *general* level of household indebtedness, but with that group, mostly young families, where debt is high, albeit temporarily because of age profile or unemployment, relative to income. Even in those cases for this group where default and repossession is avoided (leading to further contagious falls in housing prices), rising interest rates can require massive cutbacks in their other consumption expenditures, also thereby deflating demand (Mian and Sufi 2014).

The main new instrument to try to counterbalance this housing/property finance cycle has become macro-prudential regulations, for example raising loan to value (LTV) or loan to income (LTI) ratios during housing booms. While helpful, these are no panacea. The psychological impetus of a housing boom is likely to overwhelm the extent of variation that the authorities feel that they can introduce in such regulation, especially since they act in large part by preventing young families from getting onto the housing ladder, a politically sensitive issue.

The situation in the EMEs is somewhat similar, despite some important differences. Growth and sentiment among the EMEs managed to avoid the gloom in the major advanced economies in the first half of the post-crisis decade. House prices in major cities across the EME universe rose rapidly, leading to the usual bubble-like expectations of a never-ending boom in the property sector, and construction and mortgage financing all increased strongly. Among the commodity producing economies, the rise in labour income from the rapid expansion of such commodity production and a rapid inflow of capital combined to lift credit growth and the housing sector. The key urban regions of Russia, Brazil, Indonesia, Malaysia and even S. Africa experienced large increases in house prices and credit allocation to those who could access credit. Despite rising commodity prices, commodity importers also benefitted from benign global conditions that allowed easy monetary and fiscal policies to dominate the macroeconomic landscape. The result was a boom in the property sectors across Asia—not just in North Asia but also in India and the Philippines.

The subsequent economic slowdown in China and many other EMEs was accompanied by a downturn in housing and personal income growth. Unlike the AEs, EM housing had a downturn rather than a crisis (with the notable exception of Turkey and the near-miss in China), but households have nevertheless remained saddled with debt that has choked off the demand for housing and has also constrained other consumption choices. As a result, the fallout has been felt by construction companies that also remained heavily indebted and, in many cases, the banks and financial institutions that have extended these mortgages.

11.2.2 Corporates

Debt ratios of (non-financial) corporates rose substantially across EMEs, especially in China. China's state-owned enterprises (SOEs) borrowed heavily from government-owned banks. The resulting surge in growth combined with falling interest rates led to a sharp pickup in commodity prices, capital inflows into EMEs and a pickup in corporate leverage in many key economies. Besides China's SOEs, the borrowing was dominated by commodity and construction companies. The severe leverage problems that PEMEX, Petrobras and Eskom have faced are the result of the excesses during the first half of the post-GFC expansion. Across commodity-importing EMEs, such as Korea, Malaysia, Thailand, India and Turkey, leverage increased rapidly, partly because of the excesses of construction companies.

The increase in debt in the early part of the expansion was used to finance an increase in investment. The return on many of those investments, by SOEs in China, commodity producers and construction companies, fell sharply over the second half of the expansion, but the debt has largely remained on the books of the companies involved.

By contrast, fixed investment has remained relatively sluggish in developed economies, and low enough relative to earnings/profits to allow financial surpluses to emerge, as already discussed in Chapters 5 and 6. The cause of rising debt ratios in such advanced economies has, instead, been a switch from equity finance to debt finance. To some considerable extent this has been, especially in the USA, and to a lesser extent in other Anglo-phone countries, caused by the increasing incidence of buy-backs; data on the USA in Diagram 11.2. Hoisting leverage by such buy-backs is the simplest method of raising RoE. Also see J. Ford on the role of private equity in this respect, in his *Financial Times* column, 'Warren is right to worry about dangers of private equity looting', 29 July 2019, p. 8. But, just as raising leverage in banks increases the risks for other stakeholders, including the public at large, in exactly the same way buy-backs in other corporates is a risk-shifting activity.

Moreover, an increasing chunk of such corporate debt has been in lesser quality debt, levered loans and BBB debt issue. See Diagrams 11.3 and 11.4.[1]

Fundamentally, a regime of low and falling interest rates makes default on fixed income obligations less likely even if revenue growth slows down. Financially, the low risk of default makes the purchase of high-yielding securities far more attractive when the 'search for yield' dominates investment strategies. A

---

[1] Reproduced with permission from the Bank of England, July 2019 Financial Stability Report.

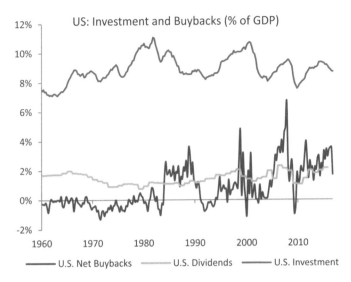

US: Investment and Buybacks (% of GDP)

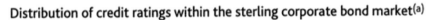

— U.S. Net Buybacks ····· U.S. Dividends —— U.S. Investment

Diagram 11.2 United States—Investment stayed weak as firms preferred to use debt to finance buybacks

Distribution of credit ratings within the sterling corporate bond market[a]

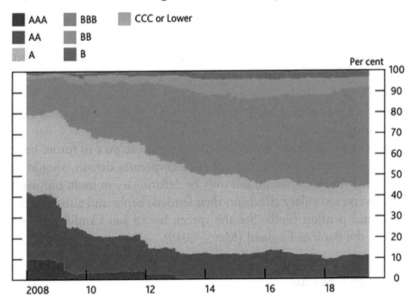

The chart shows the distribution of credit ratings, as measured by market value, of the ICE/BofAML sterling corporate bond index. This index can be used as a representative measure of the sterling corporate bond market. However, the index may not capture all sterling corporate bonds and alternative indices may contain different rating distributions.

Diagram 11.3 The share of BBB-rated corporate bonds reached record highs in 2019 (*Source* Bank of England, Financial Stability Report, July 2019)

Twelve-month rolling global gross issuance of leveraged loans[a]

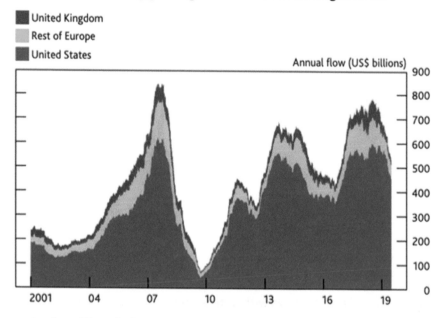

■ United Kingdom
▢ Rest of Europe
■ United States

Based on public syndication transactions, and excluding private bilateral deals.

Diagram 11.4 The leveraged loan market has been growing rapidly in recent years, although it has slowed since its peak in 2018 (*Source* Bank of England, Financial Stability Report, July 2019)

combination of the two naturally led to the rapid growth of the issuance of relatively more risky assets.

This is, perhaps, the area of greatest concern with respect to future financial fragility. If a significant number of such corporates default, should the interest burden worsen, it would not only be deflationary in itself, but would also have adverse secondary effects on their lenders, banks and also insurance companies and pension funds. See the speech by Sir Jon Cunliffe, Deputy Governor of the Bank of England (May 7 2019).

11.2.3   Public Sector

In the household sector, wealth has been increasing faster than debt. In the corporate sector, the buoyancy of profits and falling/low interest rates has kept their debt service ratio low. Similarly, in the public sector the rise in debt levels has been, almost entirely, offset by falling interest rates, leaving debt service ratios nearly constant, even in Japan, over the last couple of decades, as shown in Diagram 11.5.

So far, perhaps, so good. But what happens if nominal interest rates start to rise again? Largely because of the exceptionally low levels of interest rates, interest payments have become a tiny fraction of general government spending, so it might seem that that could be absorbed easily enough up to a point. But every little extra burden hurts, especially when the ageing of society is placing greater ineluctable pressures on the government's accounts.

Of course, if advantage had been taken of the extraordinarily low interest rates to extend the duration of the public debt, then the forthcoming rise in nominal official short-term interest rates would have less effect. But the felt need for an ever more expansionary monetary policy has led instead to

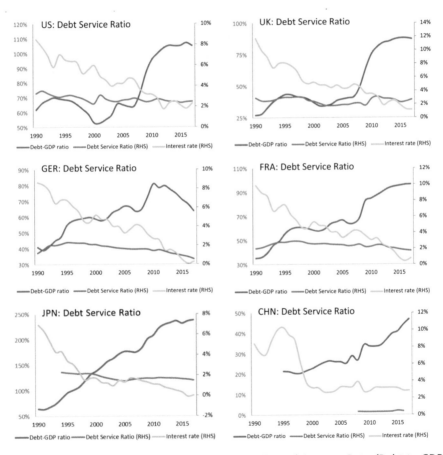

Diagram 11.5 Debt-GDP Ratio, Debt Service Ratio and Interest Rate (Debt-to-GDP ratio is on the left axis, interest rate and debt services ratios are on the right axis) (*Source* World Bank, OECD)

a significant reduction in effective durations. In particular, a combination of QE and a 'floor system' of paying interest on commercial bank deposits at the Central Bank has meant that the equivalent volume of QE, backed by such deposits, has an effective zero duration.

Thus, public sector fiscal finances will feel the full pain of any increase in official interest rates almost immediately. With corporate sector finances having become increasingly fragile, and (populist) political calls for keeping interest rates low, the Central Bank will become under intensifying pressure to keep any increases in interest rates gradual and limited. But if such interest rate increases remain gradual and small, then the present incentives to extend and expand debt finance remain in place. That is the debt trap in which so many of our countries have now become ensnared.

Moreover, as Alfaro and Kanczuk (2019) describe, in recent years 'non-Paris Club creditors, notably China, have become an important source of financing for low- and middle-income countries. In contrast with typical sovereign debt, these lending arrangements are not public, and other creditors have no information about their magnitude' and such arrangements 'greatly reduce traditional/Paris Club creditors' debt sustainability'.

11.3   Can We Escape the Debt Trap?

So how could we get out of this debt trap? The best, and most attractive, way of doing so is by faster real growth. If real growth is greater than the level of real interest rates, then, with a zero public sector deficit, the debt ratios would inevitably be falling. Indeed, if real growth is sufficiently high relative to real interest rates, the sectoral deficit can become higher, while still allowing for a fall in debt ratios.

11.3.1   Growth

The problem that the world, particularly most advanced economies, faces is that the conjuncture is highly unlikely to be conducive to growth much, if at all, in excess of real interest rates. This is for several reasons, as earlier described:

- There is going to be a strong increasing demand for public sector expenditures to provide pensions and health care and support for the sharply increasing proportion of the aged in our economies, as life expectancies have risen and could rise yet further. The prospect for such additional public expenditure in future decades is concerning [OBR 2018, pp. 75–85, especially Box 3.3]. Meanwhile the taxable capacity of those of working age is limited, see Heer et al. (2018) and Papetti (2019, p. 30).

- Meanwhile demography is bringing about not only a decline in the rate of growth of, but in many countries, e.g. in Europe and China, an absolute decline in the number of workers, as already discussed. Even if productivity were to return to the more favourable growth rates of the decades up to 2008, such declines in the workforce mean that aggregate real output will continue to grow at a slow rate. The growth of output per worker in Japan has been rising rather faster than the growth of output per worker in most other advanced economies, Chapters 3 and 9. But, nevertheless, the growth of real output in aggregate in Japan has been slow, at about 1% per annum, because of the declining workforce there in recent years. Similar problems will also weigh heavily on many European countries over future decades, though the USA and UK are in a slightly more favourable position, in part because of inward migration in recent decades.

- Real interest rates have become exceptionally low, partly because demographic pressures, particularly in China, have led to savings 'gluts', while investment ratios outside of China, as earlier argued, have remained extremely low, partly under the influence of the globalised availability of additional cheap labour. Both these factors are going into reverse. As the dependency ratio rises, personal sector savings ratios are likely to decline, unless governments consciously restrict the future generosity of their pensions and medical assistance for the aged, which could be politically challenging. At the same time the recovery in the power of labour, as workers become scarce, and taxation rises to meet extra public sector expenditures, will lead to rising real unit labour costs. In order to offset that, corporates are likely to increase their investment demand. So, the likelihood is that the balance between investment and saving, i.e. the demand and supply of loanable funds, may well lead to a recovery in real interest rates. If so, forthcoming pressures may lower growth rates, at the same time as real interest rates rise, making it increasingly difficult simply to grow out of current high debt ratios.

If we cannot grow out of the current high debt ratio levels, then debtors could meet claims on them by failing to pay back as much initially as implicitly promised. There are, perhaps, three ways of doing so:

11.3.2 Unexpected Inflation

The first, and simplest, way of reducing the real debt burden is through (unexpected) inflation; note that inflation expectations are currently 'well anchored' and held at low levels, around 2%. Such anchoring of inflationary expectations depends, considerably, on investor confidence that central banks will be able to maintain their inflation target into the foreseeable future. But will they? Over the last two and a half decades since inflation targetry became generally adopted, nominal and real interest rates have trended downwards. This has made central banks the best friend of indebted Ministers of Finance and their bosses (Prime Ministers). Central banks have been far too eager to attribute the decline in inflation to the success of their own implementation of the inflation target regime, and commentators and politicians have had no good reason to contradict that claim. If nominal interest rates are now on a rising track again, even if gradually, this will put them in conflict with the immediate desires and interests of Ministers of Finance and other politicians, as has already been evident in certain countries, such as the USA, India and Turkey. In almost every country, the central bank's independence was brought about by an act of the legislature; the exception is Europe where the independence of the ECB is enshrined in a common Treaty. Whereas the independence of the ECB would be hard to revoke, the independence of other central banks can be reversed by a further Act. If the politicians find that central bank policies to achieve price stability get in their way of objectives for faster growth and lower taxes, they may seek to end, or sharply reduce the independence of central banks. If so, that vaunted independence might ultimately prove a somewhat weak reed as protection against a more inflationary future.

11.3.3 Renegotiation

But the ECB's independence is more solidly based. In their case debtors, including national member governments, would not be able to get out of their commitments by inflating them away. The same would be true in those other countries where central bank independence (CBI) holds firm. In such cases, when the pressure of debt service becomes too great, the next possible alternative is renegotiation of promised cash flows to ease the debt service burden. Such renegotiations generally go under the heading of 'Extend and Pretend', whereby the cash flows in the form of regular interest payments are either reduced and/or pushed further back in time, thereby alleviating the immediate cash flow burden on the debtor. Normally, this is done in such a way that, although the present value of the debtors' future cash flows is reduced, the accountants feel able to leave the nominal value of such debt unchanged on the books of the creditors. In this way, debtor relief need not necessarily be accompanied by any reduction in the apparent financial strength of creditors. That is, of course, 'smoke and mirrors', but since much finance depends on confidence and trust, 'smoke and mirrors' can be a beneficial device.

11.3.4 Default

The final mechanism for debtor relief is straight default, either partial or total, writing down the nominal amounts of cash flows to be paid back to creditors. Such default, of course, prevents the debtor involved from accessing credit markets for a period of time. But the history, for example of sovereign default, implies that memories are relatively short, so that a prospective recovery of the defaulting debtor need not prevent a return to financial markets for very long. Nevertheless, in such circumstances, where there is a clear-cut default, the creditor involved has to take an offsetting immediate hit to their own balance sheet. Thus, default can have far greater systemic effects than renegotiation; the problems of the 'doom loop' between banks and sovereigns are a case in point. So, both because of the costly implications of default for borrowers, and the widening systemic effect of such default on creditors, default by borrowers is an extreme, and unhappy, response to excessive debt burdens, perhaps more so than either renegotiation or a slightly higher rate of inflation. Nevertheless, all these three alternatives, i.e. inflation, renegotiation and default, are costly and undesirable.

Finally, for completeness, rather than as a practical reality in current conditions, there is another way for crushing debt loans to be removed, in the guise of creditors forgiving part, or all, of the debts owed to them in debt jubilees. Michael Hudson (2018) has demonstrated that this was a common, regular feature of ancient empires, Babylonia, Assyria, etc., and has marked overtones in early Judaic and Christian cultures. The debts forgiven were household, *not* commercial, and were mostly owed to the King and royal palace. The King not only forgave debts owed to himself, but had the power to insist that other wealthy creditors did likewise. Such debt jubilees reinforced the social structure and communal obligations, e.g. serving in the army, of these empires, and served to prolong their existence, with such jubilees being called at the accession of a new King or at a time of national emergency.

As the power of the wider wealthy creditor class rose relative to that of the central ruler rose, so the practicality of debt jubilees declined. Indeed, those rulers who became strong enough to defy other creditors and re-impose such jubilees were often termed 'tyrants', whose precise meaning has some interesting class connotations. More generally, creditor/debtor relationships are now generally intermediated by financial institutions, so debt forgiveness could bankrupt them. Moreover, the class of creditors has so widened, e.g. via semi-obligatory pension arrangements, that questions about which creditors forgive what debts has become so complex that nowadays debt forgiveness has merged indistinguishably into the process of debt renegotiation, discussed in Sect. 11.3.3 above. For more on all this, consult Goodhart and Hudson (2018).

12

A Switch from Debt to Equity Finance?

12.1 Introduction

If growing out of debt seems improbable, and failing to meet commitments by one, or another, form of default on debtor promises is also highly undesirable, what else could be done? The argument here is that what could be done, should have been done, and has not been done is to revise the balance of the fiscal advantages of financing dramatically towards equity finance, and away from debt finance.

The benefits of equity finance are obvious, but worth reiterating. First, unlike debt, equity has no maturity and hence no looming deadline for redemption. Second, dividends are both discretionary and can be shaped to revenues or earnings in a way that fixed coupon payments cannot. Some debt instruments, like interest rate swaps and inflation indexed bonds, do show payments that are variable in nature, but the bulk of the debt universe is comprised of fixed coupon paying bonds. Missed coupon payments count as a default in a way that not paying dividends doesn't. Finally, during periods of stress around debt, an income stream of fixed payments that is supposed to protect creditors turns out to be a dubious asset at best. History is littered with episodes of default on debt that have gone hand-in-hand with macroeconomic upheaval. Thus, even the benefits to creditors from holding debt versus equity are not clear and obvious.

A switch to equity finance would be easier to execute in the future than to switch the large legacy stock of debt that the world has already accrued. Nevertheless, debt-to-equity swaps are already being used—most aggressively in China—to change the profile of the balance sheet. Even in the future, a

© The Author(s) 2020
C. Goodhart and M. Pradhan, *The Great Demographic Reversal*,
https://doi.org/10.1007/978-3-030-42657-6_12

switch from debt to equity finance would be easier to design for institutions than for households. This is perhaps easiest to see and most important in the case of corporate finance. But, first, let us consider what might be done in the cases of household and public sector finances.

How could we encourage households and mortgage lenders to switch to equity financing modes? Households borrow primarily on fixed interest mortgages, in order to buy houses. This too could be switched more onto an equity basis. During periods when housing prices were expected to rise at a rate faster than the CPI, financial institutions might be glad to provide an equity element to housing finance, but borrowers would probably be resistant. A study by the Bank of England, Benetton et al. (2019), reported that,

> A counterfactual study of homebuyers who, instead of using the equity available, relied on high loan-to-value mortgages shows that their financing choices can be rationalized by an expected rate of house price appreciation of 7.7% per year.

But the regulators might adjust the required loan-to-value ratio to give an advantage to equity finance, rather than fixed interest finance, for mortgage borrowing, in some large part on the grounds that it would protect the borrower. Such equity finance for housing would seem to require the development of future markets for housing prices wherein lenders could hedge their inflation risk exposure. This is already possible to some extent via purchases in Real Estate Investment Trusts and Asset Backed Securities (with residential or commercial property as the underlying security).

During periods when housing prices were expected to fall, relative to the CPI, even if only temporarily, lenders would not be happy to take out such equity finance. In such circumstances, the public sector might have to provide a backstop for equity finance for housing.

Over the very long run, technical innovation in building houses has lagged severely behind innovation in most other manufacturing production. Moreover, much of the price of housing relates to land values, and land is in fixed supply. Partly as a result, again over such very long periods, housing prices have generally trended above the CPI. If that should remain there in future, a government-provided equity finance backstop along the lines of the 'Help-to-Buy' scheme (i.e. already in operation in the UK) would actually provide, in the medium term, a profitable opportunity for the public sector.

A roughly similar argument can be made for student loans. That would require switching more of the cost of higher education from a fixed-interest student loan/debt basis onto an equity-type basis, whereby the lender receives a (small) share of the student's subsequent total taxable income. This could even be made an obligatory requirement for college enrolment, which would serve as a progressive, redistributional tax (and/or deter some of the wealthy from attending college). On this, see Goodhart and Hudson (2018).

Turning, briefly to the public sector, it also could turn to a more equity-based form of finance by offering nominal income bonds, in place of fixed interest debt. While such issues have been advocated from time to time, and quite frequently during recent years (see, for example, Sheedy (2014) and Benford et al., Bank of England's Financial Stability paper (2016), and the references cited therein), they have yet to be taken up on any large scale. But given the uncertainties about productivity and the availability of labour over future decades, it might well be a propitious moment for yet a further reconsideration.

It is in the corporate sector that the case for a switch from debt to equity finance holds the most promise. There are two main problems that need to be addressed fairly soon, if there should be any sustained shift by the corporate sector to equity finance.

The first of these is that debt finance has, at least for the corporate sector, considerable fiscal advantage over equity finance. This would have to be rectified and equity finance made as advantageous for corporates as debt finance already is, if there were to be any success in introducing such a shift. We discuss this in Sect. 12.2 below.

The second problem is that the combination of limited liability for all equity holders, and the alignment of the incentives of managers with their equity shareholders, has led to a tendency towards short-termism and low investment, as noted earlier, and discussed further in an associated paper by Goodhart and Lastra (2020), and also by Huertas (2019).

12.2 Levelling the Net Fiscal Advantages of Debt and Equity

There are two main sets of proposals, of which we are aware, that address the issue of removing the fiscal advantage of debt for corporates and levelling the playing field between equity and debt finance. These are, first, the Allowance for Corporate Equity (ACE), included in the Mirrlees Review, *Tax by Design* (2011), and the second is the proposal for Destination-based Cash Flow Taxation' (DBCFT), now more usually described as Border Taxes, as described in the Oxford University Centre for Business Taxation, paper of the same title

(WP17/01), January 2017, by Auerbach et al. These are further described in order below.

12.2.1 ACE—A Tax Allowance for Equities?

Tax treatment is a key reason that firms prefer debt to equity. The ACE proposal by the Mirrlees Review for the Institute for Fiscal Studies (2011, Chapter 17) attempts to rectify that imbalance. Interest expenses, an explicit line item on the corporate income statement, are tax deductible. Financing a project with equity does not generate a similar tax-deductible expense. As a result, firms prefer to return profits to their equity holders and raise more debt. What's more, the cost of issuing debt falls as inflation rises, making debt financing even more attractive during such times. The net effect is to make corporate financing riskier and less efficient.

The ACE is an attempt to replicate the tax benefits of debt for equity financed projects—by introducing an explicit (though imputed) allowance against equity that is also tax deductible, just like interest expenses. There are two issues with the implementation of the ACE that the Mirrlees Review addresses. First, equating debt to equity could be done by removing the tax deductibility of interest expenses, but this would have to be done globally. Otherwise, firms would simply relocate to other destinations that continued to allow tax deductibility. Second, introducing the ACE would mean a loss of tax revenue. While it would be tempting to raise the corporate income tax to compensate for that lost revenue, the Mirrlees Review suggests instead accepting the loss of tax revenue from this particular source and balancing it off against a review of the nation's tax structure as a whole. Thus, in an internationally competitive context, it would not be viable to remove the tax deductibility of interest payments from (say) UK firms unilaterally. So, in order to level the fiscal advantages of debt and equity, the normal return component of profits would equally have to go untaxed, thereby narrowing the corporate tax base. Although such a reform was introduced in Belgium in 2008, its main drawback is that it would have a significant revenue cost, unless the corporate tax rate was raised considerably in lieu.

The problem with the latter would be that it would raise corporate tax rates in the UK probably well above those ruling in other countries, and thereby increase the incentive for multinational firms to shift taxable profits, or even activity, outside the UK. So, the Mirrlees Review suggests that the authorities should accept that they can get less revenues from such corporate taxation and offset this by raising taxation elsewhere as part of a larger overall adjustment to the tax system.

In our own view, the benefit of rebalancing debt and equity as a source of finance is big enough, in the context of the excessive leverage that the world has inherited, to make the introduction of such a rearrangement of the tax base worthwhile. Nevertheless, political resistance to any further increases of taxation elsewhere has been such that there has been no indication, as far as we are aware, of any willingness by the Treasury or any Chancellors of the Exchequers, in the years since the Mirrlees Review was published, to give active consideration to this proposal. Whether a future crisis involving enhanced concerns about the excessive leverage of non-financial corporations might reinvigorate discussion of this issue remains to be seen.

12.2.2 Border Taxes

Destination-Based Cash Flow Taxes try to achieve a similar equivalence between debt and equity, but we think that they are more controversial.

Border taxes would make all corporate expenses, including investment, tax-free. Exports would be untaxed, while imports would be taxed. Giving relief to expenses is essentially equivalent to imposing a Value Added Tax (VAT). Border taxes would make all expenses equivalent, thereby making firms indifferent between debt and equity. Its implementation would be much easier than imputing the ACE and there would be no loss of revenue and very little economic distortion. The other important advantage of border taxes is that they make corporate tax avoidance difficult. If the same set of rules on expenses and exports vs imports are in operation in a country, firms will find geography irrelevant because they will no longer be able to exploit tax avoidance schemes like inter-company loans and holding assets in tax havens. Similarly, more and more countries will find it to their advantage to adopt such a scheme to avoid revenue loss, or perhaps to appear as competitive as other economies with border taxes in operation.

> **Border taxes, also known as the destination-based cash flow tax**
>
> The Executive Summary of 'Destination Based Cash Flow Tax' (Oxford University Centre for Business Taxation, paper of the same title (WP17/01), January 2017, by Auerbach et al.) describes the concept as follows[1]:

---

[1]Previously published in Auerbach, A., Devereux, M. P., Keen, M. and J. Vella, 'Destination-Based Cash Flow Taxation', Oxford University Centre for Business Taxation, Working Paper 2017/1. Reproduced with permission.

The DBCFT has two basic components.

- The "cash *flow*" element gives immediate relief to all expenditure, including capital expenditure, and taxes revenues as they accrue.
- The "destination-based" element introduces border adjustments of the same form as under the value added tax (VAT): exports are untaxed, while imports are taxed.

This is equivalent in its economic impact to introducing a broad-based, uniform rate Value Added Tax (VAT) - or achieving the same effect through an existing VAT - and making a corresponding reduction in taxes on wages and salaries.

The paper evaluates the DBCFT against five criteria: economic efficiency, robustness to avoidance and evasion, ease of administration, fairness and stability. And it does so both for the case of universal adoption by all countries and the more plausible case of unilateral adoption.

In contrast with existing systems of taxing corporate profit, especially in an international environment, the DBCFT and VAT-based equivalent have significant attractions:

- A central motivation for the DBCFT is to improve economic efficiency by taxing business income in a relatively immobile location - that is, the location of final purchasers of goods and services (the "destination"). The DBCFT should not distort either the scale or the location of business investment and eliminates the tax bias towards debt finance by assuring neutral treatment of debt and equity as sources of finance.
- Taxing business income in the place of destination also has the considerable advantage that the DBCFT is also robust against avoidance through inter-company transactions. Common means of tax avoidance - including the use of inter-company debt, locating intangible property in low-tax jurisdictions and mispricing inter-company transactions - would not be successful in reducing tax liabilities under a DBCFT.

   Here however the distinction between universal and unilateral adoption is important. With adoption by only a subset of countries, those not adopting are likely to find their profit shifting problems to be intensified: companies operating in high tax countries, for instance, which may seek to artificially over-price their imports, will face no countervailing tax when sourcing them by exporting from related companies in DBCFT countries.

- By the same token, the DBCFT provides long term stability since countries would broadly have an incentive to adopt it - either to gain a competitive advantage over countries with a conventional origin-based tax, or to avoid a competitive disadvantage relative to countries that had already implemented a DBCFT. It would also be resistant to tax competition in tax rates.

Given all these attractions and benefits of a DBCFT, one might reasonably ask why it has not already been adopted? It was seriously considered by the incoming Republican administration in 2017 in the USA, but then dropped. There are, however, numerous drawbacks.

- It would represent a major change in the direction and assignment of taxation. As in any such major change, it would have large groups of sizeable losers and winners. Losers usually are more vocal in remonstrating than winners are in support.
- The main losers would be importers. It would be seen, and subject to objection, as equivalent to a temporary devaluation. There may be some query whether it is acceptable under WTO rules.
- It would (temporarily) raise domestic prices, especially of goods/services with a high import content.
- While the intention is to combine the rise in VAT with a reduction in taxes on labour income, there is no certainty that this would, or could, be done so as to leave labour real post-tax incomes unchanged.
- Even more seriously, the non-working poor, e.g. old, unemployed, sick, would not be protected, and, absent a general re-rating of benefits would lose, depending in part on exchange rate effects. So the scheme could be attacked as potentially highly regressive.
- Since investment is pro-cyclical and volatile, as are corporate losses, DBCFT tax receipts would be more procyclical and volatile than the current forms of corporate tax (IMF Policy Paper, 2019).
- It could generate schemes for fraudulent loss-making, though Devereux and Vella (2019) contest this argument.

Thus, to introduce DCBFT without provoking a political storm would probably have to involve reworking much of the structure of transfer and benefit payments, as well as taxes on wages and salaries. So, it would be a massive exercise, which would dampen the enthusiasm for such a reform of most Ministers of Finance.

Rather than do this, they might prefer to explore other channels for dealing with the tax avoidance mechanisms that so many international corporations can now put in place.

While the benefits of a DBCFT are clear, the costs of making such a large jump to a new, and untried, system create a sizeable hurdle, so far preventing its acceptance.

12.3 Reforming the Incentive Structure for Corporate Managers

Current criticism of modern capitalism has several facets; it is argued that it leads to managers assuming excessive risk, being overpaid, and failing to undertake sufficient long-term investment, especially R&D.[2] The first two criticisms, excessive risk and excessive pay, were particularly levied at banks and other financial intermediaries in the aftermath of the GFC. There have been a variety of proposals aimed at checking or preventing such malfunctions. One set of such proposals has focussed on limiting the business structures of banks and other financial intermediaries. Examples of such proposals include narrow banking in various guises, ringfencing of core retail financial structures, and a variety of other regulatory measures.

Our proposal, as set out in greater length in Goodhart and Lastra (2020), instead, is to apply a distinction between a class of 'insiders', who should be subject to multiple liability, and 'outsiders', who would retain limited liability, as at present. So, for the ordinary shareholder there would be no change. Such a scheme obviously involves making a distinction, which must be inevitably somewhat arbitrary, between 'insiders' and 'outsiders'.

But how do you distinguish between these two categories? In principle, the distinction is straightforward. 'Insiders' have access to significantly greater information about the working of the enterprise than 'outsiders', and the potential to use that information to prevent excessively risky actions. In practice, of course, the distinction is not so easy to make. 'Insiders' would include all of the Board of Directors, including the externals. For employees, we would suggest a twofold categorisation, by status within the company, and by scale of remuneration. Thus any employee on the Executive Board, or who was Chief of a Division would be included. But the key players in a company are frequently indicated by the scale of their remuneration rather than by their formal position. So any employee who was earning a salary in excess of, say, 50% of that of the CEO would also be assessed as an 'Insider'. Nevertheless, if the potential sanction of multiple liability arising from failure was regarded as severe, there could be attempts to adjust titles and salaries so as to avoid being categorised as an 'Insider'. So, the regulatory authority should have the right to designate anyone in a particular company as being an 'insider', subject to judicial review.

Large shareholders are also in a position to access inside information, and to exert influence on the course that a company might follow. So any shareholder with a holding greater than, say, 5% of the company should also be regarded as an 'insider'. There is no particular key threshold, above which a large shareholders should be regarded as an 'insider'. It is arguable that one

---

[2]In an article entitled 'Rethink the purpose of the corporation' (Financial Times, 12 December 2018), Martin Wolf criticises the mantra of shareholder value maximisation, affirming that in the cases of highly leveraged banking the Anglo American model of corporate governance does not work. He refers to a number of books—including Colin Mayer's 2018 *Prosperity*—that suggest that capitalism is substantially broken.

should give shareholders holding between 2 and 5% of the value of the shares the ability to choose whether to count as an 'outsider', or as an 'insider'. If they want to count as an 'outsider', they would have to give up all voting rights, and not participate in policy discussions, e.g. at AGMs.

The base to which the liability should apply would be the remuneration of all those counted as 'insiders', cumulated from the date that they took on that role. This would apply to all forms of remuneration, except those provided in the form of bail-inable debt, with all subsequent transactions in such debt having to be notified. This would apply to the directors and employees. Shareholders would be liable according to the purchase value of their shares.

Not all 'insiders' are equal. In particular, the CEO has much more information and power than any of his subordinates, other members of the Board, or the auditors. One might think that the CEO's liability could be three times the accumulated relevant value of remuneration (ex bail-inables) from the time that he or she had taken up the role of CEO. Board members and chief officers of the company might have two-times liability, and every other 'insider' employee a single liability equal to their accumulated revenue. Similarly, large shareholders with greater than 5% holdings might have double liability, i.e. for an additional twice purchase value of their shares, while 'insider' shareholders, between 2 and 5%, might be liable to pay in an additional purchase value of their shares, roughly as in the American National Bank system before the 1930s.

That raises two further questions. The first is what should happen when an 'insider' ceases to play that role, e.g. an employee leaves the company, or a large shareholder sells their shares. The second is that an 'insider' may be aware that the company is entering dangerous territory, but cannot persuade management to change direction. In that case, how could they avoid being sanctioned for a policy that they would not themselves advocate?

In the first case, of departure from the role of 'insider', it would seem appropriate to taper the liability according to the degree of 'insider' knowledge and power. Thus, if it was agreed that the CEO should have a three times extra liability, then that liability would decline at a constant rate over the following three years, leaving the CEO with zero further liability exactly three years after they had left. By the same token, those with a two times additional liability, should have it taper at a constant rate until they were free of any further liability after two years, and so on for those with a one-time additional liability.

Then we come to the second issue, which is the question of how those with additional liability can avoid sanction in those cases where they have opposed the policy, but have failed to succeed in changing it. Our suggestion in this case is that those in such a position should address a formal, but confidential and private, letter to the relevant regulators, setting out their concerns about the policy being followed. The regulator would have to formally acknowledge receipt of such letters, and they could then be used in mitigation, or often abandonment of any sanction, should the company then fail. Moreover, in the event of the company failing, for the reasons indicated in such a letter(s), this would in turn act as a form of accountability for the regulators. All such letters would have to be made publicly available in the event of failure. It would be a legal offence for the regulator then not to publish any such letter.

There is a more difficult question, whether the regulator, having received such a private confidential letter of warning, perhaps from the auditor, or an unhappy employee, should make them public. In our view, such warnings need to be investigated further by an independent body, such as the regulator or a financial ombudsman before being made publicly available, since in many cases, they may well be groundless with the maintained policy of the company being appropriate. But if the regulator, after investigation, should feel that the warnings had merit, the first step would then be to have a private discussion with management on the merits of the case, and, if management remained unmoved, the next stage would be to publish the warning (anonymously) together with the regulator's own assessment, at the same time offering management the opportunity to state publicly their own side of the case. When the latter process had been completed, 'outsiders' would then be as well informed as 'insiders' on the merits of the issue.

Note that it puts regulators in the firing line for at least severe reputational damage, if they receive such warnings, fail to act upon them, and the warnings prove prescient.

The purpose of the exercise is to provide appropriate sanctions for failure on those with 'insider' knowledge and power. The particular illustrative numbers chosen in the above section are, obviously, somewhat arbitrary. But the exercise can be calibrated to impose appropriate sanctions for all such 'insiders', whether large shareholders, key employees or regulators. We think that this would be a better form of governance.

13

Future Policy Problems: Old Age and Taxes, and the Monetary-Fiscal Clash

"Demographic change is a key long-term pressure on the public finances,"
– The Office of Budget Responsibility, UK, July 2018.[1]

Where will we find the funds to sustain the spending needs of the aged? If you thought the amount of debt in the world today was already a problem, then the official projections of ageing-related spending in the future will make for very difficult reading.

There are no easy fixes—raising taxes on the rich or the poor is an extremely difficult strategy, for economic and political reasons, respectively. And walking away from obligations towards the elderly is not feasible either, because the swelling ranks of the voting bloc that is the elderly simply will not allow it in a democracy.

It is the path of both monetary and fiscal policy, then, that must change quite dramatically. Fiscal innovation *is* on offer—we wade through a number of promising tax regimes, including a modern day 'Domesday Book' such as the one the Normans put together in 1086. All these regimes, however, present their own particular difficulties in implementation and we think it will be desperation rather than innovation that eventually forces their adoption. In the meantime, the growing debt burden will feed the inflationary impulse we have outlined in earlier chapters.

Monetary policy will also suffer. The eager willingness with which governments have encouraged central bank independence will now reverse. For the

---

[1] Reproduced under the Open Government Licence: http://nationalarchives.gov.uk/doc/open-government-licence/version/3/.

© The Author(s) 2020
C. Goodhart and M. Pradhan, *The Great Demographic Reversal*,
https://doi.org/10.1007/978-3-030-42657-6_13

past few decades, central banks have given too much credit to their own inflation targeting regimes and too little to demography in accounting for the disinflation we have seen. As long as inflation and interest rates were falling, Ministers of Finance were happy. Will that still be the case as the ranks of the elderly swell and push inflation and interest rates higher? We don't think so. The conflict between the two has already started, but we are just at the beginning.

13.1   Introduction: The Rocky Road Ahead

Demographic trends will place huge pressure on public policies, fiscal and monetary, over coming decades. The baseline projection for the public sector's primary balance and net debt in the UK, as estimated in the OBR's, 'Fiscal Sustainability Report' (July 2018) (their Chart 2, p. 12), is reproduced below as Diagram 13.1.

The main cause of the OBR's forecast deterioration in the public finances is demographic, and especially reflects health costs (paragraph 24, page 7):

> In this year's report, we continue to assume that health spending rises to accommodate non-demographic cost pressures beyond the medium term and that this adds 1 percentage point a year to health spending growth in the long term. We assume that excess cost growth falls from the latest available estimates for primary and secondary care (which are higher than 1 percentage

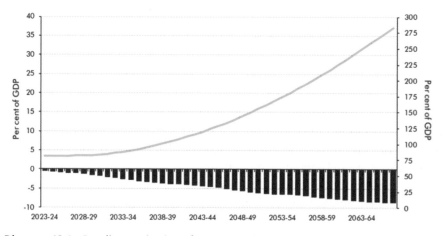

Diagram 13.1 Baseline projections for primary balance and Public Sector Net Debt: UK (Reproduced from the OBR under the Open Government Licence: http://nationala rchives.gov.uk/doc/open-government-licence/version/3/)

point) back to this long-term assumption steadily over the period to 2038-39. This approach and the values that we have chosen are similar to those used by the US Congressional Budget Office. It is important to emphasise that our health spending projections are not based on any bottom-up assessment of 'need', but rather embody a judgement that 'unchanged policy' is best interpreted as assuming that spending rises to accommodate demographic and non-demographic cost pressures over time.

Moreover, their assumption about productivity seems too comfortable to us, given the projected slowdown in the growth rate of the working population and recent trends in productivity. 'Whole economy productivity growth will average 2.0 per cent a year in steady state', in their view (paragraph 22, page 7).

Note that we argue that productivity will rise, but we are more comfortable with this view for the corporate sector, particularly in activities where firms can raise the capital-labour ratio effectively. This is harder to do in health care where the needs of the elderly (and, indeed, of patients in general) are highly idiosyncratic. Those who see US health care as the 'least efficient' sector often fail to recognise that this is because tasks in that field (as well as in education which is also 'inefficient' according to productivity metrics) do not lend themselves to duplication, and hence automation. The overall effect will be that productivity in large swathes of the corporate sector will indeed rise, but overall productivity will rise slower thanks to the nature of the expanding healthcare sector. Particularly given the weak starting point for productivity, the path towards higher economy-wide productivity may be bumpier than the OBR's benign assumption, even though the direction is correct.

Exactly the same syndrome holds for the USA. The *Congressional Budget Office Report* (2019) shows exactly the same family of fiscal trends (Figs. 1.4 and 1.8 from that report are reproduced below as Diagrams 13.2 and 13.3, respectively).

In one respect, the USA is in a rather more adverse condition than most other countries, thanks to a worse starting fiscal stance (adjusted for the stage of the business cycle). This is only partly because of the recent fiscal expansion measures deployed by the Trump administration, as their Fig. 1.3 (reproduced below as Diagram 13.4) portrays.

In another respect, however, the USA is in a rather better state than most other advanced economies, since the ratio of old to working population is both lower and growing less rapidly.

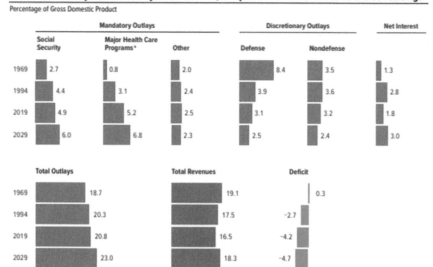

CBO's Baseline Projections of Outlays and Revenues, Compared With Actual Values 25 and 50 Years Ago

Percentage of Gross Domestic Product

	Mandatory Outlays			Discretionary Outlays		Net Interest
	Social Security	Major Health Care Programs[a]	Other	Defense	Nondefense	
1969	2.7	0.8	2.0	8.4	3.5	1.3
1994	4.4	3.1	2.4	3.9	3.6	2.8
2019	4.9	5.2	2.5	3.1	3.2	1.8
2029	6.0	6.8	2.3	2.5	2.4	3.0

	Total Outlays	Total Revenues	Deficit
1969	18.7	19.1	0.3
1994	20.3	17.5	-2.7
2019	20.8	16.5	-4.2
2029	23.0	18.3	-4.7

a. Consists of outlays for Medicare (net of premiums and other offsetting receipts), Medicaid, and the Children's Health Insurance Program, as well as outlays to subsidize health insurance purchased through the marketplaces established under the Affordable Care Act and related spending.

Diagram 13.2 CBO's baseline projections of outlays and revenues, compared with actual values 25 and 50 years ago: USA (*Source* CBO)

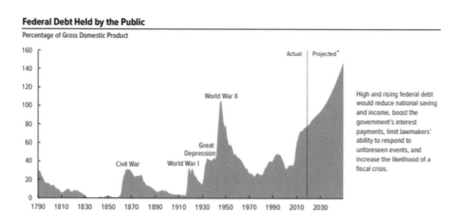

Federal Debt Held by the Public

Percentage of Gross Domestic Product

High and rising federal debt would reduce national saving and income, boost the government's interest payments, limit lawmakers' ability to respond to unforeseen events, and increase the likelihood of a fiscal crisis.

Diagram 13.3 Federal debt held by the public: USA (*Source* CBO)

13.2   Two Things Are Inevitable: Old Age and Taxes

So, on present demographic and medical assumptions the current fiscal stance is unsustainable. Of course, it may not happen. Medical science may find a way to cure dementia/Alzheimer's and to delay the ageing process, so we

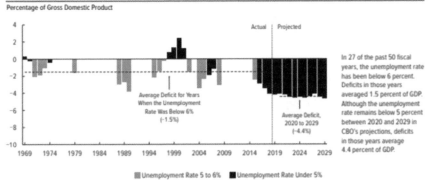

Diagram 13.4 Baseline deficits compared with deficits and surpluses when the unemployment rate has been relatively low: USA (*Source* CBO)

can all work to age 85 (and perhaps be programmed to die of sudden heart failure on a night randomly picked in the year after our 100th birthday). But it would be over-sanguine to rely on future scientific breakthroughs to resolve such problems. And even if current trends continue for only two, or three, decades more, it will put almost all our public finances in a parlous state.

Indeed, the attempt to claw back such deficits and debt ratios from levels reached in the aftermath of the GFC by austerity appears to have reached in many countries the limit of public political acceptability. Such austerity largely took the form of pruning public expenditures in fields other than health, pensions and defence. We tend to doubt whether such pruning can go any further. Furthermore, we believe that social and political pressures will continue to force medical and pension costs up in accordance with current projections, and that new and old superpower rivalry will keep defence spending up.

So, what seems almost inevitable is that the maintenance of public sector solvency will require higher taxation. But on what? The geographical mobility of (skilled) people, financial wealth and corporate headquarters can make steeply progressive income taxes, general wealth taxes and much higher standard-form corporate taxes largely self-harming. On the other hand raising income taxes at the lower end of the spectrum could worsen inequality and cause workers to demand higher pre-tax wage rates.

The Upper Bound Threshold to Taxation on the Working Population

Heer, Polito and Wickens (2018) seek to estimate the upper bound threshold of taxation on the working population. They conclude, pages 40/41, that,

> The main challenge to the sustainability of state pension systems is population aging. Although a world-wide phenomenon, aging is a particular problem for advanced economies where the ratio of pension recipients to contributors to the pension system - the dependency ratio - are among the highest in the world, and are projected to double over the next 85 years. Moreover, many of these countries are close to the limits of what tax policy can do to relieve the situation....
>
> There are significant differences in thresholds levels, distances and probabilities among these countries. The outlook for most of the European countries is of particular concern. Compared to the United States, all have, on average, smaller fiscal spaces, more generous pension systems, are older and are projected to age much faster. The European countries are therefore found to be much closer to the threshold than the United States in 2010 and are predicted to reach the threshold well before 2050. In contrast, the United States is found to maintain a positive distance until 2100.

In contrast, Kotlikoff's General Gaidar Model (GGM) has opposite conclusions. Thus he writes (2019, pp. 34/35),

> Thus, the GGM suggests, quite surprisingly, no long-term fiscal problems arising from ageing in China, Japan, South Korea, or Western Europe. Indeed, in each of these regions, consumption tax rates are much lower at the end of the century than at the beginning. According to the GGM, the country with the biggest fiscal problem arising, in large part, from ageing is the US. The share of elderly in the US is now 17%. By 2100, it will be 27%. In the GGM, the US doesn't experience catch-up productivity growth, since all catch-up is relative to the US.

Also, see Conesa et al. (2019), Laitner and Silverman (2019), and Börsch-Supan (2019), all in Bloom (editor), *Live Long and Prosper* (2019).

While we are not fiscal experts we would make four suggestions where higher tax revenues might be found, i.e. corporation tax; land value taxation; carbon tax; a destination-based cash-flow tax (DBCFT)—the latter having already been mentioned in Chapter 12, Sect. 12.2.2.

13.2.1   Reforming the Basis of Corporation Tax

There has been much Base Erosion and Profit Shifting (BEPS), the latter from international competition, notably via tax havens, especially in the case of companies providing digital services, in recent decades. This has severely cut the proceeds of corporation taxes, particularly in large economies, and probably well below the social optimum.

The OECD's main proposal ('Secretariat Proposal for a "Unified Approach" Under Pillar One', October 2019) is to shift the nexus of such corporate taxation, at least for digital companies, from physical presence to sales within the country. If this reform becomes adopted, which will not be known by the time this book goes to print, it could sharply raise the tax take from corporate taxation in most large economies, and lessen the attraction of tax havens.

13.2.2 A Land Tax

A canal cruise in Amsterdam usually raises eyebrows. Not just for the famously tilted buildings, but also when one realises that buildings were taxed by their width and the size of the windows. The most tax-efficient buildings along the canal are thus ones with barely a few feet for the front façade. The idea (presumably) was to tax dwellers for their access to public roads and appropriating sunshine for their own personal use. The idea is amusing in the modern age, but is it justifiable and fair?

Our proposal has some Dutch elements, but not quite.

We propose a tax on land as it bestows wealth upon owners 'in their sleep', but not to tax the effort of construction on that land. Land and construction upon it extracts benefits from the infrastructure and other land and construction near it. In other words, it imbibes positive spillovers and hence taxing those spillovers makes sense. Urban and rural land will also have to be treated differently. Such a tax regime will create social benefits and could also be designed to avoid sudden discrete jumps in property values.

The evolution of the thinking on land tax

Once societies became agrarian, land ownership became the main source of power and wealth. That continued largely unchanged until the Industrial Revolution. Even though power and wealth have now become more broadly distributed towards human, financial and technological capital, land ownership remains a key index of one's standing in society. Real estate also remains by far the economy's largest asset—so large that it absorbs about 80% of bank credit in many countries, with such credit thereby raising housing and other real estate prices, adding to the economy's debt overhang.

Unlike other forms of wealth, land is fixed, not mobile. The disincentives arising from taxation in reduction of effort, transfer abroad, etc. that apply to most other forms of wealth tax do not apply to land. With a few exceptions (e.g. polders in Holland), land, unlike other forms of wealth, was not created by human labour. There is also an ethical case for land taxation that does not apply to most other forms of wealth (at least, not to the same extent). A large proportion of any site's land value is created by beneficial externalities. Most of these result from public spending, e.g. on transportation, parks, schools and other amenities, as well as investment by private developers in the neighbourhood.

In particular the State provides peace and security via law, defence and police. Without these services, as Hobbes (*Leviathan*, 1651—a must-read which is now available in Wordsworth Classics of World Literature, 2014) noted, not only would life be brutish and short, but land values would be low and uncertain. Again, the State provides a wide range of services, e.g. the value of a property and neighbourhood depends on the quality of the above-mentioned schools, hospitals, road and rail transport. Finally, land value depends on the degree to which others want to live and work in the area.

As Adam Smith (1776, now available 1982),[2] John Stuart Mill (1848, now available 2016) and other great economists have explained for over two centuries, the owner of urban or raw undeveloped land has done little or nothing to create the bare land value on which a building may be placed. As Mill (*Principles of Political Economy*, Book V, Ch. II §5) pointed out, the landlord enjoys a rising rental income and hence market price for property 'in his sleep'.[3] And, of course, there is Henry George (notably *Our Land and Land Policy*, 1871, now available 2016).

By contrast, capital investment in construction and related development entails a real expense, and as such is less appropriate than land as a subject for taxation. Taxing the bare land value rather than an overall property tax (i.e. land plus building) would provide an incentive to develop and supply new housing more rapidly by effectively *reducing* the average tax paid per square foot of the land.

The same argument cannot be used for rural land. The shape and appearance of the countryside in Europe, for example, is mostly a man-made

---

[2]'Landlords love to reap where they have not sown, and demand a rent even for its (the land's) natural produce' (*Wealth of Nations*, Book I, Ch. 6, §8). Landownership privileges 'are founded on the most absurd of all suppositions, the supposition that every successive generation of men has not an equal right to the earth … but that the property of the present generation should be … regulated according to the fancy of those who died … five hundred years ago.' (Book III, Ch. 2, §6).

[3]In *Principles of Political Economy, with Some of their Applications to Social Philosophy* (1848, now available 2016), Book V, ch. II §5, Mill described rent-yielding properties as enabling their holders to demand payment from society 'without any exertion or sacrifice on the part of the owners … Landlords … grow richer, as it were in their sleep, without working, risking, or economizing. What claim have they, on the general principle of social justice, to this accession of riches?'.

artefact. It would be idiotic to place a tax on national public parks. What could be done would be to assess the broad social value of different forms of rural land usage so as to qualify the land tax. This may sound difficult and bureaucratic, but it would only be an extension of the subsidy procedures for agriculture already in place in many countries (e.g. the Rural Payment Agency, RPA, in the UK). In so far as farm land prices did fall, this could enable a younger and more diverse set of farmers to come into the profession. Estimating bare land values would be difficult, but no more so than for many other objects of value, e.g. art collections. Also, expenditures whose purpose is to maintain/improve the value of the land, e.g. hedging/ditching, fertilising, weeding, gardening, could offset such a land tax.

One of the first fiscal and governance measures taken by the Normans after their conquest of England (1066) was to do a comprehensive survey of land ownership in the *Domesday Book* (1086). Not only the UK, but all other advanced economies need a modern equivalent. Satellite imagery has often been misinterpreted, mistaking bunkers for atomic facilities, but we can be sure they would be more successful at distinguishing construction from land in a cheap, efficient and comprehensive manner. More relevant, associated data, such as the availability of public infrastructure, especially public transport, climate details, would also be easy to catalogue.

So, our preference would be for a land tax based on pure land values, with a property tax as a fallback.

The beneficial impact on land and property prices

Such a tax would bring two immediate benefits. First, it would immediately lower market prices for land, and hence for housing and commercial properties. Second, to the extent that constructions are not taxed, it would incentivise owners of land to build more in order to reduce the tax burden per square foot of their land. Since the threat of such a levy would distort and disrupt valuations and transactions, it might seem logical to impose an initially affordable but steadily rising tax on (bare) land (or property) values, rather than an immediate stochastic jump.

There should be some who are concerned that the future increases in tax rates would be immediately reflected in today's prices in a discounted manner. This may happen, but the case of Miami provides significant evidence to the contrary. A considerable part of the urban landscape of Miami will inevitably sink below the water line in the next 50 years. That has deterred neither construction nor house prices from rising in that great city.

Unless there is to be a general financial crisis, the path of least resistance to the land tax, advocated by most classical economists, would have to be gradual, but steadily rising. A regular, low tax rate applied to such land valuations would require such valuations to be kept up-to-date, and would therefore be bureaucratically onerous, but technologically easy, and far less onerous than trying to introduce a broader wealth tax. And because land is immobile, it would have less distortionary effects on the economy, while redistributing wealth from the current owners of land to a property-owning society.

13.2.3   A Carbon Tax, Aka, Let's Put a Smile on Greta's Face

For many, perhaps most, people their main existential worry is not worsening dependency ratios or demographic change, but rather climate change, and all the problems that that could bring with it. The declining birth rates (except in Africa), and slowing population growth, is welcomed by climate change activists as reducing the need for fossil fuels.

But a carbon tax would serve both causes. It would raise funds to pay for the growing need to care for the old, while at the same time using market forces to reduce fossil fuel usage where it was less valuable. Despite the advocacy of such a tax by many leading economists, a recent example being Kotlikoff et al. (2019), 'Making Carbon Taxation a Generational Win Win', it has not figured as a rallying cry by such activists, who seem to imagine that direct regulatory controls would be less distortionary (or fall on some unspecified other set of people), than a tax/subsidy-based system. This is a common fallacy.

Nevertheless, tax increases are always unpopular, and Macron's difficulties with the 'gilets jaunes' in France in 2019 are a well-known case in point. The argument was that the poor in rural France, ill-served by public transport, would be badly hit, while rich Parisians could take the Metro.

This is again where a modern 'Domesday Book' could come in. The land could be divided into areas where public transport was in different categories, e.g. excellent, satisfactory, poor, almost non-existent. Then the tax rate on petrol/gasoline could vary from area to area. In the USA, differing State taxes on gas cause garages to congregate at certain State borders, but the distortion seems relatively minor. By the same token the tax rate on heating bills could be made to vary conditional on the average temperature. Already in many countries special account is taken of the heating needs of the elderly.

What we need is a carbon tax, but one that is more cleverly designed to ease the pressures on the poor, the elderly and those whose way of life prevents them from adjusting flexibly to the new tax.

13.2.4 DBCFT

We have already discussed this in the previous chapter (in Sect. 12.2.2), and we keep the discussion brief here. Its great advantage is that corporations cannot avoid it by the many tax dodges that they have perfected, and it can therefore be increased to raise additional funding without fear of business shifting abroad. Its great disadvantage is that it takes the form of an indirect tax on consumption, a generalised VAT, and is consequently regressive in its incidence.

So, the introduction of a DBCFT would have to buttressed with detailed efforts to ensure that the poor were not disadvantaged. It is not enough to reduce the taxes imposed on wages and labour incomes at the same time. The (relative) income of the old, the unemployed, single mothers, and all other benefit recipients would have to be protected also from the increase in prices, including notably on imported foodstuffs, that the introduction of such a tax would bring, even if only temporarily.

In summary, this section argues that there are additional forms of tax that could be introduced to meet the crisis of fiscal unsustainability that looms ahead. But all will meet with opposition, especially from those most affected, and would need to be introduced both gradually, and with carefully designed offsets and protection for the most vulnerable.

Given public opposition to increased taxation, we doubt whether politicians will do enough either to maintain the macro-economy in balance, as the household and corporate sectors swing back into deficit, or to address the concern about ever-rising public sector debt ratios. The result, as emphasised earlier, will be a revival of inflationary pressures. This leads on to the question of what monetary policy and Central Banks could do in this new context.

13.3 Monetary Policy

Politicians and their economic advisers have consistently underestimated the deflationary pressures forced upon the world's economies by the joint forces of globalisation and demography over the last three decades (since the early 1990s). In doing so, they have also over-estimated the amount of success to be allocated to their inflation-targeting policies, and their control over inflation in general.

Those countries that could do so, especially Germany, much preferred to balance their economies by running large current account surpluses, rather than via public sector deficits and debt accumulation. This, of course, placed greater pressure on the equivalent deficit countries, where such deficits were partly, or largely, blamed on their own fiscal incontinence (rather than on the policies of the 'more prudent' creditor countries).

In this context of globally sub-optimal fiscal deficits, expansionary monetary policies were required to balance the global economic books. Such policies had the additional implication in that they benefited almost all the most powerful sectors of society. Central Banks, and their Chairs/Presidents/Governors, became best friends of those in the Ministry of Finance, as well as corporations, households with outstanding mortgages, and the rich and the old. By holding down the interest costs of debt, central banks encouraged a rise in asset prices. Only the young and poor did less well directly. Even then, it can be, and has been, argued that they benefited more from the higher aggregate demand and employment that such expansionary monetary policies generated.

But what will happen when the tide turns, and the Great Reversal gets underway?

Just as global fiscal policies were systematically insufficiently expansionary over the last three decades, so they will, most likely, be insufficiently contractionary over the coming three decades, 2020–2050. If so, monetary policy would have to take the strain of reining back demand in order to defend their inflation targets. This would involve higher nominal, and real, interest rates. This would be counter to the interests of all those who benefitted from loose monetary policy of the past decades.

Meanwhile, just as central banks had less to do with the disinflation of the last decades than they have claimed, they are likely to have little success in keeping inflation low without hurting growth even more. The genesis of long-term inflation trends of the past and future decades will turn out to be quite a non-monetary phenomenon.

Rather naturally, Central Bank independence (CBI) is likely to fall into jeopardy, but not necessarily in an uniform manner. CBI is likely to be far better protected in countries (or zones) with left-leaning governments. Not only are such governments less concerned with the welfare of those who benefit from ever-rising asset prices, but also they want to protect their backs against financial panics, rising credit risk premia, being shut out of the ability to borrow on the bond market, etc. For such leftist governments, an independent Central Bank provides a much-needed surety of financial rectitude in an environment of rising inflation. Right-wing, particularly populist, governments feel no such need for that protection since the rich and powerful are, in general, already in their constituency. It is therefore under the ascendency of these regimes that CBI is likely to suffer the most.

In fact, the right-wing, populist, backlash against CBI is already happening (Bianchi et al. 2019). Tellingly, the leading article of *The Economist* (April 13–19, 2019) was entitled 'Interference Day: Independent central banks are under threat. That is bad news for the world'. CBI is in most cases a 'paper tiger'. Such independence has usually been brought about by a legislative act; what one Parliament has enacted, another can repeal. Even when leaving the original Act in place, governments can generally either so change the mandate or the appointees to its management in order to bend the Central Bank to its will. Central Banks are inherently political institutions, and they know that, whatever their current constitutional position may be.

The one exception is the European Central Bank, which is protected by a Treaty, which requires unanimity to revise. But even in this case the ECB knows that it would be hazardous to adopt policies that are strongly opposed by several of its major constituent countries.

The glory years of Central Bank independence may be coming to a sticky end.

14

Swimming Against the (Main)Stream

Understanding the past is very important to preparing for the future. Policies, financial market conditions and preparations for the future are a natural consequence of the mainstream thinking of the time. Some of this also has to do with the duration of a trend—the longer it lasts, the more convinced everyone is that it is here to stay. Once established, conventional thinking is extremely hard to dislodge, particularly at turning points. We are at such an inflexion point right now—and mainstream models are unable or unwilling to change direction. Where and how do we differ from such models? And what are the consequences of conventional thinking getting things wrong?

Since World War II the advanced economies of the world have been subject to two such consecutive strong and persistent trends in nominal variables, inflation and interest rates. This is most dramatically shown in Diagram 14.1 for the nominal interest rate on UK long-term Consols from 1694 until 2018. Such rates were remarkably constant from 1694 until about 1950, ranging between 2.5 and 5%. But then they rose steadily to a peak of about 15% in 1973/1974 before falling, equally steadily to their current, abnormally low, levels of under 1%.

Year to year inflation was considerably more variable in the earlier centuries, mostly influenced by periods of war and the vagaries of harvests. But wars were usually expected to be short-lived, sometimes incorrectly so, as in 1914, and harvests were stochastic. So, as this diagram indicates, longer-term inflation expectations and real interest rates remained rather stable over these centuries.

What, then, changed so sharply after World War II that we have had persistent trends in nominal variables, and what caused these two, strong

© The Author(s) 2020
C. Goodhart and M. Pradhan, *The Great Demographic Reversal*,
https://doi.org/10.1007/978-3-030-42657-6_14

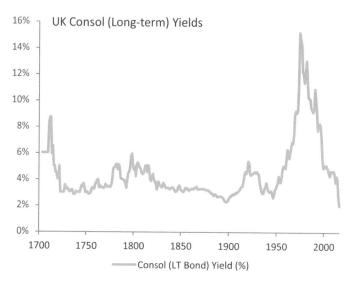

Diagram 14.1 Consol (Long-term bond) yields in the United Kingdom (*Source* FRED, Bank of England)

but opposite, successive trends? The answer to these questions is important because we want to know if we are simply going back to the pre-war era of stability, or if there is a third trend coming? And if there is a third trend, what does the future hold?

The mainstream approach to inflation has been based on monetarism and Keynesian demand management. To a monetarist, or to a gold-enthusiast, the answer to explaining such trends is straightforward. Advanced economies moved from a gold standard regime to a fiat money regime. Fiscal dominance allowed politicians to bribe the electorate with their own money and inflation ensued. Then stagflation took over in the horrible 1970s, and conditions got so bad that a move to Central Bank Independence (CBI) restored some vestiges of monetary constraint on politicians.

There is, of course, considerable truth in this assessment, but it is not the whole story. Thus, in the first period of upwards trends, 1950–1979, the economics profession believed that they could control the pressure of demand via fiscal policies in order to obtain the optimal, social, trade-off between unemployment and inflation, along the Phillips curve. After the awful experiences of the 1930s, when the post-war policymakers had been young, they wanted to err (asymmetrically) in going for the lower end of the feasible range of unemployment. And if that caused higher inflation than desired, then try direct measures via prices and incomes policies. Well intentioned, but it did not work.

Moreover, the policies of virtually guaranteed full (or over-full) employment strengthened the bargaining power of labour, for example the National Union of Mineworkers (NUM) in the UK and the UAW, Union of Auto Workers, in the USA. Trade union membership and labour militancy increased. A consequence of the strengthening of labour's bargaining power was that the Natural Rate of Unemployment was rising in the background, an ironic side effect of the deployment of Keynesian demand management to raise the average level of employment.

But the events and problems of these earlier decades (1950–1979) are not our focus. Instead, we concentrate on the second half of the post-war period (1980–2018), and what is yet to come in future.

Here the mainstream monetarist tale, and even more so that of the gold-enthusiast, is even less satisfactory, especially for the years after 2007. Inflation, it is regularly repeated, is a monetary phenomenon, and Central Banks can create money. How, then, can we have a persistent problem of lower than targeted inflation?

Of course, we are told that this problem is due to the zero, or effective, lower bound to nominal interest rates. But when inflation remains around 1%, as now in 2019, the ELB only becomes a serious constraint when the equilibrium real interest rate, r^*, itself becomes negative, falling far below its prior typical values of 2.5 to 3.5%. And that is a real, and not just a nominal, monetary problem.

The mainstream explanation of our times is precisely that, an r^* that has indeed become negative. The secular stagnation thesis involves a variety of arguments (inequality and even the need for ageing societies to invest less are in the mix), to explain why r^* has fallen and will remain low for the foreseeable future. Empirical estimates of r^* regularly show estimates that are negative or very close to zero, backing up the claims of the secular stagnationists.

The broader argument is that we are stuck in a world of low aggregate demand and inflation. Low inflation and an even lower r^* means that aggregate demand can never really recover, condemning economies to keep generating low inflation because of the slack in their economies.

There is a reason for the popularity of this line of thinking. The attempts of the Federal Reserve to raise interest rates, only to be forced to lower them rather unceremoniously again, and the inability of central banks to raise inflation despite extraordinary policies certainly fit the story.

However, the theory falls short upon closer examination on at least three counts.

- First, deflationary pressure arising from excess capacity problems is a problem that is more easily associated with China than to the USA. The argument does not pretend to explain the period before the GFC, in which growth was sound and inflation and real interest rates were falling, which means understanding both pre- and post-crisis dynamics requires two separate explanations—that's possible, but unsatisfying as an approach to understanding long-term trends.
- Second, the estimates of r* that are generated from the so-called unobservable components or Kalman filter models assume that the path of r* and the path of potential growth are determined by a common factor, productivity. Empirical examination of the link between growth and real interest rates shows no such link (Hamilton et al. 2015). That makes the estimates themselves questionable at best.
- Finally, and perhaps most importantly, the explanation for the path of r* takes inequality and low investment as given. Yet, both of these phenomena in turn depend largely on globalisation and demographic factors (as we have argued in Chapter 1). Using them as causes for falling interest rates then fails to identify a clear picture of what exactly is the driving force.

14.1   Our Approach and Main Thesis

The main thesis of this book is that the evolution of the real trends in the economy (continued real output growth coexisting with deflationary headwinds) has been caused by a combination of demography and globalisation, leading to the largest ever upwards supply shock to the availability of labour (assisted by labour saving technology). Almost inevitably in this context, the real return to labour, except for high-skilled workers complementary with capital, has gone down, while the return to capital, profitability, has gone up. Labour has increasingly lost its bargaining power, under threat from offshoring and immigration. Behind the scenes the Natural Rate of Unemployment (NRU) has been steadily falling.

Apart, perhaps, from our view that variations in NRU (u*) are at least as important, and more variable than, variations in the natural real interest (r*) or growth (g*) rates, see Chapter 8, our analysis of the long-term trends over the last three decades is relatively mainstream. Where this book does diverge from the mainstream is being much more global in outlook, and in particular by ascribing the greatest importance for the world's macroeconomic developments to the role of Asia, and of China in particular. We record the enormous importance of China in this respect in Chapter 2. Most economists focus on their own countries or regions, and most economists in the West come from North America or Europe. There is a token reference to global factors and a discussion of China somewhere in their notes, but neither plays a role that is strong enough to dominate domestic developments. Nowadays that is too narrow a canvas to do justice to our macroeconomic story.

Then, in Chapter 3 and subsequently, we turn to the future. Here the first big story is that the previously highly favourable demographic developments in the fastest growing areas in the world, e.g. East Asia and Europe, are currently and sharply reversing. As a result of the demographic changes of the past, the myriad of left-behind workers with dampened expectations are turning to nativist, populist politicians on the right. The policies they espouse to limit immigration and protect local industries chime with the views of the disillusioned workers (Chapter 7). They may have lost bargaining power, but they have retained political power. This is the Great Reversal of our title.

Although one can query how far globalisation is now in retreat, the basic outlines of this Great Reversal are undeniable. If, as we claim, favourable demography and rampant globalisation was largely, but not wholly, responsible for the faster growth, and much lower nominal variables, i.e. inflation and interest rates, over the last three decades, then it simply stands to reason that the next three decades will see lower growth and faster inflation and higher nominal interest rates, than recently.

14.2 Where and Why Does the Mainstream Disagree with Us?

Whereas we believe that these background demographic and structural issues provide a critical backdrop to future macroeconomic developments, especially at turning points, such as now, they rarely get mentioned in the greater bulk of economic forecasts, which have a horizon of two years, or less. This is in some large part because, over such short horizons, both demography and structure can be usually taken as given and constant. As a result, forecasts, however much fancied up by some form of mathematical model, usually involve some combination of continuation of current outcomes (momentum) plus a partial reversion to an estimated equilibrium level (return to normal). But if the equilibrium itself is changing, what is the model reverting to? Conventional forecasting approaches may be insufficient at a time when the Great Reversal is taking place.

Thankfully, there is a small but increasing band of economists who focus on demographic variables and undertake longer run forecasts. But even that small group tends to predict a much longer time gap before nominal variables and the real interest rate start to reflate than we do (Papetti 2019).

Our approach differs from the mainstream in this field on at least three important issues.

- First, we are not as sanguine about the future of personal savings as the mainstream. The consumption assumptions of their models simply do not match the consumption dynamics that an ageing society will display.
- Second, we are more optimistic on corporate investment when faced with a declining workforce. We agree with Andrew Smithers that a serious governance problem in capitalist economies has hindered investment, particularly in the USA.
- Finally, the mainstream view sees debt and demography singing from the same hymn sheet in driving growth, inflation and interest rates lower for the foreseeable future. We see the two in conflict, with debt a gigantic block that the irresistible forces of demography will eventually move out of its way. In turn, that will put monetary and fiscal policymakers in conflict with each other.

The mainstream envisages a perfect foresight process of life-time consumption smoothing. We do not. Such an assumption would involve a triumph of theory over practical experience. While there certainly is some smoothing, see the past high personal savings ratio in China, it is only partial; so making this assumption implies a huge future jump in savings.

Since real output per head will still be growing, a life-cycle smoothing assumption implies that relative consumption should be declining, slowly, as age increases. This does not happen in advanced economies; instead consumption tends to rise in the final decade of life. This is primarily because of medical expenses which are concentrated at the end of life. Such medical, and caring, expenses are going to become much more of a burden, absent a medical miracle, not yet on any horizon, since dependency, especially dementia, is an exponentially rising function of age, and care for dementia is currently scandalously underfunded. We not only take this into account, but also the steady upwards rise in the age of having a first child (we know of no other paper that discusses the economic effects of this latter).

Even putting to one side the extra burden of dependency on our ageing population, the weight of pensions and medical care costs is bound to rise, at a time when real growth will be slowing, thereby reducing taxable capacity. So, the mainstream often assumes that the retirement age will rise, perhaps even faster than life expectancy, and that the relative generosity of pensions will be cut. Until now, most economies have been moving strongly in the opposite direction. We accept that the pressures are such that countries will have to go down this road. But it is politically extremely unpopular to do so, and we contend that upwards movements in retirement age, and downwards moves in relative pension generosity, will be gradual and limited. President Macron can vouch for this!

In most mainstream models, all investment takes place in the corporate sector, ignoring housing. The old find it painful to move, and do not have to do so, having paid off their mortgages. Consequently, in an ageing society, there will be more households and a maldistribution of space. Currently the larger number of old living apart is being offset (on the number of households) by more young living with their parents, owing to the high cost of separate accommodation. Even here, calls on the bank of Mum and Dad will reduce savings for retirement, as in Chapters 5 and 6.

For all these reasons, we believe that mainstream theorists have been too sanguine about the strength of future personal savings ratios.

Turning next to the corporate sector, we believe that the main problem is to understand why corporate investment in the advanced economies has been so sluggish in recent years. Until one understands the past, how can one predict the future? Given high profitability, and rock-bottom funding costs, one might have expected much higher investment.

Part of the answer is that investment, like production, has been off-shored to emerging Asia, see especially Chapter 9 on Japan. If so, the curtailment of globalisation will bring some boost to domestic investment. Another part of the answer could be that the weakness of labour bargaining power has allowed employers in the non-traded services sector to raise profits by lowering wages in the gig economy, rather than going through the more difficult process of raising employee productivity, notably via investment (see Chapters 5, 6, 7 and 9). Again, if so, the strengthening again of labour power and minimum wages (see the box on minimum wages in Chapter 7) could have the effect of encouraging domestic investment and productivity. So, we are less pessimistic than most of the mainstream about the prospective decline in the workforce leading to an equivalent fall in corporate investment.

But we share the view that Andrew Smithers has so eloquently put forward, that a further reason for the stagnation of investment ratios has been a governance problem in capitalist economies, notably in the USA. Giving corporate executives eye-wateringly huge bonuses if they can manage to raise short-term equity valuations encourages them to raise leverage, issuing debt to buy back equities, and to use available funds to increase dividends now, rather than undertake longer-term (and risky) investment. The temptation to feather one's own nest while the going is good is both natural and overwhelming. The result has been a large increase in corporate debt ratios, especially in Asia, though the reasons for this there are rather separate from the factors driving debt ratios up in the USA and Western Economies. Be that as it may, non-financial corporate debt ratios are generally now much higher than they were in 2008/2009.

Debt will play a significant role, but not in the way that the mainstream believes. If one thinks that nominal interest rates will remain rock-bottom for the foreseeable future, then there is little reason to worry since debt service ratios will remain low. The same holds for the public sector, perhaps even more so. Given the unusual move into surplus of the corporate sector, while the household sector remained in surplus, the public sector had to move into deficit to maintain macroeconomic balance (Chapters 3, 5, 6 and 11), more so in countries with a current account deficit, e.g. USA, UK; less so in countries with a surplus, e.g. Germany, China. But with the extreme counter-example of Germany, most other advanced economies found their public sector debt ratios rising over the last couple of decades at a faster rate than ever before, outside of war time, Chapters 1, 3, 5, 6 and 11.

Moreover, the ageing of our societies implies simultaneously that calls on public expenditures will be rising fast, at a time when the growth of real incomes to provide taxable capacity to meet it is falling. All this has been largely obscured in recent decades by an offsetting decline in nominal interest rates, leaving debt service ratios constant. But the future projections of such debt ratios, e.g. by the OBR in UK and CBO in the USA, on the basis of current policies, are scary (Chapters 1 and 11). Have such debts already grown so large that Central Banks can hardly now raise nominal interest rates without setting off a financial collapse? Are we caught in a debt trap, whereby low interest rates, plus the structure of capitalism, have so raised debt that interest rates cannot be raised much, thereby encouraging the accumulation of yet more debt?

The mainstream doesn't see much of a change in the relationship between fiscal and monetary policy. That is primarily because the forecast of low infla-tion and nominal interest rates far into the future imply that refinancing debt and running deficits will create very little friction between the two.

We review how we might try to escape the debt trap in Chapters 11 and 12. This should involve reducing the fiscal advantages of debt over equity and preventing corporates from avoiding tax by using tax havens. It will probably also have to involve some new sources of tax, e.g. on land values (not wealth) and air pollutants, such as a carbon tax, see Chapters 12 and 13. The basis for remunerating corporate executives especially the CEO will also need to be reconsidered.

Clearly policymaking will become much more difficult if we should be correct and wage-costs and inflation start to rise significantly in future. Our view that this may well happen is countered by a variety of arguments. The first is that the Phillips curve has become much more horizontal. We address this in Chapter 8. The second is that it has not happened in Japan; we address this in Chapter 9. The third is that the China effect of producing tradeables cheaply for world consumption, thereby keeping down inflation and wage costs elsewhere, could now pass to India and Africa, where demographic developments remain highly favourable. We discuss this in Chapter 10. In this same chapter, we also review the possibility of raising participation rates among the elderly and automation/robotics/AI, as a means of compensating for the slowdown in the workforce (as also in Chapter 3).

So what, to conclude, are the implications for policies, fiscal and monetary (Chapter 13) and for real interest rates (Chapters 6 and 13)?

Policymaking is always difficult. But if our version of the future is correct, it will soon become more so. Public expenditures will rise as ageing leads to more pensions and greater medical/caring costs, at a time when real income growth, and taxable capacity, is slowing. We review possible ways of increasing tax revenues in Chapter 13.

In recent decades Central Banks have been the best friends of Ministers of Finance, lowering interest rates to ease fiscal pressures and to stabilise debt service ratios. When inflationary pressures resume, as we expect in due course, such prior harmony will revert to mutual hostility, as the Central Bank tries to defend its inflation target, while the politicians want faster growth and lower debt services. We can guess who will win. If the politicians win, as we expect, real interest rates will remain low, since inflation rates will rise by more than nominal interest rates; vice versa if Central Banks should dominate. Even if politicians win, we doubt central banks will simply walk away without a fight for their inflation targets in which they believe. Inevitably, that will bring about a period of policy uncertainty, and volatility.

Mainstream thinking takes for granted that both debt and ageing will keep nominal and real variables at rock bottom levels. In large part, these are lessons the mainstream has incorrectly gleaned from Japan's experience, a misstep that we address in Chapter 9.

We see these two, demography and debt, as standing more in conflict than in alliance. As demography starts to pressure inflation and interest rates higher, economies and/or sectors with unsustainable debt will one by one be bullied into submission. The shock to debt will undoubtedly create periods of weaker growth and even recessions or crises—the experience of Turkey and Argentina in 2018 shows as much. These periods will also generate lower inflation and interest rates cyclically. However, underneath those cyclical slowdowns, inflation and interest rates will structurally resurface to remove the obstacle of indebtedness from their path. When exactly these battles will be fought, and won and lost, is impossible to say, but we will need all the luck we can get to navigate our way forward.

Postscript: Future Imperfect After Coronavirus

Our book was mainly written in 2019, and the typescript delivered to our publisher, before anyone was aware of the impending coronavirus pandemic. The overall impact of the pandemic will be to accelerate the trends we have outlined in this book. China will become more inward-looking and less deflationary globally, and inflation itself will rise much earlier and faster than we had anticipated. Meanwhile, the pandemic has already had, and will continue to have, dramatic repercussions on the world economy. In practice, it has not been so much the medical implications, serious though they were, but rather the (necessary and correct) policy responses that has had the major, even if hopefully short-run, impact on our economies.

Indeed, if one was a cold-hearted economist, whose sole aim was to maximise GDP, or even better GDP per head, then one's advice on the best way to respond to the coronavirus pandemic would have been to do absolutely *nothing*, to ignore it entirely and let it take its course. It primarily affects the elderly; the average age of death so far in the UK has been about 80; and even then the younger deaths are mainly amongst those with other severe medical problems, co-morbidity in the jargon. This is a group largely dependent on others to help with daily living, and thus stopping their carers from producing goods and other services to swell GDP per head. The original, herd immunity, strategy of Boris Johnson might, it was at the time suggested, have raised deaths in the UK by 250,000 in 2020, but this needs to be set against the normal total deaths of nearly 500,000 p.a., an increase of some 50/60% in one year. Given the age and frailty of those likely to die, this increased death toll in 2020 would have been almost entirely offset by sharply lower death tolls over the subsequent decade.

While one should keep such an analysis in mind, such a cold-hearted policy would have been morally wrong, and socially and politically entirely unacceptable. Indeed, deprived of sport, the press kept giving us daily league totals of national deaths. So the response was almost inevitably quarantines and lock-downs. Meanwhile, as all too usual in a crisis, international cooperation gave way to national *sauve qui peut*. What this has represented is a self-imposed supply shock of immense magnitude. Such a supply shock reduces output and raises prices. Nor is the demand from this period entirely recoverable. Particularly when it comes to services, some of the consumption is permanently lost. The daily commute to work, or the horrifically executed haircuts at home, will not be demanded twice over whenever normal life resumes.

The authorities, like most of the rest of us, were caught short by the sudden advent of the pandemic, and rightly rushed to limit unnecessary deaths. But in so doing, they imposed a massive supply shock.

In their praiseworthy and correct aim to reduce the immediate devastating effect of such a lock-down supply shock on incomes and expenditures, the authorities, quite rightly, opened the floodgates of direct fiscal expenditures and indirect encouragement to banks to extend lending to all borrowers with cashflow problems. This will have, as intended, mitigated losses of incomes and some expenditures, but will naturally have to be balanced by economic consequences further on.

In the short run, the inflationary consequences of this massive adverse supply shock will have been counter-balanced by a collapse in non-food commodity prices, much aggravated by the disastrously timed oil war. It will also have been matched by the commensurate decline in demand, some voluntary, some enforced, some permanent, some simply delayed. In any case, at a time when the basket of goods and services that we buy was so suddenly distorted out of all recognition, it will have become almost impossible over the months from March 2020 until an approximate resumption of normality to put together sensible and meaningful data for CPI, RPI, or any other inflation series.

But what will then happen as the lock-down gets lifted and recovery ensues, following a period of massive fiscal and monetary expansion? The answer, as in the aftermaths of many wars, will be a surge in inflation, quite likely more than 5%, or even on the order of 10% in 2021, (assuming that the pandemic gets tamed by the end of this year—the longer the outbreak takes to tame, the weaker will be the ensuing surge in real activity and then inflation).

However, warnings about inflation were also sounded when QE was launched in the aftermath of the Great Financial Crisis. Those fears weren't realized, why should they be any more real now? For three reasons. First, the design of QE meant that most of the injections remained within the banking system in the form of excess reserves. They were never able to filter through to broader aggregates of money which matter for inflation. Today's policy measures are injecting cash flows that will directly raise the broader measures of money. Second, the speed with which the global economy could recover to the level of output just before the outbreak. The stronger the recovery, the more these policy injections will look procyclical. Third, China's role in the global economy has now changed from being an exporter of deflation to a more neutral one now and increasingly inflationary into the future.

What will the response of the authorities then be? First, and foremost, they will claim that this is a temporary, and once-for-all blip. Second, the monetary authorities will state that this is a, quite desirable, counterbalance to the years of prior undershooting of targets, entirely consistent with average inflation, or price-level targeting. Third, the disruption will have been so great that it will take time to bring unemployment back down towards 2019 levels and large swathes of industry, (airlines, cruise ships, hotels, etc.), may still be in difficulties. Does it make any sense, having propped up industry in such a widespread manner in 2020, to let much of that same industry go to the wall in 2021 as a result to rising interest rates and fiscal retrenchment? In any case, the borrowing lobby (government, industry, those with mortgages) is much more politically powerful than the savings lobby.

But if such a surge in inflation is to be (quickly) halted, some people's real incomes have to suffer. Who might that be? The ordinary worker's real income has been rather stagnant over the last 30 years. We ascribe that, in the previous chapters here, to the huge positive labour supply shock that was caused by globalisation and favourable demographic effects. That enabled employers to threaten to move jobs to Asia or to more compliant migrants coming to home territory, unless workers moderated their demands; and this was a credible threat.

A combination of Trump-type policies, populism, barriers to migration and now the coronavirus pandemic has now defanged that threat to workers.

The balance of bargaining power is now swinging back to workers, away from employers; current, more socialist, political trends are reinforcing that. Following the recovery, whenever that happens, wage trends will change. The likelihood is that wage demands will then match, or even perhaps exceed, current inflation, despite the inevitable pleas for moderation in the context of a 'temporary blip' in inflation. The coronavirus pandemic, and the supply shock that it has induced, will mark the dividing line between the deflationary forces of the last 30/40 years, and the resurgent inflation of the next two decades.

The losers will be savers, pension funds, insurance companies, and those whose main financial assets take the form of cash. It will no longer be fiscally feasible to protect the real value of pensions from the ravages of inflation. The folly of responding to the crisis of excessive debt in 2007–2009 by encouraging all borrowers (except banks) to take on more leverage and debt, will become apparent.

So what will happen? Inflation will rise considerably above the level of nominal interest rates that our political masters can tolerate. The excessive debt, amongst non-financial corporates and governments will get inflated away. The negative real interest rates that may well be necessary to equilibrate the system, as real growth slows in the face of a reversal of globalisation and falling working populations, will happen. Even if central banks feel uncomfortable with such higher inflation, they will be aware that the continuing high levels of debt make our economies still very fragile. And if they try to raise interest rates in such a context, they will face political ire to a point that might threaten their 'independence'. Only when indebtedness has been restored to viable levels can an assault on inflation be mounted. Next time, can we reform capitalism, ideally as outlined in Chapters 11 and 12, so that we do not encourage excessive debt expansion every time that our economy hits a soft spot?

Any such inflationary impulse in the last few decades would have had to overcome the deflationary effects that China's integration produced. China, however, no longer stands in the way of global inflation. The difficult geopolitical terrain that emerged from President Trump's trade war in 2018 has become even more tricky since the onset of the pandemic. National policies have become increasingly inward looking and global flows of physical capital are likely to follow suit, particularly when it comes to the strategic bone of contention between the US and China, i.e. global dominance in technology. The inevitable conclusion is that China will have to raise productivity from here on primarily on the basis of domestic innovation.

Economically, protecting the domestic economy has become the first priority, particularly in China where the social compact between the Communist Party and the population implies ensuring a stable economy and employment protection. Like most other economies around the world, China's fiscal expansion will require it to tap into its pool of savings. In China's case, that might eventually mean tapping into the considerable savings of its SOEs that have been the mainstay of China's national savings over the last few decades.

In both cases, China has the resources to protect its future, but the impact it had on the global economy will no longer be the same as in the past.

As we move deeper into de-globalisation, the temptation will be to think of the world as a collection of local entities, a temptation that would lead one to erroneous conclusions. Slowing globalization remains entirely consistent with the global transmission of shocks, particularly when the underlying change is as uniform across the major economies of the world as ageing.

As this book was finally going into print, an important and relevant new paper became available by Stansbury and Summers, entitled 'The Declining Worker Power Hypothesis: An Explanation for the Recent Evolution of the American Economy', NBER Working Paper 27193, May 2020. This paper, like ourselves, places a great deal of emphasis on the declining bargaining power of workers, and is in many respects similar and supportive of our own work.

But there is one crucial difference. This is that they deny that the decline in such bargaining power has been due to globalisation. On this latter point, they rely, as we do, on the work of Peter Schott, with various colleagues, i.e. Bernard, Bradford Jenson, and Schott, (2006), 'Survival of the best fit: Exposure to low-wage countries and (uneven) growth of US manufacturing plants', Journal of International Economics, and also Pierce and Schott (NBER Working Paper 18655, December 2012), which latter, surprisingly, Stansbury and Summers do not reference. What these papers show is that plants and employment were most adversely affected in those industries where import growth from low-wage countries was most in evidence. But, Stansbury and Summers then argue that such competition from low-wage countries would have the result that 'returns to capital would fall alongside rents to labor, and [also] that the total rents in the industry - profits, plus labor rents - would be falling'. However, this would be so only in the case when the competition from abroad took the form of sales of products produced by companies headquartered in the low-wage country.

Contrary to the arguments of Stansbury and Summers, globalisation largely took the form of companies resident in the developed economy, i.e. the USA, outsourcing the physical production of the good or service abroad, but maintaining control of the final sales, and the overall infrastructure, capital, managerial expertise, and intellectual property. In fact, Pierce and Schott (2012) provide microeconomic evidence to show quite conclusively that the "surprisingly swift decline in US manufacturing" was due to the offshoring of the production of labour-intensive goods to China. Similarly, and very famously, China and Taiwan account for the bulk of the supply chain in the production of iPhones; but Apple remains headquartered in California. The rise of Chinese companies has been spectacular in many cases, but they have been far more successful in dominating China's domestic market than the global marketplace. In such cases, we would certainly expect the returns to capital in the developed economy to rise relative to rents to labour there.

Thus, we think that the test for globalisation undertaken by Stansbury and Summers is simply mistaken. Instead, Stansbury and Summers can only suggest that the driving force for the declining bargaining power of labour was a growing ruthlessness of businessmen. Indeed, businessmen were more ruthless, but that largely took the guise of outsourcing production to other countries, thereby undercutting labour strength domestically. Globalisation, working with the global surge in labour supply, was calling the shots. That will still hold true when the global workforce shrinks in the decades that lie ahead of us.

In summary, an imperfect, inflationary future is coming to our doors faster than we had expected, thanks to the pandemic. Slowing globalization amidst a global trend of ageing will ensure that the future is nothing like the past.

References

Chapter 1

Congressional Budget Office. (2019). *The Budget and Economic Outlook: 2019 to 2029*. https://www.cbo.gov/system/files?file=2019-03/54918-Outlook-Chapter1.pdf.

Friedman, M. (1968, March). The Role of Monetary Policy. *The American Economic Review, 58*(1), 1–17.

Gutiérrez, G., & Piton, S. (2019, July). *Revisiting the Global Decline of the (Non-Housing) Labor Share* (Bank of England Staff Working Paper No. 811).

International Monetary Fund. (2017, October). *Fiscal Monitor: Tackling Inequality*. Washington, DC: IMF.

King, M. (2003, October 14). Speech, Bank of England, East Midlands Development Agency/Bank of England Dinner, Leicester. https://www.bankofengland.co.uk/-/media/boe/files/speech/2003/east-midlands-development-agency-dinner.

Krueger, A. B. (2018). Luncheon Address: Reflections on Dwindling Worker Bargaining Power and Monetary Policy. In *Changing Market Structures and Implications for Monetary Policy: A Symposium Sponsored by The Federal Reserve Bank of Kansas City* (pp. 267–282). Kansas City: Federal Reserve Bank of Kansas City.

Obstfeld, M. (2019, July 22). *Global Dimensions of U.S. Monetary Policy* (Centre for Economic Policy Research Discussion Paper DP1388).

Office for Budget Responsibility. (2018). *Fiscal Sustainability Report*. https://obr.uk/fsr/fiscal-sustainability-report-july-2018/.

Piketty, T. (2014). *Capital in the Twenty-First Century*. Cambridge, MA and London, UK: Harvard University Press.

Schwellnus, C., Pak, M., Pionnier, P.-A., & Crivellaro, E. (2018, September). *Labour Share Developments Over the Past Two Decades: The Role of Technological Progress, Globalisation and "Winner-Takes-Most" Dynamics* (OECD Economics Department Working Papers No. 1503).

Chapter 2

Agarwal, I., Gu, G. W., & Prasad, E. S. (2019, September). *China's Impact on Global Financial Markets* (National Bureau of Economic Research Working Paper 26311).

Jiang, K., Keller, W., Qiu, L. D., & Ridley, W. (2018). *Joint Ventures and Technology Transfers: New Evidence from China*. Vox CEPR Policy Portal, voxeu.org.

Lardy, N. R. (2001, May 9). *Issues in China's WTO Accession*. The Brookings Institution. https://www.brookings.edu/testimonies/issues-in-chinas-wto-accession/.

Ma, G., & Fung, B. S. C. (2002, August). *China's Asset Management Corporations* (Bank for International Settlements Working Paper No. 115).

Nabar, M. (2011, September). *Targets, Interest Rates, and Household Saving in Urban China* (International Monetary Fund Working Paper WP/11/223).

Pierce, J. R., & Schott, P. K. (2012, December). *The Surprisingly Swift Decline of U.S. Manufacturing Employment* (National Bureau of Economic Research Working Paper No. 18655).

Rodrik, D. (2011, October). Unconditional *Convergence* (National Bureau of Economic Research Working Paper No. 17546).

Chapter 3

BBC News. (2018, August 29). *Russia's Putin Softens Pension Reforms After Outcry*. https://www.bbc.co.uk/news/world-europe-45342721.

Börsch-Supan, A., Härtl, K., & Ludwig, A. (2014). Aging in Europe: Reforms, International Diversification, and Behavioral Reactions. *American Economic Review: Papers and Proceedings, 104*(5), 224–229.

Button, P. (2019, May). *Population Aging, Age Discrimination, and Age Discrimination Protections at the 50th Anniversary of the Age Discrimination in Employment Act* (National Bureau of Economic Research Working Paper 25850).

Cravino, J., Levchenko, A. A., & Rojas, M. (2019, September). *Population Aging and Structural Transformation* (National Bureau of Economic Research Working Paper 26327).

Maestas, N., & Jetsupphasuk, M. (2019). What Do Older Workers Want?, Chapter 5. In D. E. Bloom (Ed.), *Live Long and Prosper? The Economics of Ageing Populations*. London: A VoxEU.org eBook, CEPR Press.

United Nations. (2015). *World Population Ageing*. Department of Economic and Social Affairs, Population Division, United Nations. https://www.un.org/en/dev elopment/desa/population/publications/pdf/ageing/WPA2015_Report.pdf.

Chapter 4

Bauer, J. M., & Sousa-Poza, A. (2015). Impacts of Informal Caregiving on Caregivers: Employment, Health and Family. *Journal of Population Ageing, 8*(3), 113–145.

Bauer, J. M., & Sousa-Poza, A. (2019). Employment and the Health Burden on Informal Caregivers of the Elderly, Chapter 3. In D. E. Bloom (Ed.), *Live Long and Prosper? The Economics of Ageing Populations*. London: A VoxEU.org eBook, CEPR Press.

Cavendish, C. (2013). *The Cavendish Review: An Independent Review into Healthcare Assistants and Support Workers in the NHS and Social Care Settings*. Department of Health, London. https://assets.publishing.service.gov.uk/government/uploads/ system/uploads/attachment_data/file/236212/Cavendish_Review.pdf.

Cavendish, C. (2019). *Extra Time: 10 Lessons for an Ageing World*. London, UK: HarperCollins.

Dwyer, J. (2019, November). *Innovative Approaches to Increasing Investment in Alzheimer's Research, Treatment and Cure*. Presentation at the 6th Annual Lausanne Conference on Preparing the Alzheimer's Ecosystem for a Timely, Accurate and Compassionate Diagnosi.

Eggleston, K. (2019). Understanding 'Value for Money' in Healthy Ageing, Chapter 12. In D. E. Bloom (Ed.), *Live Long and Prosper? The Economics of Ageing Populations*. London, UK: A VoxEU.org eBook, CEPR Press.

Financial Times. (2019, June 25). *How the World Deals with Alzheimer's and Dementia—In Charts* (Financial Times Special Report: FT Health—Dementia Care).

Financial Times. (2019, July 16). Foreign Operators Take on Chinese Elderly Care, p. 14.

Financial Times. (2019, June 10). Robots/Ageing Japan: I, Carebot. *Lex Column*, Monday, p. 22.

Gratton, L., & Scott, A. (2016). *The 100 Year Life—Living and Working in an Age of Longevity*. London: Bloomsbury.

Green, D. (2019, April 29). *Fixing the Care Crisis*. Centre for Policy Studies.

Kingston, A., Comas-Herrera, A., & Jagger, C. (2018). Forecasting the Care Needs of the Older Population in England Over the Next 20 Years: Estimates from the Population Ageing and Care Simulation (PACSim) Modelling Study. *The Lancet Public Health, 3*(9), e447–e455.

Kingston, A., Robinson, L., Booth, H., Knapp, M., & Jagger, C. (2018). Projections of Multi-Morbidity in the Older Population in England to 2035: Estimates from the Population Ageing and Care Simulation (PACSim) Model. *Age and Ageing, 47*(3), 1–7.

Kingston, A., Wohland, P., Wittenberg, R., Robinson, L., Brayne, C., Matthews, F. E., et al. (2017). Is Late-Life Dependency Increasing or Not? A Comparison of the Cognitive Function and Ageing Studies (CFAS). *The Lancet, 390*(10103), 1676–1684.

Kivipelto, M., Ngandu, T., Laatikainen, T., Winblad, B., Soininen, H., & Tuornilehto, J. (2006, September). Risk Score for the Prediction of Dementia Risk in 20 Years Among Middle Aged People: A Longitudinal, Population-Based Study. *Lancet Neurol, 5*(9), 735–-741

Kydland, F., & Pretnar, N. (2018). *The Costs and Benefits of Caring: Aggregate Burdens of an Aging Population* (NBER Working Paper 25498).

Kydland, F., & Pretnar, N. (2019). Who Will Care for All the Old People?', Chapter 2. In D. E. Bloom (Ed.), *Live Long and Prosper? The Economics of Ageing Populations*. London: VoxEU.org eBook, CEPR Press.

Lancet Commissions. (2017, December 16). On Dementia Prevention, Intervention, and Care. *The Lancet, 390*, 2673–2734.

Lex. (2019, June 10). Robots/Ageing Japan: I, Carebot. *Financial Times*, Monday, p. 22.

Livingston, G., Sommerlad, A., Orgeta, V., Costafreda, S. G., Huntley, J., Ames, D., et al. (2017, December 16). Dementia Prevention, Intervention, and Care. *The Lancet, 390*, 2673–2734.

Mayda, A. M. (2019, June 19). Discussion of *Demographic Changes, Migration and Economic Growth in the Euro Area* by A. Börsch-Supan, D. N. Leite, & J. Rausch, European Central Bank Sintra Forum, Portugal.

Norton, S., Matthews, F. E., Barnes, D. E., Yaffe, K., & Brayne, C. (2014, August). Potential for Primary Prevention of Alzheimer's Disease: An Analysis of Population-Based Data. *Lancet Neurol, 13*(8), 788–794.

Patterson, C. (2018). *World Alzheimer Report 2018: The State of the Art of Dementia Research: New Frontiers*. London, UK: Alzheimer's Disease International (ADI).

Prince, M., Wilmo, A., Guerchet, M., Ali, G.-C., Wu, Y. T., & Prina, M. (2015). *World Alzheimer Report 2015: An Analysis of Prevalence, Incidence, Cost and Trends*. London, UK: Alzheimer's Disease International (ADI).

Scott, A. (2019). A Longevity Dividend Versus an Ageing Society, Chapter 11. In D. E. Bloom (Ed.), *Live Long and Prosper? The Economics of Ageing Populations* London: A VoxEU.org eBook, CEPR Press.

Vradenburg, G. (2019, November). 'Welcome Remarks' at the 6th Annual Lausanne Conference on *Preparing the Alzheimer's Ecosystem for a Timely, Accurate and Compassionate Diagnosis*.

World Alzheimer Report. (2016). *World Alzheimer Report 2015: An Analysis of Prevalence, Incidence, Cost and Trends*. London, UK: Alzheimer's Disease International (ADI).

World Alzheimer Report. (2018). *The State of the Art of Dementia Research: New Frontiers*. London, UK: Alzheimer's Disease International (ADI).

World Alzheimer Report. (2019). *Attitudes to Dementia*. London, UK: Alzheimer's Disease International (ADI).

World Dementia Council. (2012, December). *Defeating Dementia: The Road to 2025*. worlddementiacouncil.org.

Chapter 5

Aksoy, Y., Basso, H. S., Smith. R. P., & Grasl, T. (2015). *Demographic Structure and Macroeconomic Trends* (Banco de Espana, Documentos de Trabajo No. 1528).

Autor, D., Dorn, D., Katz, L. F., Patterson, C., & Van Reenen, J. (2017). Concentrating on the Fall of the Labor Share. *American Economic Review Papers and Proceedings, 207*(5), 180–185.

Autor, D., Dorn, D., Katz, L. F., Patterson, C., & Van Reenen, J. (2019, May). *The Fall of the Labor Share and the Rise of Superstar Firms* (National Bureau of Economic Research Working Paper No. 23396).

Bernanke, B. S. (2005, March 10). *The Global Saving Glut and the U.S. Current Account Deficit*. The Federal Reserve Board, Speech. Available at https://www.fed eralreserve.gov/boarddocs/speeches/2005/200503102/.

Button, P. (2019, May). *Population Aging, Age Discrimination, and Age Discrimination Protections at the 50th Anniversary of the Age Discrimination in Employment Act* (National Bureau of Economic Research Working Paper 25850).

Congressional Budget Office. (2019). *The Budget and Economic Outlook: 2019 to 2029*. https://www.cbo.gov/system/files/2019-03/54918-Outlook-3.pdf.

Covarrubias, M., Gutiérrez, G., & Philippon, T. (2019, June). *From Good to Bad Concentration? U.S. Industries Over the Past 30 Years* (National Bureau of Economic Research Working Paper No. 25983).

Crouzet, N., & Eberly, J. (2019, May). *Understanding Weak Capital Investment: The Role of Market Concentration and Intangibles* (National Bureau of Economic Research Working Paper No. w25869). Available at SSRN https://ssrn.com/abs tract=3394650.

Hernández-Murillo, R., Ott, L. S., Owyang, M. T., & Whalen, D. (2011, May/June). Patterns of Interstate Migration in the United States from the Survey of Income and Program Participation. *Federal Reserve Bank of St. Louis Review, 93*(3), 169–185.

Hundtofte, S., Olafsson, A., & Pagel, M. (2019, October). *Credit Smoothing* (National Bureau of Economic Research Working Paper 26354).

Juselius, M., & Takáts, E. (2016, April 6). *The Age-Structure-Inflation Puzzle* (Bank of Finland Research Discussion Paper No. 4/2016).

Kalecki, M. (1954). *Theory of Economic Dynamics: An Essay on Cyclical and Long-Run Changes in Capitalist Economy*. London: George Allen & Unwin.

Liu, E., Mian, A., & Sufi, A. (2019, August). *Low Interest Rates, Market Power, and Productivity Growth* (National Bureau of Economic Research Working Paper No. 25505).

Mayhew, L. (2019, June/July). A Home Alone Explosion, Cass Business School, *Financial World*, 13–15.

McGovern, M. (2019). Life Cycle Origins of Pre-Retirement Financial Status: Insights from Birth Cohort Data, Chapter 10. In D. E. Bloom (Ed.), *Live Long and Prosper? The Economics of Ageing Populations.* London: A VoxEU.org eBook, CEPR Press.

Meen, G. (2005). On the Economics of the Barker Review of Housing Supply. *Housing Studies, 20*(6), 949–971.

Melitz, J., & Edo, A. (2019, September). *The Primary Cause of European Inflation in 1500–1700: Precious Metals or Population? The English Evidence* (Centre for Economic Policy Research Discussion Paper DP14023).

Office for Budget Responsibility. (2018). *Fiscal Sustainability Report.* https://obr.uk/fsr/fiscal-sustainability-report-july-2018/

Papetti, A. (2019, March). *Demographics and the Natural Real Interest Rate: Historical and Projected Paths for the Euro Area* (European Central Bank Working Paper No. 2258).

Philippon, T. (2019). *The Great Reversal: How America Gave Up on Free Markets.* Cambridge, MA and London, UK: Belknap Press of Harvard University Press.

Schön, M., & Stähler, N. (2019). When Old Meets Young? Germany's Population Ageing and the Current Account (Deutsche Bundesbank, No. 33/2019).

Smithers, A. (2009). *Wall Street Revalued: Imperfect Markets and Inept Central Bankers.* Hoboken, NJ: Wiley.

Smithers, A. (2013). *The Road to Recovery: How and Why Economic Policy Must Change.* Chichester, UK: Wiley.

Smithers, A. (2019). *Productivity and the Bonus Culture.* Oxford: Oxford University Press.

Wood, J. (2019). *Retirees Will Outlive Their Savings by a Decade.* World Economic Forum. Available at https://www.weforum.org/agenda/2019/06/retirees-will-outlive-their-savings-by-a-decade/.

World Economic Forum. (2018). *How We Can Save (for) Our Future.* Available at https://www.weforum.org/whitepapers/how-we-can-save-for-our-future.

World Economic Forum. (2019). *Retirees Will Outlive Their Savings by a Decade.* Available at https://www.weforum.org/agenda/2019/06/retirees-will-outlive-their-savings-by-a-decade/.

Chapter 6

Brand, C., Bielecki, M., & Penalver, A. (Eds.). (2018, December). *The Natural Rate of Interest: Estimates, Drivers, and Challenges to Monetary Policy* (European Central Bank Occasional Paper, No. 217).

Caballero, R. J., Farhi, E., & Gourinchas, P.-O. (2017). The Safe Assets Shortage Conundrum. *Journal of Economic Perspectives, 31*(3, Summer), 29–46.

Davis, S. J., Haltiwanger, J. C., & Schuh, S. (1996). *Job Creation and Destruction.* Cambridge: MIT Press.

French, E. B., Jones, J. B., McCauley, J., & Kelly, E. (2019, August). *End-of-life Medical Expenses* (Centre for Economic Policy Research Discussion Paper DP13913).

Gordon, R. J. (2012, August). *Is U.S. Economic Growth Over? Faltering Innovation Confronts the Six Headwinds* (National Bureau of Economic Research Working Paper, No. 18315).

Hamilton, J. D., Harris, E. S., Hatzius, J., & West, K.D. (2015, August). *The Equilibrium Real Funds Rate: Past, Present and Future* (Natural Bureau of Economic Research, No. 21476).

Heise, M. (2019). *Inflation Targeting and Financial Stability: Monetary Policy Challenges for the Future.* Cham, Switzerland: Springer.

Kalemli-Özcan, S., Laeven, L., & Moreno, D. (2019, February). *Debt Overhang, Rollover Risk, and Corporate Investment: Evidence from the European Crisis* (European Central Bank Working Paper No. 2241).

Laubach, T., & Williams, J. C. (2003, November). Measuring the Natural Rate of Interest. *The Review of Economics and Statistics, 85*(4), 1063–1070.

Marx, M., Mojon, B., & Velde, F. R. (2019, July 9). *Why Have Interest Rates Fallen Far Below the Return on Capital* (Bank for International Settlements Working Paper, No. 794).

Mokyr, J., Vickers, C., & Ziebarth, N. L. (2015). The History of Technological Anxiety and the Future of Economic Growth: Is This Time Different? *Journal of Economic Perspectives, 29*(3, Summer), 31–50.

Rachel, L., & Smith, T. D. (2015, December). *Secular Drivers of the Global Real Interest Rate* (Bank of England Staff Working Paper No. 571).

Rachel, L., & Summers, L. H. (2019, March 4). *On Falling Neutral Real Rates, Fiscal Policy, and the Risk of Secular Stagnation* (Brookings Papers on Economic Activity, BPEA Conference Drafts).

Smithers, A. (2009). *Wall Street Revalued: Imperfect Markets and Inept Central Bankers.* Hoboken, NJ: Wiley.

Smithers, A. (2013). *The Road to Recovery: How and Why Economic Policy Must Change.* Chichester, UK: Wiley.

Smithers, A. (2019). *Productivity and the Bonus Culture.* Oxford: Oxford University Press.

Chapter 7

Autor, D. H. (2019). Work of the Past, Work of the Future. *AEA Papers and Proceedings, 109,* 1–32.

Boehm, C., Flaaen, A., & Pandalai-Nayar, N.(2019, May). *Multinationals, Offshoring and the Decline of U.S. Manufacturing* (National Bureau of Economic Research Working Paper 25824).

Bayoumi, T., & Barkema, J. (2019, June). *Stranded! How Rising Inequality Suppressed US Migration and Hurt Those "Left Behind"* (IMF Working Paper WP/19/122).

Blinder, S. (2015). Imagined Immigration: The Impact of Different Meanings of 'Immigrants' in Public Opinion and Policy Debates in Britain. *Political Studies, 63,* 80–100.

Borella, M., De Nardi, M., & Yang, F. (2019, March). *The Lost Ones: The Opportunities and Outcomes of Non-College-Educated Americans Born in the 1960s* (Opportunity and Inclusive Growth Institute, Working Paper 19).

Bratsberg, B., Moxnes, A., Raaun, O, & Ulltveit-Moe, K.-H. (2019, April). *Opening the Floodgates: Industry and Occupation Adjustments to Labor Immigration* (Centre for Economic Policy Research Discussion Paper 13670).

Compertpay, R., Irmen, A., & Litina, A. (2019, March). Individual Attitudes Towards Immigration in Aging Populations (CESifo Working Paper 7565).

Desmet, K., Nagy, D. K., & Rossi-Hansberg, E. (2018). The Geography of Development. *Journal of Political Economy, 126* (3), 903–983.

Duffy, R., & Frere-Smith, T. (2014). *Perceptions and Reality: Public Attitudes to Immigration.* London: IPSOS-MORI Social Research Institute.

Durant, W., & Durant, A. (1968). *The Lessons of History.* New York, NY: Simon & Schuster Paperbacks.

Federal Reserve Bank of Kansas City. (2018). *Changing Market Structures and Implications for Monetary Policy: A Symposium Sponsored by The Federal Reserve Bank of Kansas City.* Kansas City: Federal Reserve Bank of Kansas City.

Gbohoui, W., Lam, W. R., & Lledo, V. (2019). The Great Divide: Regional Inequality and Fiscal Policy (IMF Working Paper, WP/19/88).

George, A., Lalani, M., Mason, G., Rolfe, H., & Rosazza, C. (2012). *Skilled Immigration and Strategically Important Skills in the UK Economy*, Migration Advisory Committee.

Hainmueller, J., & Hiscox, M. J. (2007). Educated Preferences: Explaining Attitudes Towards Immigration in Europe. *International Organization, 61*(2), 399–442.

Hainmueller, J., & Hiscox, M. J. (2010). Attitudes Toward Highly Skilled and Low-Skilled Immigration: Evidence from a Survey Experiment. *American Political Science Review, 104,* 61–84.

High Pay Centre. (2019). *No Routine Riches: Reforms to Performance-Related Pay.* http://highpaycentre.org/files/No_Routine_Riches_FINAL.pdf.

Immervoll, H., & Richardson, L. (2011, December). *Redistribution Policy and Inequality Reduction in OECD Countries: What Has Changed in Two Decades?* (Institute for the Study of Labor (IZA) Discussion Paper No. 6030).

International Monetary Fund. (2017, October). *Fiscal Monitor: Tackling Inequality.* IMF: Washington, DC.

Ipsos MORI. (2018). *Attitudes Towards Immigration Have Softened Since Referendum But Most Still Want to See It Reduced.* https://www.ipsos.com/ipsos-mori/en-uk/attitudes-immigration-have-softened-referendum-most-still-want-see-it-reduced.

Kaufmann, E. (2017). Levels or Changes? Ethnic Context, Immigration and the UK Independence Party Vote. *Electoral Studies, 48,* 57–69.

Krueger, A. B. (2018). Luncheon Address: Reflections on Dwindling Worker Bargaining Power and Monetary Policy. In *Changing Market Structures and Implications for Monetary Policy: A Symposium Sponsored by The Federal Reserve Bank of Kansas City* (pp 267–282). Kansas City: Federal Reserve Bank of Kansas City.

Mayda, A. M. (2019, June 19). Discussion of *Demographic Changes, Migration and Economic Growth in the Euro Area* by A. Börsch-Supan, D. N. Leite, & J. Rausch, European Central Bank Sintra Forum, Portugal.

Migration Advisory Committee. (2018). *EEA Migration to the UK: Final Report*. London: MAC.

Milanovic, B. (2016). *Global Inequality: A New Approach for the Age of Globalization*. Cambridge, MA and London, UK: The Belknap Press of Harvard University Press.

Philippon, T. (2019). *The Great Reversal: How America Gave Up on Free Markets*. Cambridge, MA and London, UK: Belknap Press of Harvard University Press.

Piketty, T. (2014). *Capital in the Twenty-First Century*. Cambridge, MA and London, UK: Harvard University Press.

Rachel, L., & Summers, L. H. (2019, March 4). *On Falling Neutral Real Rates, Fiscal Policy, and the Risk of Secular Stagnation* (Brookings Papers on Economic Activity, BPEA Conference Drafts).

Rodrik, D. (2018). Populism and the Economics of Globalization. *Journal of International Business Policy, 1*(1), 12–33.

Rolfe, H. (2019, May). Challenges for Immigration Policy in Post-Brexit Britain: Introduction. *National Institute Economic Review, 248,* R1–R4.

Rolfe, H., Ahlstrom-Vij, K., Hudson-Sharp, N., & Runge, J. (2018). *Post-Brexit Immigration Policy: Reconciling Public Attitudes with Economic Evidence*. Leverhulme Trust, NIESR.

Rolfe, H., Runge, J., & Hudson-Sharp, N. (2019, May). Immigration Policy from Post-War to Post-Brexit: How New Immigration Policy Can Reconcile Public Attitudes and Employer Preferences. *National Institute Economic Review, 248,* R5–R16.

Scheidel, W. (2017). *The Great Leveler: Violence and the History of Inequality from the Stone Age to the Twenty-First Century*. Princeton: Princeton University Press.

Stiglitz, J. (2019). *People, Power, and Profits: Progressive Capitalism for an Age of Discontent*. London: Allen Lane.

Chapter 8

Engles, F. (2018). *The Conditions of the Working Class in England in 1844*. London: Forgotten Books.

Engels, F., & Marx, K. (2018). *The Communist Manifesto*. London: Arcturus.

Flemming, J. S. (1976). *Inflation*. London: Oxford University Press.

Forbes, K. J. (2019, June). *Has Globalization Changed the Inflation Process?* (Bank for International Settlements Working Paper No. 791).

Friedman, M. (1968, March). The Role of Monetary Policy. *The American Economic Review, 58*(1), 1–17.

Hooper, P., Mishkin, F. S., & Sufi, A. (2019, May). *Prospects for Inflation in a High Pressure Economy: Is the Phillips Curve Dead or is It Just Hibernating?* (National Bureau of Economic Research Working Paper, No. 25792).

Lindé, J., & Trabandt, M. (2019, April 23). *Resolving the Missing Deflation Puzzle* (Centre for Economic Policy Research Discussion Paper DP13690).

McLeay, M., & Tenreyro, S. (2018). *Optimal Inflation and the Identification of the Phillips Curve* (Discussion Papers 1815, Centre for Macroeconomics [CFM]).

Mojon, B., & Ragot, X. (2019, March). *Can an Ageing Workforce Explain Low Inflation?* (Bank for International Settlements Working Paper 776).

Phelps, E. S. (1968). Money-Wage Dynamics and Labor-Market Equilibrium. *Journal of Political Economy, 76,* 678–711.

Phillips, A. W. (1958, November). The Relation Between Unemployment and the Rate of Change of Money Wage Rates in the United Kingdom, 1861–1957. *Economica, 25*(100), 283–299.

Robertson, D. H. (1959, December). A Squeak from Aunt Sally. *The Banker*, CIX, p. 720.

Stock, J. H., & Watson, M. W. (2019, June). *Slack and Cyclically Sensitive Inflation* (National Bureau of Economic Research Working Paper 25987).

Chapter 9

Ahmadjian, C. L., & Robinson, P. (2001, December). Safety in Numbers: Downsizing and the Deinstitutionalization of Permanent Employment in Japan. *Administrative Science Quarterly, 46*, 622–654.

Bank of Japan. (2019, July). *Japan's Balance of Payments Statistics and International Investment Position for 2018*. International Department. https://www.boj.or.jp/en/statistics/br/bop_06/bop2018a.pdf.

International Monetary Fund. (2011, July). *Japan: Spillover Report for the 2011 Article IV Consultation and Selected Issues* (International Monetary Fund Country Report No. 11/183).

Johnson, C. (1982). *MITI and the Japanese Miracle: The Growth of Industrial Policy, 1925–1975*. Stanford: Stanford University Press.

Kang, J. S., & Piao, S. (2015, July). *Production Offshoring and Investment by Japanese Firms* (International Monetary Fund Working Paper WP/15/183).

Kiyota, K. (2015, September/October). Trends and Characteristics of Inward and Outward Foreign Direct Investment in Japan. *Japan SPOTLIGHT*, Japan Economic Foundation. https://www.jef.or.jp/journal/pdf/203rd_Cover_04.pdf.

Kuroda, H. (2014, August 23). *Deflation, the Labour Market, and QQE*. Remarks at the Economic Policy Symposium held by the Federal Reserve Bank of Kansas City. https://www.bis.org/review/r140825a.pdf.

METI. (2011). *White Paper on International Economy and Trade.* Policy Planning and Research Office, Trade Policy Bureau. https://www.meti.go.jp/english/report/data/gWT2011fe.html.

Ministry of Economy, Trade and Industry (METI). (1997–2019). *Survey of Overseas Business Activity.* Published Annually. https://www.meti.go.jp/english/statistics/tyo/kaigaizi/index.html.

Ogawa, K., Saito, M., & Tokutsu, I. (2012, July). *Japan Out of the Lost Decade: Divine Wind or Firms' Effort?* (International Monetary Fund Working Paper WP/12/171).

Sakura, K., & Kondo, T. (2014). *Outward FDI and Domestic Job Creation in the Service Sector* (Bank of Japan Working Paper No. 14-E-3).

Chapter 10

Benzell, S. G., Kotlikoff, L. J., LaGarda, G., & Sachs, J. D. (2018). *Simulating U.S. Business Cash Flow Taxation in a 17-Region Global Model.* https://kotlikoff.net/wp-content/uploads/2019/03/Simulating-U.S.-Business-Cash-Flow-Taxation_0.pdf.

Börsch-Supan, A. (2019, June 17–19). *Demographic Changes, Migration and Economic Growth in the Euro Area.* ECB Forum on Central Banking, Sintra, Portugal.

Börsch-Supan, A., Härtl, K., & Ludwig, A. (2014). Aging in Europe: Reforms, International Diversification, and Behavioral Reactions. *American Economic Review: Papers and Proceedings, 104*(5), 224–229.

Börsch-Supan, A. H., & Wilke, C. B. (2004). *Reforming the German Public Pension System* (Center for Intergenerational Studies Discussion Paper 226). Institute of Economic Research, Hitotsubashi University.

Button, P. (2019, May). *Population Aging, Age Discrimination, and Age Discrimination Protections at the 50th Anniversary of the Age Discrimination in Employment Act* (National Bureau of Economic Research Working Paper 25850).

Desmet, K., Nagy, D. K., & Rossi-Hansberg, E. (2018). The Geography of Development. *Journal of Political Economy, 126*(3), 903–983.

International Monetary Fund. (2015, April). *How Can Sub-Saharan Africa Harness the Demographic Dividend?* IMF African Department.

Kotlikoff, L. J. (2019). Ageing in Global Perspective, Chapter 4. In D. E. Bloom (Ed.), *Live Long and Prosper? The Economics of Ageing Populations.* London: A VoxEU.org eBook, CEPR Press.

The World Bank. *Human Capital Project.* https://www.worldbank.org/en/publication/human-capital.

The World Bank. (2018, October 11). *Human Capital Index.* The World Bank Group. https://www.worldbank.org/en/publication/human-capital.

The World Bank. (2019). *Doing Business 2019: Training for Reform* (16th ed.). The World Bank Group. https://www.doingbusiness.org/content/dam/doingBusiness/media/Annual-Reports/English/DB2019-report_web-version.pdf.

Chapter 11

Alfaro, L., & Kanczuk, F. (2019, October). *Undisclosed Debt Sustainability* (National Bureau of Economic Research Working Paper 26347).

Altavilla, C., Boucinha, M., & Peydró, J.-L. (2018, October). Bank Profitability. *Economic Policy, 96*, 531–586; earlier (2017) in (ECB Working Paper No. 2015).

Borio, C., Gambacorta, L., & Hofmann, B. (2017). The Influence of Monetary Policy on Bank Profitability. *International Finance, 20,* 48–63.

Borio, C., Rungcharoenkitkul, P., & Disyatat, P. (2019, October). *Monetary Policy Hysteresis and the Financial Cycle* (Bank for International Settlements Working Paper No. 817).

Brunnermeier, M. K., & Koby, Y. (2018, December). *The Reversal Interest Rate* (National Bureau of Economic Research Working Paper No. 25406).

Cunliffe, J. (2019, May 7). *Financial Stability Post Brexit: Risks from Global Debt.* Bank of England Speech.

Eggertsson, G. B., Juelsrud, R. E., Summers, L. H., & Wold, E. G. (2019, January). *Negative Nominal Interest Rates and the Bank Lending Channel* (National Bureau of Economic Research, Working Paper 25416).

El-Erian, M. A. (2016). *The Only Game in Town, Central Banks, Instability, and Avoiding the Next Collapse.* (Penguin Random House).

Ford, J. (2019, July 29). Warren is Right to Worry about Dangers of Private Equity Looting. *Financial Times*, p. 8.

Goodhart, C. A. E., & Hudson, M. (2018, January 16). *Could/Should Jubilee Debt Cancellations be Reintroduced Today?* (CEPR Discussion Paper DP12605).

Goodhart, C. A. E., & Kabiri, A. (2019, May 23). *Monetary Policy and Bank Profitability in a Low Interest Rate Environment: A Follow-Up and a Rejoinder* (Centre for Economic Policy Research Discussion Paper DP 13752).

Heer, B., Polito, V., & Wickens, M. R. (2018, June). *Population Aging, Social Security and Fiscal Limits* (CESifo Working Paper No. 7121).

Heider, F., Saidi, F., & Schepens, G. (2019, October). Life Below Zero: Bank Lending Under Negative Policy Rates. *The Review of Financial Studies, 32*(10), 3728–3761.

Hudson, M. (2018). *…and Forgive Them Their Debts: Lending, Foreclosure and Redemption from Bronze Age Finance to the Jubilee Year.* Glashütte: ISLET-Verlag Dresden.

Kalemli-Özcan, S., Laeven, L., & Moreno, D. (2019, February). *Debt Overhang, Rollover Risk, and Corporate Investment: Evidence from the European Crisis* (European Central Bank Working Paper No. 2241).

Mian, A., & Sufi, A. (2014). *House of Debt: How They (and You) Caused the Great Recession, and How We Can Prevent It from Happening Again*. Chicago: University of Chicago Press.

Office for Budget Responsibility. (2018). *Fiscal Sustainability Report*. https://obr.uk/fsr/fiscal-sustainability-report-july-2018/.

Papetti, A. (2019, March). *Demographics and the Natural Real Interest Rate: Historical and Projected Paths for the Euro Area* (European Central Bank Working Paper No. 2258).

Xu, T., Hu, K., & Das, U. S. (2019, January). *Bank Profitability and Financial Stability* (International Monetary Fund Working Paper WP/19/5).

Chapter 12

Auerbach, A., Devereux, M. P., Keen, M., & Vella, J. (2017, January). *Destination-Based Cash Flow Taxation* (Oxford University Centre for Business Taxation, WP 17/01).

Benetton, M., Bracke, P., Cocco, J. F., & Garbarino, N. (2019, April). *Housing Consumption and Investment: Evidence from Shared Equity Mortgages* (Bank of England Staff Working Paper No. 790).

Benford, J., Best, T., & Joy, M (2016, September). *Sovereign GDP-Linked Bonds* (Bank of England, Financial Stability Paper No. 39).

Devereux, M., & Vella, J. (2018). Gaming Destination Based Cash Flow Taxes. *Tax Law Review, 71,* 477–514.

Goodhart, C. A. E., & Hudson, M. (2018, January 16). *Could/Should Jubilee Debt Cancellations Be Reintroduced Today?* (CEPR Discussion Paper DP12605).

Goodhart, C. A. E., & Lastra, R. (2019, January 28). Equity Finance: Matching Liability to Power (CEPR Discussion Paper, DP 13494).

Goodhart, C. A. E., & Lastra, R. M. (2020, March 11). *Journal of Financial Regulation.* Published Online. https://academic.oup.com/jfr/advance-article-abstract/doi/10.1093/jfr/fjz010/5802863.

Huertas, T. (2019, May 22). *'Rebalance Bankers' Bonuses: Use Write-Down Bonds to Satisfy Both Supervisors and Shareholders.* SSRN. Available at SSRN https://ssrn.com/abstract=3336186 or http://dx.doi.org/10.2139/ssrn.3336186.

Institute for Fiscal Studies (Ed.). (2011). *Tax by Design: The Mirrlees Review.* Oxford: Oxford University Press.

International Monetary Fund, Fiscal Affairs Department. (2019, March 10). *Corporate Taxation in the Global Economy* (IMF Policy Paper No. 19/007).

Mayer, C. (2018). *Prosperity: Better Business Makes the Greater Good*. Oxford: Oxford University Press.

Mirrlees Review, Institute for Fiscal Studies (Ed.). (2011). *Tax by Design: The Mirrlees Review.* Oxford: Oxford University Press.

Sheedy, K. (2014, April). *Debt and Incomplete Financial Markets: A Case for Nominal GDP Targeting* (Brookings Papers on Economic Activity, pp. 301–373).

Wolf, M. (2018, December 12). Rethink the Purpose of the Corporation. *Financial Times*.

Chapter 13

Bianchi, F., Kung, H., & Kind, T. (2019). *Threats to Central Bank Independence: High-Frequency Identification with Twitter* (National Bureau of Economic Research Working Paper, No. w26308).

Bloom, D. E. (Ed.). (2019). *Live Long and Prosper? The Economics of Ageing Populations*. London: A VoxEU.org eBook, CEPR Press.

Börsch-Supan, A. (2019). Pension reform in Europe, Chapter 19. In D. E. Bloom (Ed.), *Live Long and Prosper? The Economics of Ageing Populations*. London: A VoxEU.org eBook, CEPR Press.

Conesa, J. C., Kehoe, T. J., Nygaard, V. M., & Raveendranathan, G. (2019). Macroeconomic Effects of Ageing and Healthcare Policy in the United States, Chapter 7. In D. E. Bloom (Ed.), *Live Long and Prosper? The Economics of Ageing Populations*. London: A VoxEU.org eBook, CEPR Press.

Congressional Budget Office. (2019). *The Budget and Economic Outlook: 2019 to 2029*. https://www.cbo.gov/system/files?file=2019-03/54918-Outlook-Chapter1.pdf.

George, H. (2015). *Our Land and Land Policy and Other Works*. Rutherford: Fairleigh Dickinson University Press.

Heer, B., Polito, V., & Wickens, M. R. (2018, June). *Population Aging, Social Security and Fiscal Limits* (CESifo Working Papers 7121/2018).

Hobbes, T. (2014). *Leviathan*. London: Wordsworth Classics of World Literature.

Kotlikoff, L. J. (2019). Ageing in Global Perspective, Chapter 4. In D. E. Bloom (Ed.), *Live Long and Prosper? The Economics of Ageing Populations*. London: A VoxEU.org eBook, CEPR Press.

Kotlikoff, L. J., Kubler, F., Polbin, A., Sachs, J. D., & Scheidegger, S. (2019, April). *Making Carbon Taxation a Generational Win Win* (National Bureau of Economic Research Working Paper No. 25760).

Laitner, J., & Silverman, D. (2019). Population Ageing and Tax System Efficiency, Chapter 17. In D. E. Bloom (Ed.), *Live Long and Prosper? The Economics of Ageing Populations*. London: A VoxEU.org eBook, CEPR Press.

Mill, J. S. (2016). *The Principles of Political Economy: John Stuart Mill*. Scotts Valley: CreateSpace Independent Publishing Platform.

OECD Secretariat. (2019, October). Secretariat Proposal for a "Unified Approach" Under Pillar One, Public consultation document, OECD.

Office for Budget Responsibility. (2018). *Fiscal Sustainability Report*. https://obr.uk/fsr/fiscal-sustainability-report-july-2018/.

Smith, A. (1982). *The Wealth of Nations: Books I–III*. London: Penguin Classics.

The Economist (2019, April 13). Interference Day: Independent Central Banks are Under Threat. That is bad news for the world.

Chapter 14

Hamilton, J. D., Harris, E. S., Hatzius, J., & West, K.D. (2015, August). *The Equilibrium Real Funds Rate: Past, Present and Future* (Natural Bureau of Economic Research, No. 21476).

Papetti, A. (2019, March). *Demographics and the Natural Real Interest Rate: Historical and Projected Paths for the Euro Area* (European Central Bank Working Paper No. 2258).

Postscript

Bernard, A. B., Jensen, J. B., & Schott, P. K. (2006, January). Survival of the Best Fit: Exposure to Low-Wage Countries and the (Uneven) Growth of U.S. Manufacturing Plants. *Journal of International Economics, 68*(1), 219–237.

Pierce, J. R. & Schott, P. K. (2012, December). *The Surprisingly Swift Decline of U.S. Manufacturing Employment* (National Bureau of Economic Research Working Paper 18655).

Stansbury, A. & L.H. Summers, L.H. (2020, May). *The Declining Worker Power Hypothesis: An Explanation for the Recent Evolution of the American Economy* (National Bureau of Economic Research Working Paper 27193).

Index

© The Editor(s) (if applicable) and The Author(s), under exclusive license to Springer Nature Switzerland AG 2020
C. Goodhart and M. Pradhan, *The Great Demographic Reversal*,
https://doi.org/10.1007/978-3-030-42657-6